Trans
Figured

MY JOURNEY FROM BOY TO GIRL TO WOMAN TO MAN

BRIAN BELOVITCH

Skyhorse Publishing

Skyhorse Publishing books may be purchased in bulk at special discounts for sales promotion, corporate gifts, fund-raising, or educational purposes. Special editions can also be created to specifications. For details, contact the Special Sales Department, Skyhorse Publishing, 307 West 36th Street, 11th Floor, New York, NY 10018 or info@skyhorsepublishing.com.

Skyhorse® and Skyhorse Publishing® are registered trademarks of Skyhorse Publishing, Inc.®, a Delaware corporation.

Visit our website at www.skyhorsepublishing.com.

10 9 8 7 6 5 4 3 2 1

Library of Congress Cataloging-in-Publication Data is available on file.

Cover design by Rain Saukas

Print ISBN: 978-1-5107-2964-3
Ebook ISBN: 978-1-5107-2965-0

Printed in the United States of America

For Gloria and Paul

"There are only two ways to live your life.
One is as though nothing is a miracle.
The other is as though everything is a miracle."

Albert Einstein

CONTENTS

CHAPTER 1

Sex Work Singer

Broke, busted, and disgusted at having spent every last dime, I needed more cash. Still buzzed from yet another nasty binge after the Limelight show, my days now seemed pretty mundane. It was spring 1986, and trying to wake up and muster enough energy to shower was sometimes all I could do. Or maybe I'd just skip it, I thought, opting instead to linger by the phone. Now I knew how a dog felt begging for table scraps, desperate as I was to catch a trick, a date, a john. My miniscule Hell's Kitchen studio apartment on West Forty-Fifth Street was becoming more like a cellblock.

Queen crack had a way of making you feel that way.

Barely a month ago, I had been planning my big birthday party at the Saint, calling up Andy Warhol to invite him personally.

"Andy, hi. It's Tish. Tish Gervais," I said.

"Oh, hi, Tish," he said in his instantly recognizable flat tone.

"I'm calling because I'd be so honored to have you as one of the hosts on the invitation for my thirtieth birthday party at the Saint."

"Gee thanks. Sure."

Thrilled, I thanked him and hung up, knowing any further conversation with the pop icon was futile. He was especially shy and his assistant had told me that I scared him. I couldn't say I blamed him, though I was certainly no Valerie Solanas.

Still, I couldn't help thinking about how quickly my situation had changed since I made that phone call. Johnny R., my former sugar daddy, had stopped paying my rent, and there were few if any work options for trans women back then so I had registered with two escort agencies for more sex work. Somehow sashaying in and out of fancy hotels like the Plaza, the Waldorf Astoria, and the St. Regis lessened the sting of shame. As long as I didn't have to splash my ass in a back-page sex ad in the *Village Voice* or *Screw*, it helped me retain the fantasy that my life didn't suck and left me with a sliver of dignity intact.

Plain and simple, I'd been whoring my whole life. It wasn't the end to my means nor did I want to claim it as a career choice. Not that there was anything wrong with sex work—it's just that I always had bigger dreams for myself. But my acting and party-promoting career was practically zilch by then. Indeed, the only acting I was doing was acting like everything was fine when it fact it wasn't. Word had gotten out in my nightclub circle of friends that I was hitting the crack pipe pretty much twenty-four seven, so most people knew they couldn't rely on me any more for parties or performing gigs.

Getting up at two or three in the afternoon, mind you, wasn't the ideal time of day to get much done. I'd click on the TV, not even knowing if I had cable because Johnny had stopped paying the bill. Several hours would pass with me channel surfing, chain smoking, and praying that the phone would ring.

Sure enough the phone rang.

It was Freddie. "Hello!" I spoke with as much fake enthusiasm as I could muster. "Where have you been?"

"Oh, you know me, busy with the wife, kids, work and all. Hey, listen, Natalia, let's say you and I get together tonight. I want to take you out. Get dolled up real nice and we'll take a ride to Atlantic City. It's going to be a real special time, just the two of us. I'll get a suite, champagne, dinner—the works."

I laughed, thinking, *What did I do to deserve this sheer act of generosity?*

Freddie was notoriously cheap with the girls with something extra. That's what I called myself instead of a "chick with a dick." More ladylike. He was a forty-year-old frustrated married man, short, kind of stocky, not bad looking in a Tony Soprano kind of way.

Freddie liked to get fucked, but he just couldn't come out and say it. It was an endless game of how to find things to stick up his bum: candles, cucumbers, dildos, you name it. I even kept frozen bananas in the freezer just in case. I knew once I whipped out the banana, stuck it in him, he'd get off and go. He was notoriously tedious and stingy; you had to really work hard for any extra cash. Sometimes at least he'd be generous with bling or drugs.

But the thing is, he always had the purest coke.

"Sure, Freddie. Sounds like fun. What time?"

• • •

At 8:00 p.m. on the dot, the buzzer rang. I pressed the intercom and in a sultry voice said, "Who is it?"

"Who the hell do you think it is, little red fucking riding hood?" Freddie yelled back in his thick Brooklyn accent. Buzzing him in, I ran into the bathroom and ripped the rollers out of my thick brunette mane, brushed it, and tossed it back. I grabbed some perfume and sprayed heavily.

Earlier, I had rummaged through my closet to fish out something to wear for the trip to Atlantic City. I didn't have much, for I had sold a lot of my best clothes to other girls or to my dealer for more drugs. What I found was a fuchsia silk wrap dress and black patent leather pumps. This was another thing about Freddie: he had a foot fetish, so before he arrived I spent a half hour working on my feet to get them into perfectly worshipful shape.

Freddie Romano was a small-time hood. I knew he had some connections, but I wasn't sure with whom because I never wanted to know. He carried a gun and made money fencing stolen merchandise and dealing drugs on the side. A lot of the other pre-op girls liked him because, even though he was a real piece of work, if he liked his time with you, he'd tip you with a nice piece of bling or some coke.

I opened the door and there was Freddie, flowers in hand and all dressed up in a gray, pin-striped, double-breasted suit and tie. He looked unusually handsome, though the suit hung on him like it belonged to someone a size larger.

"Hello, gorgeous," he said. "You look great, babe. Turn around." He whistled as I swirled around like Maria in *West Side Story*, and bent down to kiss my feet. "You're looking hot, doll."

Freddie plopped his black attaché case on the kitchen counter.

"Close your eyes, babe." I did, hearing the snap, snap of the case opening. "Surprise," he said. My eyes widened when I saw a big pile of gold, diamond, and pearl jewelry. Like a cherry on top of a sundae was a giant baggy full of coke.

"You like?" he asked. "I have to bring this to Atlantic City. Got another baggy? Let me split a little off for the ride down."

He opened the bag and dipped into it with his diamond-adorned pinky to scoop out a hearty bump for me to try.

Sniffing hard and long, my head swelled and my body tingled from my head to my toes. "Ooh, this is so good. Shall I bring my pipe? I can cook some up real quick for the ride."

"Nah, I just wanna sniff, if you don't mind." *Oh, here we go,* I thought. Here comes the creepy control freak that he is. "Wait till we get to Atlantic City, ha!"

I felt dejected because sniffing didn't really do it for me anymore. I loved to smoke and was sure that at some point in the evening I would be able to get him to give me some to cook up. Without him looking, I tossed my butane torch, small Pyrex bottle, stem, and a baggie with baking soda into my purse and snapped it shut. I dashed into the bathroom for a quick fluff of my hair and a swipe of red lipstick and off we went.

Strutting out with Freddie in tow, I saw a shiny black stretch limousine parked on the curb and barely noticed the driver hold open the door for us. It wasn't my first time in a limo. Once inside, I checked the wet bar to see if it was fully stocked because I really needed a drink if I were going to spend several hours putting up with Mr. Romano.

"Oh, goodie," I said after sliding open the wet bar to discover its contents full. This would take the edge off the coke jitters.

Freddie told the driver to raise the tinted partition. "Don't open it unless I tell you to, buddy."

The partition slid up, the driver turned on the ignition, and soon we were rolling out of Hell's Kitchen down Ninth Avenue and into the Lincoln Tunnel. I leaned back and said, "Freddie, be an angel and pour me a drink. How about a nice vodka martini? Two olives, please."

• • •

When we arrived at the casino, Freddie grabbed my arm and paraded me into the Trump Hotel lobby as if I were his wife. I waited patiently as he registered for the room, which was a lavish suite with a full dining room, a bedroom, and a gorgeous view of Atlantic City.

"My, how fancy we've become, Mr. Romano," I said once we were inside.

"Hey, nothing's too good for you, babe. After all, it's a very special night."

I was thinking, *Jesus, this is so cheesy. I must be one of God knows how many girls he's run this game on.* "Yes, honey, it is very sweet of you."

"What do you say I run a bath and order some food before we go downstairs to the casino?" he suggested.

"Sure," I responded, though food and gambling were the last things on my mind. I wanted to get my hands on more of that coke. "Let me have some blow, Freddie. I'd like to cook up a little to smoke."

"Don't you think you can wait till we get back to the city?" he asked me. "I really don't want you to smoke here, if it's okay."

"Aw, come on. Don't tell me you dragged me all this way to be such a bore." I was not happy with this new development and was determined to get some of the coke to cook up and freebase. That was my thing. He knew it. It was odd that he was resisting. Usually we'd smoke for hours. It helped loosen him up so that I could begin the parade of toys to stuff up his bum.

"If you don't mind," he said, "I'd really wish you could wait, just this once, for me. Don't worry, I'll take care of you later." He served up a few more lines. I guess I'd just have to follow the script I had been given.

He then headed to the bathroom and started to run a bath. Hours had slipped away and I had no idea what time it really was. Freddie called for me to come into the bathroom, where he was naked, sitting in the tub.

"Come here," he says. "Wanna grab that washcloth and wash my back?"

Oh my God, I thought, *Am I really playing the subservient little mob gal role?* I started to wash his back and he said, "Oh, honey, that feels so good," and then I noticed that his shoulders were shaking and he was stifling a sob.

"What's wrong, Freddie? Did I do something to upset you? I'm sorry about the smoking."

"There's something I have to tell you, but you mustn't ever tell anyone else about it, okay? Can you promise me that?"

"Sure, no problem. What is it?"

He was sobbing again, wiping his tears away with his nubby hands. He looked like an overgrown child who had been very naughty. He looked me in the eye and proceeded to tell me why he had brought me there that night.

"It's the last time you'll ever see me. You're one of my favorite girls. We always have a good time. You have a good heart and you never try and take advantage of me like some of the others."

"Thanks," I said. "I just try to make you happy, that's all. You've been good to me, too. What do you mean I won't ever see you again? Are you going away? Moving? What?"

"Natalia, I made a very, very big mistake and now I am going to have to suffer the consequences. In a little while, my number will be up. Someone's on the way here to make me pay the price."

He was going to be killed! I began to panic. This fucking trick had just so much as told me that I might become an accessory to murder! I wasn't at all considering what he had just said was going to happen to him. I started screaming.

"Get the fuck out of that bath tub right now, Freddie, and get dressed. Call your driver and have him pick me up. I want to go back to the city, now!"

"Shh! Be quiet before they call downstairs to the front desk, be quiet."

"Quiet? Are you out of your fucking mind? Pay me what you owe me and get me the hell out of here. That's what I want and then I'll be quiet." Well, so much for my fantasy of being a hooker with a heart of gold.

Wrapping a robe around him, Freddie walked out of the bathroom. "All right. I'm sorry I told you but I had to tell someone. I'll call the driver. Calm down." He grabbed his pants and pulled out a couple of hundred-dollar bills and handed them to me. I stuffed the money in my purse.

"What about the coke? You said you would give me some for later."

"I can't give you any more. I have to turn that and the jewelry over when they get here." Handing me a pretty little diamond pendant on a gold chain, he said, "Take this." I was now thinking that the ride back would be brutal but at least I could sell the little trinket for an eight ball when and if I got back home.

"Here's one more thing I'd like you to have." He reached into another pocket and handed me a small bullet. I was so high at this point and so relieved that I was getting the hell out of here that I took it without thinking, tossing it into my purse.

Calmer now, I said, "Thanks," and gave him a hug.

He picked up the phone and rang for the driver. "He'll be waiting downstairs. Car fifty-four."

I slipped into my dress, snapped open my bag, checked my face, applied some fresh lips, fluffed my hair, and turned to Freddie. "Good luck with all this." I didn't know what else to say.

Freddie looked sad and somewhat bewildered as the door closed behind me. Up until this point, I had managed to avoid any serious run-ins with the law and this was something I wanted nothing to do with.

I made a swift exit from the hotel to find car fifty-four. I slid in as the driver slammed the door shut. The sound of the ignition signaled we were off. It happened so fast I couldn't tell you what the driver looked like. All I knew was that I was out of that hotel. Halfway to New York, my mind started playing tricks on me. I realized I might never even make it back to my own private hell in Hell's Kitchen. The coke continued to make me increasingly paranoid. I began to imagine the driver, who I hadn't spoken to or for that matter even got a really good look at, was taking me somewhere to finish me off.

I opened my purse, grabbed one of the last cigarettes I had, and saw the bullet that Freddie had given me. I was now certain that I'd been set up. Freddie had given me the bullet so that I'd be found with it and blamed for his death. I felt that that it would be an act of divine intervention if I ever saw my freedom again. I finished off the bottle of vodka and gratefully I passed out.

I woke to the sound of the limousine door being yanked open. "Here you are, miss. Three-Forty-One West Forty-Fifth Street," the driver said.

I couldn't believe it. There was my front door. Feeling a bit unsteady, I stumbled out onto the sidewalk. I nearly knelt to kiss the ground, so certain I had been that I wouldn't make it back. *There must be a God after all*, I thought.

"Thank you very much," I said to the driver as I wobbled toward my lobby door.

The slowly rising sun reminded me the night was nearly over but that wasn't enough to convince me my little noir adventure had ended. Oh no, I knew I'd have a buyer for this diamond pendant. In minutes, I was banging on my dealer Sonia's apartment door on the third floor of my building. I knew she'd be able to straighten me out.

After scoring my coke from her, I headed back upstairs to cook up a fierce witch's brew of hard rock to smoke away the rest of the night. I was shaking and sweating when I finally plunked the rock into my pipe and torched it with a crackling blaze of butane. Snap, crackle, and pop, I inhaled the smoke deeply into my lungs and held it in as long as I could until I felt my body go numb. A sultry, tingling sensation seeped slowly through my body, relieving me of the fear and all the emptiness I felt. My problems slipped away in a cloud of smoke and now I was content, calm knowing that my true lover had arrived to comfort me.

The next day when I finally woke up I reached for the remote. *Oprah* was on so it had to be late afternoon. Immediately, I remembered the one pressing thing I had to attend to. The bullet. It was still in my purse. Grabbing some newspaper, I wrapped it up. I wrapped a scarf around my messy hair, slipped on a pair of dark sunglasses, and left the building and walked toward Ninth Avenue, a few blocks from my apartment. When I was far enough away, I tossed the newspaper into a trash can.

Then I remembered that tonight was the opening of *Ginger & Fred*, the new Fellini film at MoMA. Dinah Prince of the *Daily News* had invited me. . . .

CHAPTER 2

Miss Gendered

Click, clack, click, clack went my mother Del's spring-o-lator pumps as she dragged me down the rickety wooden steps of our house and into the car for our weekly shopping trip to downtown Fall River, Massachusetts. I was too young to stay behind with my brothers, but just thought she liked having me along. My brothers loathed these shopping trips, but I for one appreciated them each and every time. It was an adventure. On these little outings, if I behaved, I'd be treated to a banana split at the Woolworth's soda fountain. And if I were really lucky, I'd get to pop one of those multi-colored balloons hovering over the counter enticing kids like me to do just that. Hopes were high that I'd win the treat for a lower price or free. Even at five, I knew a good bargain when I saw one.

We didn't have much money, but whatever profits my father made running the local crap games allowed us to have a nice car. Our big old 1959 black Buick Special sat in the yard waiting to take Del and me downtown. To prepare for the trips, she'd swipe the brightest shade of red lipstick on her full Portuguese lips, spray perfume, and wrap her bleached blond hair up in a scarf.

Exiting the car, I'd run through the revolving doors at Woolworth's, spinning one too many times before my mother grabbed me by the collar to stop. While she headed to the women's lingerie department, I'd stray over to the makeup counter. I loved peeking into all the cases with their bright, multicolored packages and, if I stood on tippy-toes, I could usually reach the top of the counter. This time a saleslady popped up from behind the counter and indulged me in my curiosity, asking, "Where did you get those eyelashes, honey?"

"From my mommy," I answered proudly.

It was 1961 and Elvis Presley's music was everywhere, even in Woolworth's. Whenever I heard any type of music, I'd automatically stop and start swaying my little five-year-old hips to the beat. So there I was, on this sunny afternoon in Woolworth's, without a care in the world, when I heard Elvis crooning, *Oh, let me be your teddy bear, put a chain around my neck and lead me anywhere, oh, let me be, oh, let me, your teddy bear.* Without missing a beat, I started dancing and swaying my hips and soon a small crowd of ladies had gathered to watch my impromptu performance.

"How cute. Oh, what beautiful curls this kid has," said one lady.

"Oh, yes, and those long eyelashes! I'd kill for them!" said another.

Just then my mother appeared, looking flustered. "There you are," she said. "I've been looking all over for you and here you are shaking your ass!"

One lady then said to my mother, "Excuse me, ma'am. What beautiful eyelashes she has."

My mother grabbed my hand hard and pulled me away. "It's he, not she!" she said to the woman. "And it's none of your goddamned business!" Shocked at her outburst, the ladies turned away, while Del pulled me along. "What did I tell you? I told you to stay close by me and there you were shaking your ass like a little girl. Wait till I get you home and tell your father!"

Confused and hurt, I felt tears fall from my big brown eyes, making my lashes even thicker.

"Stop that crying, before I really give you something to cry about!" she said. Shoving me into the car, she slammed the door and started up the engine, and we sped off toward home. I couldn't help feeling upset for not understanding what it was that I had done wrong. I loved music, it made me happy, and I loved dancing. What could possibly be wrong with that? It was too much for my little five-year-old brain to comprehend, but one thing that was easy to understand was that once again I had been mistaken for a girl. My mother's hysterical reaction proved it couldn't be a good thing!

Much of my early life was spent in Fall River. It was there so many odd years ago that my life would take many unexpected twists and turns. As a young person growing up in a barely-working class family in New England, I couldn't imagine what my future would bring. The roller-coaster ride through the often uncertain and unpredictable world of gender identity was something my family and I could never have prepared for.

Third born out of seven kids, I was assigned male at birth. In Fall River, I was raised with two older brothers, three younger brothers, and one sister: Joseph, Randall, Jeffery, the twins, Todd and Sheila, and our half-brother, David. It was a chaotically challenging household. As best I can recall, and God forbid that I risk cliché, I always felt different, separate from everyone. By the age of five I remember feeling that, hey, it was a good thing. Until I discovered that my feeling different would soon be distorted and turned against me. It didn't help that my natural personality was bright and enthusiastic and that I was curious, precocious, and a real rascal, interested in everything. I was also interested in something children might be better off learning about later in life: sex.

Growing up in a butch brood of five hypermasculine brothers, I often felt inadequate around them physically. According to my mother, as an infant I spent weeks in oxygen tents before I came home from the hospital. My breathing problems as a child would limit the amount of physical exercise I could participate in before getting winded or short of breath.

Every night in our house there were television wars over my viewing preferences for shows like *Walt Disney's Wonderful World of Color, Cinderella,* or *Peter Pan.* Instead, my brothers preferred the shoot-'em-up bang-bang series like *Bonanza, Gunsmoke,* or *The Wild Wild West.* Often it became physical with my mother coming to the rescue. Although suffering through *The Wild Wild West* viewing Robert Conrad's revealing skintight pants and fabulous footwear was bearable, there was something much more comforting about the Rodgers and Hammerstein version of *Cinderella* with Leslie Ann Warren singing "In My Own Little Corner." Stuart Damon as the prince was dreamy and one of my earliest crushes.

Early on I knew I wasn't heterosexual like my brothers. The anxiety I felt as a child and in adolescence about how I would function sexually was always present. It was drilled into me that if you weren't hetero-identified and didn't desire to sleep with women, then something must be seriously wrong with you. I strongly rejected this whole idea proliferated in my household. In order to be a man, you must grow up, screw a lot of girls, eventually get married, and have a ton of kids. From where I stood, I found this to be an absolute impossibility. I knew I wanted none of it.

Embedded in my psyche was the idea that using my penis for sex with anyone other than a female was wrong. Although I did just that, I couldn't escape the shame and disgust that was projected onto me from my family and society as a whole. And, of course, this wasn't an idea exclusive to the Belovitch family. It was permeated throughout contemporary society. The sexual revolution had begun like gangbusters for heterosexuals, but moved at a snail's pace as far as gay and trans matters were concerned.

Fall River had had a prosperous past due to its successful textile industry coming from mills that were first built there in 1811. It was also famous for one of the most notorious murder trials in American history. Lizzie Borden, an heiress in her own right, was charged with murdering her father and stepmother with an ax in 1892. *Poor Lizzie must have been in a tizzy when she was accused of giving her mother forty whacks. When she saw what she had done she gave her father forty-one.* The O. J. Simpson of her day, Lizzie was acquitted and lived out the rest of her life as a recluse in Fall River.

To this day, I don't know how or where my parents met in Fall River, but my father was much older—by nineteen years—when they married. My mother, Delores Arruda, hailed from a large family of first-generation Portuguese immigrants; she was one of eight children, two of whom were twins who had died in a tragic fire on my grandparents' farm in Somerset, Massachusetts, just across the bridge from Fall River. The fire that killed the twins could have happened on any day of the year, but coincidentally it happened on April 10, the same day many years later, in 1956, when I was born. It was a well-known fact that when I was born my mother desperately wanted a girl. Growing up knowing that her wish hadn't been fulfilled, I often felt that I had done something wrong. Even in the womb, I was already being conditioned to be a mistake.

Tragedy wasn't unfamiliar to the Arruda family. My maternal grandfather, Manuel Arruda, was a notorious alcoholic who, one night in a drunken stupor, tried to rape my mother, then barely fourteen years of age. As a result, my mother ran away from home as soon as she could. She made it all the way to Oklahoma before she was caught and returned to her family. He was also physically abusive to my grandmother and his other children.

The Belovitch side of the family hadn't fared much better, though they ended up being more prosperous than my mom's. My paternal grandparents, Louis Belovitch and Jenny Schindler, had emigrated here from Riga, Latvia, in 1888. It's been said that ancestors of the Belovitch family in Ukraine were servants to the Czar of Russia. They were expert leather craftsmen who provided beautiful boots and saddles for the Czar and his army. Prior to the pogroms that would occur against Jews in Russia, the Belovitch family was allowed to leave Russia because of their service to the Czar. My father would never speak to me about any of this.

"What do you want to know that for?" he'd ask. "It was a long time ago and it doesn't matter what happened then. Forget about it."

Such a message would be permanently imprinted in my young psyche. If things were too painful or difficult to discuss, it was better to just ignore them or leave them alone or, as my mother did, run away.

Physically, my parents were a striking couple. My father was tall and strong with beautiful sensitive hazel eyes that I always wished I'd inherited. He had a typically Slavic face, in that his nose was long and strong and his forehead wide. He, too, was one of eight children and his mother had died young, leaving his oldest sister, Sally, to raise the younger siblings. With money she inherited, Aunt Sally bought a small pushcart and used to sell fresh fish on the streets of Fall River. My grandfather, Louis, owned a salvage business on a few acres of land on Rodman Street with two tenement houses on it.

For us kids, this place was a private playground, filled with abandoned junk like empty truck backs, rubber tires, and all sorts of odd metal defunct machinery. It was my job to gather all the kids in the neighborhood together to convince, or in some cases force, them to join me in my thespian aspirations. We would put on little shows anywhere we could. Tossing a sheet over a rope gave us an instant curtain in our backyards. We made use of the back of those abandoned trailer trucks in the junkyard.

We lived in a three-bedroom apartment on the first floor of a three-story tenement on Rodman Street. My parents shared their bedroom with the newborn twins, Todd and Sheila, and my brothers and I shared the other two bedrooms. My dad squeaked out a living as a fruit and produce vendor. He owned a small weathered pickup truck, which he'd load up early in the morning at the farmers market and drive around the neighborhoods throughout Fall River and New Bedford to make whatever money he could. When he wasn't hustling fruit and produce, he was organizing local crap games with my Uncle Tony, my mother's brother-in-law, who lived with her sister Evelyn on the third floor. I didn't know it then, but it turns out that Aunt Evelyn had left Uncle Tony because she caught him with another woman, who was the ex-girlfriend of Henry Arruda, my mom's youngest brother.

One day, Aunt Evelyn and my mother had driven to the ex-girlfriend's house to give her a good ass-kicking. When they had driven up to the house and rang the doorbell, they'd discovered that they were outnumbered because the house was full of the woman's family. "Quick, Del, make a run for it before they gang up on us!" Evelyn had yelled.

Fighting was the thing to do back then and, throughout my upbringing, I perceived it as something you just did and never questioned. *Beat or be beaten* could be my family motto.

My mother didn't work because she had her hands full with four boys. The twins and David weren't born yet. Del had a sparkling personality, a great sense of humor, and a beautiful, winning smile. She had big, brown, flashing eyes, and dark hair, though sometimes she bleached her hair blond. Her body was strong with broad shoulders and a curvy figure, and she wasn't shy about bragging about her million-dollar legs that would make even Betty Grable jealous. While she did have legendary legs, sadly she lacked the ambition, education, or desire ever to move further in life. Her mood changes would come without warning. We never knew what was headed our way. One minute she'd be cheerful or downright hilarious, yet within moments any little thing could flip her over into the darkness. After all she was a Gemini, sign of the twins, but at times her personality seemed more than split. But to hear her tell it, she was the sharpest, smartest person anyone would ever get to know. It was what she wanted us to believe.

• • •

Fall was approaching and soon I would be starting school at the Brayton Avenue School, which was just a short walk from our house on Rodman Street. My older brother Randall had been assigned to take me to school on the first day, and he wasn't happy about it. Before my birth, Randall had been the baby and the sole focus of my parents' attention, but now he was often stuck having to care for me. Randy always seemed to be in his own world, a bit lost. He was a quiet kid, kind of a loner. Early on, he displayed an aloof quality, a pattern that would continue well into his adult life. In a sense, it was his way of staying on the outskirts of the chaos in our family.

The school had separate entrances for each gender, so Randy and I lined up outside of the boys' entrance. I looked across at the girls' entrance and saw that all the little girls were already starting to file in while we still waited. It was confusing to me why we were separated by gender even back then.

"Why do we have to stay over here?" I asked my brother.

"Because the girls enter over there and the boys enter here," Randy said emphatically.

"But why? Why can't we be together?" I continued in the way any annoying little brother would.

"Brian, I don't know. What difference does it make? Forget about it, come on, we're going in."

In school, we'd play the game musical chairs. In one corner of the classroom was an old upright piano, on which my teacher, Miss Preprimary, would plunk out the familiar tune "Pop Goes the Weasel." The other kids would squeal with delight as we got closer and closer to the finish. One day I was close to being the last kid standing when the music stopped. I just barely missed the seat and remember feeling increasingly anxious. Catching my reflection in a mirror across the room, I saw that my face was flushed the brightest shade of red. The rest of the children were pointing and laughing at me. The more laughter I heard, the hotter my face felt. Certainly they were laughing at me, not with me. This became a pivotal moment in my early childhood . . . the idea that failure was something that should never happen, because if it did, ridicule would almost certainly follow.

It didn't help that these were the messages I was getting at home. As a gender-fluid child, my personality drew constant scrutiny. Everything about me was fair game, especially where other children were concerned.

The first time I was exposed to sex was when I was four years old. Strange sounds coming from my parents' bedroom woke me from my afternoon nap. Crawling out of my bed and tottering out of my room, I saw that their door was slightly ajar. Pushing it open, I stood there for a second and saw my father naked on top of my mother. I didn't know what it was they were doing, but it looked as if they were playing so I giggled as young children do. My father came over to me, slapped me hard on the ass, and told me to go back to bed and then slammed the door. I cried and rocked myself back to sleep. What I remembered then was that sex hurts.

Realizing at a very early age that I was indeed different from most other kids, I never quite knew what to make of it. What child does, even if the child is lucky enough to have parents sane enough even to explain the complexities of sexual behavior? Let me tell you, my parents were far beyond ever being able to explain anything. If things made them uncomfortable, they'd cover it up with anger or ridicule.

By five years old, I'd begun my thieving career, too. It began with stealing candy bars from DeViller's drug store, which was just up the block from our house. Although I got caught and my father gave me a good whack, it was only a temporary respite from my burgeoning life of crime. As a teenager, I'd graduate to larger priced items, especially comic books. Never growing up with an actual allowance, I just stole the Archie and Vampira comics that I loved so much. The older I got, the more select I was about what I stole. Eventually, I hit the liquor store with assistance from friends. One friend would go up to the counter to distract the clerk and I would grab whatever was closest to the door, usually beer or Boone's Farm Apple Wine.

My one hard-and-fast rule was that I would never steal from friends, but anything else was up for grabs: records, clothes, food, bedding, whatever I could slip under my coat or into a bag. We were poor and if I wanted something or even if I asked for it, I probably wouldn't get it from my parents. One weekend, when my brother Jeffery and I were visiting my father after my parents' divorce, we got caught in the big department store downtown stealing sneakers. My father had to come get us out. He was pissed and both of us got our asses kicked.

When I became an adult, it continued and it was something that I was good at. I had no guilt about it, since I felt it was my right because I had been deprived of so much as a child. Which, of course, I know today isn't the case.

• • •

There are many things to remember about our home on Rodman Street. Our upstairs neighbor, Frank D., an older dark-skinned man from the Cape Verde islands, regularly dispatched me to Freitas Market across the street to get him cigars, which I loved to do because it made me feel important and he often let me keep the change. He sometimes came to the door dressed only in his robe and would fumble around in his pockets for change. The robe often slipped open and I'd see his huge penis just dangling there.

It was quite a curious sight. I don't know why I was so interested in it at the time, but why wouldn't I be? One time he actually left the robe open as I stood there staring at his crotch. He eventually grabbed and closed the robe to stop me from staring, but part of me felt that he was exposing himself on purpose, that he may have wanted me to touch it but was scared to initiate anything himself.

Even though my mother would leave my dad and move away from Rodman Street, Mr. D. remained there for many years. Whenever I'd visit my father there, I'd sprint upstairs and knock on Mr. D.'s door, knowing that I could make some money if I went to the store for him. I never told anyone in my family about this, but recently a therapist asked me when I turned my first trick. I had thought it was when I was thirteen or fourteen, but then realized that it was at the tender age of five that I had learned that sex equals money.

Although I was naive about the sexual intrigue with Mr. D., it didn't matter to me. What mattered the most was that someone was paying attention to me. Being neglected and unsupervised by my parents left me vulnerable to many similar situations.

One day I was riding my tricycle in and out of the entrance to our yard without any adult supervision. Peddling like a demon racer, I drove right into a parked Cadillac car in the driveway and smashed my forehead into the sharp fins of the fender. Luckily, I hit my hard head instead of gouging out an eye. Another time my brothers and I were playing by the garbage area in the junkyard. I slipped and fell and cut my pinky finger on a broken bottle. Who lets their toddler kids play amongst garbage and broken glass? My finger was dangling and bleeding profusely as I traipsed up the porch steps to show my mother what had happened. She wrapped a bandage around it when, clearly, I might have needed stitches.

One day, as soon as my father was out the door, my mother called Aunt Evelyn to come down and help her pack. Sitting on the cool linoleum floor, I was bewildered by this sudden flurry of activity. As I watched Del and Evelyn hastily pack and haul bags out to the old pickup truck in the yard, I started to cry, but no one paid much attention to me as they were hurriedly moving things out of the house.

Before long, everything was packed and I hadn't budged from my place on the floor. Aunt Evelyn gathered the other kids and put them into Del's Buick parked alongside the truck. Sliding in behind the steering wheel, she waved Del into the truck. After a quick final check of the apartment, my mother scooped me up from the floor as she headed out to the yard.

"Where are we going?" I asked.

"As far away from here as we can get," she said.

When my mother left my father in 1961, she became a single parent raising six kids. We moved across town to a house on a very steep hill on Lincoln Avenue facing the Taunton River. My grandfather's Sunshine Bakery was at the bottom of the hill on North Main Street. It didn't enhance our relationship in any way or make us closer to him. For the brief time we lived there, I think I went into his bakery once. It was one of my few pleasant childhood experiences. The smell of delicious Portuguese bread baking in the ovens, the many different metal trays and cooling racks in the back of the shop. A child couldn't understand the hatred my mother had for her father, but I could feel the tension on that visit. Sadly, I never got to know any of my grandparents, but I cherish the memory of that day.

After the experience of Mr. D. exposing himself to me, intentionally or not, I began to repeat the same behavior to others, which isn't unusual for kids who witness similar things. My favorite thing to do with the other kids in the neighborhood was to show off to them all the adult things I had learned to do. Squeezing under the lattice below the porch at Lincoln Avenue, we could slip under the stairs and be submerged in total darkness, except for the slivers of light shining through the slats that covered the bottom of the porch. I'd lure the Jones kids, our neighbors, to come under the porch with me, intent on playing sexual games with them.

"We can play Mommy and Daddy," I'd say before instructing Jeanne Jones to pull down her pants and show me her private parts. I'd then lie on top of her and say, "Now, I'm your daddy." We didn't know what the hell we were doing, but just as monkeys learn by imitation, that was what we would do. Boys or girls, it didn't matter. I was intent on getting into everyone's pants.

One day, Jeffery and I were playing alone on the first-floor porch. We were teasing each other, as little kids do; I was five and he was three. I climbed onto the porch railing, teetering on the edge. Jeffery was upset by something I had said and came rushing towards, me, shoving me backwards. Losing my balance, I fell backward over the railing and through the wide-open cellar door below. Suddenly, I felt a sharp, stabbing pain on my left side. An empty clothesline hook had gouged into me as I tumbled down the cellar steps. Ten stitches later, I would have a scar that remains to this day, a visual reminder of how things can go wrong when kids are left unattended.

Another time I stole matches from my mother's purse, and Jeffery and I went outside to play with them. I placed some leaves and sticks next to the side of our house so I could block the wind when I lit them on fire. Not only did I succeed in lighting my little fire, but I also managed to set the side of the house on fire in the process.

Seeing the flames race up the side of the house, Jeffery and I were so scared that we ran and hid under the porch next door. Huddling in the darkness, we heard the fire trucks race toward our house. The entire side of the house was now engulfed in flames.

Soon my father arrived at my mother's request and eventually dragged us out from under the porch next door and this time we both received quite a beating. Physical punishment was the ultimate result of any misbehavior. While Del wasn't shy about hitting us, she often deferred the duty to my father. My misbehavior was clearly a sign that my anger as a little boy had manifested in such a way that I was now finding ways to act out. Whether it was conscious or not, this was only the beginning of my delinquent behavior.

We didn't stay at Lincoln Avenue much longer, and my mother always swore it was because of me that we were evicted, but she probably just didn't pay the rent. The fire wasn't my last foray into violence at the Lincoln Avenue house. One day when Randy kept teasing me, calling me "Mary" and "sissy," I grabbed a pair of scissors and threw them at him. They struck him in the ankle and were sticking into his foot. He needed to go to the hospital to get stitches. Again, my father showed up to give me a hell of a beating. It seemed as if the only time my father showed up was to punish one of us. That would soon change, however, because my mother was planning to move us even further away from my dad and Fall River.

Mom finally broke away from Fall River and relocated to Providence, Rhode Island, so she could be closer to her new boyfriend, Louis Voccola, a stubborn, jealous Italian American man from Federal Hill who owned a small newspaper stand and a tobacco store downtown. Before long, my mother was pregnant with her seventh child, my half-brother David.

It wasn't far enough from my dad because, like clockwork, nearly every Sunday until the time of his death he would arrive with a box of Dunkin' Donuts and spend the day with us. That dozen donuts throughout the years became a symbol of my father's undying love for my mother. I suppose for the rest of us, too. Perhaps he felt it was the least he could do, having failed so miserably as a father and a husband. To this day, whenever I eat a Dunkin' Donuts Boston Kreme donut I think about my dad's Sunday visits.

It was 1962 and I was now six years old and in the first grade. Much to Lou's dismay, my mother had taken a job at the YMCA a short distance from our house on Colfax Street. She worked nights as cashier part time at the Y's coffee shop. My older brother Joey was an angry, moody teenager and strongly resented the fact that he now had to take care of all us when my mother was at work. It was a time when teenagers across the country were listening to Elvis, Buddy Holly, and The Beatles, so who would want to have to babysit not one, but six, younger siblings? On rare occasions, we did have an actual babysitter, but only when Del could afford it. Joey was so angry he'd turn a bit sadistic. While he resented the role of father figure, he enjoyed the immense sense of power he had over the rest of us. Fourteen going on fifteen, he was very handsome and tall for his age. Resembling young Johnny Cash, his hair was jet black and an ebony shock of curl was always dangling over his forehead. He had learned to play the guitar and sang a bit, which impressed the girls. He was so physically fit that I always felt inadequate next to him. He was physically perfect in every way.

My brother enjoyed boxing and liked to make Jeffery and me spar with his gloves. We'd often box in our underwear and T-shirts until one of us ended up in tears, usually me. I hated it. Another one of Joey's favorite games was to make us take turns standing up against the door so he could practice throwing knives at us, just like in the circus.

Joey liked the circus. He would get on all fours pretending he was an elephant. We'd hop on his back, as he'd crawl around the slippery lino-leum floor. Usually in his boxer shorts, he'd think nothing about exposing himself at any opportunity. He'd laugh and think it was funny and tell me to go ahead and get underneath him to get a good look. It was embarrass-ing, yes, but nevertheless I was curious to see what my older brothers looked like. He loved to expose himself to me and continually taunted me. He'd go as far as to shake his manhood at me and tell me to "come and suck it cause you know you want it." Was it what I wanted, really? It cer-tainly wasn't to have sex with my brother. But how did he know something I didn't? Still, I was only a child, not even a teenager.

He constantly ridiculed me for my effeminate ways and had quite a few girly names for me. Liberace was so obviously gay that he was used as a code name for fag, so my brother called me Liberace. My middle name was Neil so he called me Neil Sedaka, who was also a gay suspect. I loved Hayley Mills so he called me Hayley. Under normal circumstances, you'd think my oldest brother would be a mentor or a protector. Instead, Joey joined the ranks of a long line of perpetrators.

To this day, when he calls me once or twice a year and I hear his voice on the phone, it brings me back to those awful days. Recently during a visit and bolstered by the support of my husband, I confronted Joey about the abuse.

"I don't know what you're talking about," he said. "I never did that." As if I had made it all up.

To make matters worse, I was a smart kid who had an answer for everything. I'd challenge my mother or tell her what Joey was doing to us. But my mother rarely did anything about it. She needed a man in her life and at the time my brother Joey fit the bill just fine. She never understood how to foster a sense of closeness between her children. My parents had a habit of pitting us against one another—using one of us as an example—which only caused more bad feelings and resentment between us.

Randy, who was closest in age to Joey, managed to escape this bizarre horseplay. He was mainly off by himself and didn't need much super-vision. But Jeffery, Todd, Sheila, and I all suffered under Joey's cruel torture.

Since we shared a room, it was hard not to notice my older brothers jerking off under the sheets in their beds. And there was no way to avoid seeing them naked when they'd get in and out of the bath. Boundaries were non-existent in our home; my mom would run around in her bra and panties so the rest of my siblings would follow suit. But I instinctively felt ashamed about my body. I was already learning that some of the feelings I had were not only wrong but also sick. Moreover, I never quite measured up to the other boys in my family. As a pretty, slightly cherubic boy with long, thick eyelashes, a high-pitched voice, and a little swivel in my hips, I had everything going against me.

CHAPTER 3

Farewell Innocence

In 1963, the sight of a moving truck arriving at our new house on Stanwood Street was beyond exciting for us. We were still in the South Providence section, which was great because I could attend the same school. It was here where I would spend the best and worst of my childhood. My brothers and I roamed through the spacious empty house as the movers filled the main room with boxes. We hurried up to the second floor to stake out our bedrooms. Mom managed to save a little money and purchase a beautiful nine-room cottage with a large fenced-in backyard. It was ringed with mature lilac bushes and fruit-bearing pear trees. There were four bedrooms upstairs, a double parlor, large paneled dining room with a working fireplace, and at some point, my mother would put in an aboveground pool. Compared to our previous apartment, this place was a palace.

Now free from Louis as well as my dad, Del was seeing someone who was, like my dad, much older. His name was Charlie—we were told to call him "Uncle Charlie"—and he was a married man who lived with his wife in Somerset, Massachusetts, not far from Providence. Charlie was a successful businessman and ran his own construction company. He also was crazy about my mother, as was the case for many men. Del was naturally sexy. She had a great figure, was attractive and charming, and her smile was infectious and could warm the coolest of characters. If I had to choose which positive influence she did have on me it would've been her charm. As a trans woman, I'd inherit that as well as my own self-designed sexy figure.

School was within walking distance, allowing me to stay at the Lexington Avenue Elementary School where I was now in second grade, along with my older brother, Randy, and my younger brother, Jeffery. Our neighborhood was a mix of Italian and Irish working-class families. Directly across the street from our house was an old abandoned barn. We figured out a way to get in there. The barn door hinges rolled back and forth when you shook them and we were skinny enough to slip through. We spent hours of playtime there with other kids from the neighborhood. Away from the not-so-watchful eyes of adults, it was another place where we could feel some sense of independence, which I particularly enjoyed.

It provided another opportunity to further experiment with my sexuality. I hadn't outgrown the promiscuous and provocative nature I'd acquired earlier in childhood. In fact, now that I was a bit older I always found ways to get others to join in my experimentation. Boys weren't shy about showing off to one another, I learned. It isn't uncommon for children who were sexually abused to become promiscuous themselves at an early age and I was well on my way. There was another large family of boys a few houses up the block. I was friendly with them and had developed a crush on the oldest brother, Keith. Tall and lean with jet-black hair, he reminded me of a Jet from *West Side Story*: "When you're a Jet you're a Jet all the way, from your first cigarette to your last dyin' day." Swoon. He was much older than me. He never knew how I felt about him, but it was crystal clear to me I had no interest in girls. This was an unsettling feeling. I really didn't know why or what to do at such a young age with such feelings, and it wasn't as if someone was teaching me about them. Naively, I believed that perhaps everyone must feel this way and maybe it would change when I grew older, though never did I ever feel anyone else was like me, which contributed to the awful sense of loneliness I felt about my sexuality.

Uncle Charlie came to visit at least once a week. He'd give Randy money to take us across the street to Jerry's Spaghetti House for lunch so he could be alone with my mother. When I was older, it became my turn to take the younger kids over there as well. Of course, age brings with it a certain ability to see things as they are so I figured out what my mother was doing with Uncle Charlie. It was confusing, though, because why would my mother be having sex with someone we called Uncle? Yes, another messy idea about sex.

Moving through elementary school, I became angrier. Being raised by a single mom who had no job and living on welfare didn't seem like other kids I knew. Most had two parents and one or both of them worked. I was increasingly aware that other kids and teachers viewed our family as different. Kids were cruel and so were some of my teachers. Many things happened to me in elementary school, but I felt too embarrassed to talk about them at home.

Three incidents were integral to my already fairly skewed view of the world. The first involved a rather abusive friendship with an older kid named Louie P. A year older than me, he was a bit of a thug and was always hitting me up for my lunch money. He smoked cigarettes, which I thought was the coolest thing. He eventually taught me how to smoke. Now I was a fourth grader and he was in my class. After school, I'd go to his house and we would have sex. At first it was more experimental and then eventually he wanted me to give him blowjobs.

One afternoon as I was walking up the crowded stairwell between classes, Louie was ahead of me on the steps. When he turned around and saw me, I froze and then slowed my pace so he could get ahead of me but before I could he kicked me right in the face and I fell backwards.

"You dirty little faggot, you better come up with some money or I will be waiting for you after school," he said. All the other kids kept moving up the stairs and acted as if nothing happened. Louie just continued up the stairs laughing with his friends. I had nowhere to turn and in some strange way felt perhaps I deserved what was happening to me. It was because of how different I felt and how deeply ashamed I was because of it, so much so that I couldn't ever tell anyone about this until now.

Sometimes on Saturdays, Ma let us go to the movies, especially if she had won some extra money at the racetrack. I loved to go to downtown Providence to the Loews Theater; a grand, old movie house with an ornately decorated lobby and gilded framed floor-to-ceiling mirrors, marble floors, and pillars. One day in 1966, Randy, Jeffrey, and I were excited to see a double feature of *The Trouble with Angels* with my favorite actress at the time, Hayley Mills, and *The Ghost and Mr. Chicken* with Don Knotts from the TV show *Mayberry, R.F.D.* We filed into the theater and took our seats up in the mezzanine balcony near the concession stand and the restrooms. Halfway into the movie, I leaned over and whispered to Randy, "I have to pee."

"Go ahead. What are you telling me for?" he said. He hated these movies and thought they were faggy, but my mother made him take us because he was older than us.

In the cavernous men's room, there was a smoking lounge with large overstuffed chairs and, as you ventured further in, you passed huge marble sinks and mirrors. My footsteps echoed on the shiny black-and-white tiled floor. In the next section, there were rows of urinals and all the way in the back were six bathroom stalls. I entered one of the stalls, pulled down my pants, and sat on the toilet. As I did, I noticed there was a hole about the size of a large plum in the side of the stall. Looking down, I saw the feet of someone in the next stall. Intrigued, I leaned forward and peeked through the hole. Right away I saw a man sitting upright and stroking his dick. I immediately recoiled but was still intrigued so I took another look. He grinned and waved me over to him. I didn't know what to make of this but, A) I found it exciting because I knew it was something I probably shouldn't be doing, and B) the idea that someone was paying attention to me was key.

He leaned over to the hole and whispered, "Stand up and put your thing through the hole for me." He put his finger through the hole and rubbed it back and forth. I was terrified and thought, *what he if bites it off?*

I didn't know what oral sex felt like, but had thought about it and I knew Louie seemed to enjoy it. I was both excited and incredibly fearful.

The men's room was empty except for one other guy who had been smoking a cigarette when I walked in. I stood up, shaking a bit, and proceeded to do as the man asked. His mouth felt warm as he put my penis into his mouth. It did feel good; no wonder Louis liked it when I did it.

He stopped so I sat down again. "Why don't you come over here? It will be easier," he whispered. Little did I know just how much easier it would be. As if in slow motion, I pulled my pants up, exited my stall, and moved in front of his. The door to his stall slowly creaked open and he waved me in. I saw that the other man was still smoking. I was scared but nevertheless moved in and was excited to get my first real blowjob.

Lowering my pants, I let him take me in his mouth again. Just as I did, the other man, who had been smoking, slid up behind me and began grinding on my buttocks. This startled me, but the man on the toilet was making me feel so good I didn't seem to mind. It was only when I felt the second man rubbing himself on my butt that I began to panic. I reached down to pull my pants up but before I could the second man shoved his penis against me from behind. He clamped his hand over my mouth and whispered, "Relax, relax," as he raped me while the other man continued to go down on me. It all happened so fast I had very little time to protest; plus, the guy was bigger and stronger than a chubby ten-year-old. The dialogue from *The Trouble with Angels* faintly trickled into my head and I thought to myself, *If there really are angels, send one now, please.*

The man forcing himself into me from behind hurt me. It reminded me of the time when I was even younger and had seen my parents making love and thought that if this is what adults do for fun, I wanted no part of it. He finished with a muffled grunt and pulled up his pants and hurried away.

As painful as it was, something had happened to me and I wasn't sure what it was, but I did have a feeling of euphoria. I guess I had had my first orgasm. When the second man finished, I quickly pulled up my pants and went back to my stall. Not sure what to do next, I felt wet in my backside and reached over to grab some toilet paper to wipe myself. Seeing the blood on the paper really freaked me out. Frantically, I kept wiping, wiping, and wiping myself till eventually it disappeared.

Relieved that I wouldn't have to go to the hospital, I heard the toilet next to me flush. Then the stall door slammed, indicating that the first man had left. I heard the clicking of his heels echoing on the shiny black-and-white tile. Still trying to comprehend what happened, I sat there for a minute before returning to the mezzanine.

Taking my seat, I remained calm. I didn't want my brothers to think anything was wrong. They didn't know what happened during that Saturday matinee nor would anyone else. Watching Rosalind Russell reprimand the younger novices for smoking paled in comparison to what I had endured. It made me long for my own mother.

My secret was safe. I never told a soul. Instead, I kept it to myself and realized that this was just something that guys did with each other and, although it wasn't consensual, the rape I had experienced that day confirmed for me what I feared all along: That everything my family, teachers, and other kids were saying about me was true.

• • •

Although my harrowing experience in the men's room was extremely frightening, it didn't stop me from returning to the movie theater many times in my adolescent years. Now that I knew where to look, I discovered there were other places like the men's room in downtown Providence, and that other glory holes held the dubious distinction of being a gift and a curse. Given any opportunity, I would often find myself lingering in men's rooms much more frequently hoping to connect with others like myself.

Problems in school hadn't changed, except now I had this additional unpleasant experience to try and wrap my little immature brain around and try to make sense of. It had become increasingly difficult for me to focus in class. Other kids enjoyed my clowning around and I talked to them whenever I felt like it. I was unaware at the time, but in retrospect it's possible it was the result of the trauma I had suffered. There was a simmering inner rage within me that I never understood or knew how to express. Would any young boy? At times I would just explode and act out in a variety of different ways.

I often spent more time in the principal's office than in class. The school had contacted my mother more than once to complain and would send notes home with my report card saying, "Brian is a very angry young man. When he does apply himself, he does well," or "Brian is disruptive to the class and is not focusing on his studies." The warnings did nothing to address the more serious and confusing emotions I was experiencing at the time. And while my mother could be very intimidating, I knew how to appeal to her better nature. She would yell or threaten me, but that didn't do any good; it only encouraged me to do it more. After all, it was getting me some kind of attention, albeit negative, but attention nevertheless.

Another incident occurred one day when I was feeling particularly rambunctious. I was disruptive in class, making jokes and basically being defiant to Miss Emerjian, my homeroom teacher, who probably dreaded dealing with me as much as I did with having to be in her class. With her bright red lipstick, perfect Marlo Thomas "That Girl" flip, and pointy, rhinestone-studded eyeglasses, Miss Emerjian appealed to me, but she just didn't know how to handle me and my behavior exasperated her. As usual I was having trouble focusing on the lesson she was trying to teach. By talking loudly to other students and cracking jokes, I pulled attention toward myself. The class grew noisier because of my constant interruptions. On this particularly sunny spring day, she had had enough.

"Brian, get up and go and stand over there in the corner," she demanded. "I'm not going to put up with your foolishness anymore. Get over there until you are ready to behave like the others do!"

I felt my face turn beet red and said, "No!" And then more words flew from my lips. "Fuck you! I'm not standing in any goddamned corner and not you or anyone else is gonna make me."

The class giggled uncomfortably and now Miss Emerjian's face turned as red as mine. She raised her voice and said, "Get up from your desk and come with me out into the hallway!"

"No!" I said. I just don't know where I got the courage to say no and to become so defiant, but I did.

Next thing I knew she was darting toward me like a bullet trying to grab me by the arm. I resisted and pulled away. What happened next probably never happened in that school ever again. I got away from her as she chased me around the class. The kids were hysterical, out of control laughing. I had them on my side for once. I felt flushed, hot, and so incredibly angry and embarrassed that this was happening. Yet again I felt that it was because of how conflicted I felt about my home situation and my inability to express how incredibly unhappy I was. I felt hotter and hotter and Miss Emerjian could not catch me as I ran around the perimeter of the class. Now I began to knock over empty chairs and desks and shove books to the floor. I was totally out of control as I felt tears falling over my flushed cheeks.

At this moment, all the anguish and sadness I had held inside for so long had become overwhelming. It was finally bubbling to the surface and I couldn't stop it. I was swearing at Miss Emerjian, saying, "I don't fucking care what you or anyone else wants me to do, I will not stop." She left the room to find the principal. As she did, I grabbed the closest chair, lifted it up and hurled it through the classroom window. Just as I did, the principal came through the door and scooped me up from behind, dragging me from the room.

He hauled me down to his office and made me calm down. "You are in some serious trouble, young man," he said. "I'm going to call your mother to come and get you. Stay here and do not move until I get back."

As soon as he left and I knew he was out of sight, I bolted from his office. I ran out of the building and started to get as far away from the school as I could. With tears falling down my chubby cheeks, I just couldn't stop crying. Not knowing where to go, I began walking through South Providence toward Highway 95. I don't know why or how I came to the decision, but somehow I was headed in the direction of Fall River, Massachusetts, and I knew the way by heart. I became convinced that my father would rescue me. He would be able to comfort me in some way. I didn't know how but instinctually I felt that maybe, just maybe for once someone would actually take the time to find out what was wrong with me.

As I made my way onto the highway, cars whizzed by with a deafening sound. It was as if I were invisible. No one paid any attention to me as I made my way over the bridge and toward East Providence, then into Seekonk, Massachusetts. Walking and walking for hours, the sun shining, I busied myself by noticing the discarded things along the roadside, like cigarette butts and candy wrappers. My stomach began to rumble and I didn't know when I would eat again. Fumbling in my pockets, I found a single stick of Juicy Fruit gum, which would have to do.

Soon it was getting darker and I had already made my way to Swansea, Massachusetts, which was at least ten miles away from Providence. I wondered if my mother had noticed that I hadn't come home from school. Dinner was probably on the table by now. But I couldn't think of that because it only made me hungrier. I had to keep moving if I wanted to be in Fall River in no time. Funny and strange that no one ever pulled over to ask where I was going. Or if I was lost or if I needed a ride. Not that I wanted one. Just ahead, I saw a rest area and thought I would get off the highway for a bit. In the distance, I could see a restroom. Perhaps I could get some water as I was very thirsty and hunger was tapping on my empty belly. I had been walking for so long that I had lost all sense of time.

As I approached the restroom, I noticed a car pulling into the rest area. All I could see where headlights, not the car, since darkness had arrived. It rolled up next to me and I saw the emblem of the Swansea Police on the door. A fucking police car! Unaware of what was happening, I didn't realize how my situation appeared to the cop. I knew that I didn't want anyone to interrupt my trek to Fall River, let alone a cop.

The officer rolled down his window and asked, "What are you doing out here all by yourself, young man? Are you headed somewhere?"

"I'm on my way to my father's house in Fall River."

"Why don't you hop in and I'll give you a ride the rest of the way?"
Did I really have a choice? If I ran, he could certainly outrun me or maybe

even shoot me like on TV. So I obliged and decided to let the police officer take me to my father. Soon everything would be all right.

I got into the police car and told him my name and my dad's address. He brought me to the police station and gave me some chocolate milk and cookies while he called my father. Before I knew it, my father walked in. Relieved and happy to see him, I watched him sign some papers as he told me to "go outside and wait in the car" which I did. His big Oldsmobile was parked right at the entrance. I jumped in, giddy to be sprung from my first run-in with the law.

Soon my dad stormed out of the station. His ever-present cigar dangling from his lips, he opened the car door and slid into his seat. I felt safe at last and hoped he would take me back to Fall River with him.

He reached over and smacked me so hard in the face that my head slammed into the car window. "Jesus Christ, Brian, what the hell is wrong with you? Didn't I tell you not to keep giving your mother a hard time? The school called her and told her they kicked you out. Wait till I get you home, you little son of a bitch!"

My face stung as tears began to fall. My disappointment overwhelmed me. How could I ever tell my father what had really happened to me? How badly I was treated at school? Not only did other kids make fun of me but the teachers mistreated me as well. I could never tell him what happened to me at the movie theater; he would only become angrier and hate me more than I felt he already did at that moment.

Silent, I cowered close to the car door and feared that this was not the last smack that was going to come.

"Do you think I have nothing better to do than come and get you at a police station in Swansea, boy?" Still silence.

Once we turned on the highway, I knew where we were headed: back to Providence and my house on Stanwood Street. In what seemed like an eternal ride from hell, we finally got to the house. Bounding out of the car, I ran up the porch steps and upstairs to my bedroom. I had no idea what was going to happen next. I could hear my parents arguing downstairs and then I heard my father's heavy footsteps slowly creeping toward my room and knew I was really in for it. Rolling off my bed where I had been crying in the dark I crawled under the bed. The lights were out and my father called out for me when he entered the room. "Where are you, Brian? Come out from under there!"

He got down on the floor, reached under the bed, and dragged me out. He held a large rubber hose that he must have retrieved from the back seat of his car. He began to hit me mercilessly.

I screamed and begged, "Daddy, please. Please don't hit me. I'm sorry. I really am. I promise I will never do anything like that again!"

His hand with the hose came crashing down. I was screaming so loud, it's a wonder the neighbors didn't call the police. He didn't stop after the first blow. Hitting me again, he whacked across my back, my legs, wherever he could, all the time yelling at me and telling me how I was "good for nothing but trouble" and if I ever did anything like this again I was going to be sent away.

The beating continued until finally my mother came running up the stairs and got him to stop. I cried and cried and rocked myself to sleep. All I was seeking was comfort, I thought to myself, some care for me from what had been a traumatic experience. What I got instead was a brutal beating. This was another scar, a deep emotional wound that would take nearly a lifetime to heal. The next day the local newspaper ran a story. The headline read: BOY, TEN, RUNS AWAY TO FIND DAD.

CHAPTER 4
Bullying and Friendship

Though I remained sore from the beating with the hose for weeks, eventually things got back to normal, whatever that was. I made it through the rest of elementary school dodging any more serious outbursts and managed to get passable grades. While I was never a straight "A" student, I was certainly capable if I applied myself. All my teachers through the years had basically said the same thing. Soon I would be going to junior high and entering the seventh grade. Gilbert Stuart Junior High School was just a few blocks away from our house and my brother Randy was already enrolled there.

As fate would have it, I had Randy's former teacher Mr. Greenstein. Tall, handsome, and with a square jaw, he had thick red hair and a deep, commanding voice. I daydreamed about what it would be like to have him holding me. I fantasized about many of my male teachers. All kids must go through this, I thought. However, if I was having thoughts like this perhaps there must have been some mistake about my gender. Maybe I wasn't a boy at all? Maybe what everyone had been saying all along was true. In junior high, I began to question my attraction to men in an entirely different way: *If I'm attracted to men, then perhaps I really am supposed to be the opposite gender?* Christine Jorgenson had recently been in the news—she was the first American male-to-female sex change—so I knew changing my gender was possible. Secretly, I checked her autobiography out from the library.

Unsurprisingly, Mr. Greenstein was uncomfortable with my effeminate ways. He was yet another macho teacher who found anything that was the slightest bit different appalling. Often, he'd single me out and ridicule me in front of the class. By this time, I had gotten used to it and had developed a thick skin. Defiance was becoming more of a comfortable character trait. My voice was high and I began to let my curly hair grow long, mostly to protest my father's insistent nagging to get a haircut. It was 1969. I was thirteen. The Woodstock era had arrived, and it was all about being free. Rebelling was the new normal.

During this time, I had developed severe bronchitis and was receiving allergy shots on a weekly basis, which made me ineligible for gym class. This was a great relief as I was becoming increasingly embarrassed in the locker-room. Staring at other boys too long could be a problem. Besides, I felt insecure about my own still chubby and developing body.

My health excuse enabled me to sit in the library where I not only found a safe haven with books, but was also introduced to Mrs. Wholey, the school librarian. A gentle soul with silver hair, sparkling blue eyes, and a melodious, soothing voice, she had taken a special liking to me and taught me all about the library and how it worked. Soon, I was her pet project and she would let me sit at the front desk and check books in and out for other students. There I was front and center for the first time.

Mrs. Wholey often told me stories about her son Dennis, who had his own radio show in New York City. Watching her beam with pride whenever she spoke of Dennis made me glad to know that such strong love between a mother and a son existed in the world. How different my life might have been had my mother taken a modicum of pride in me. Mrs. Wholey was instrumental in securing my first after school job as a page at the local library. For the first time in my young adult life, I felt worthwhile and as if I had something of value to do. While many of the messages and signals I received from others had been negative, it was Mrs. Wholey who viewed me as someone who had intelligence, initiative, and a willingness to succeed. She never had any idea of what an impact she made on my life at a time when there was nothing but chaos and incredible confusion.

Many years later, I corresponded with her son, Dennis Wholey, who had become a TV talk show host and a successful author, ironically enough of self-help books. I wrote to him explaining how important his mother was to me and how grateful and lucky I was to have been affected by her interest in me at the time. He and his family were so moved and thankful to hear from me, as Mrs. Wholey had recently passed.

My position as a library page provided another temporary refuge, although the woman for whom I worked, Mrs. Turner, wasn't nearly as nice as Mrs. Wholey. In fact, she could be a real bitch. Critical and controlling, she thought nothing of calling attention to any mistake I made. One day she herself made the same mistake as Mrs. Emerjian did back in the fifth grade and I reacted very badly, basically telling her she could go fuck herself and stick the job up her ass. She was shocked, to say the least, and saw to it that I was never to return and actually had me banned from the library.

On the way to and from Gilbert Stuart Junior High, I'd pass the Peter Pan Diner, one of those really cool fifties diners filled with stainless steel, neon, and mirrors. Soon I became aware that it was a gathering place for some of the more colorful characters of the neighborhood, including a small group of queens and trans women who would go there regularly. One of the queens, Monica Nunez, was a striking redhead of Cuban descent that resembled a young Faye Dunaway. I later learned she was the rival of every queen in Providence because she was so "real" looking. I knew this because one day my older brother Joey pointed her out when we were walking along the avenue.

"Brian, see those girls over there across the street?" he said, pointing to a gaggle of three suspiciously tall women from afar. "One day, if you're not careful, you'll end up like them." He laughed as he said this.

"What do you mean *like them*?" I asked.

"The pretty one with the red hair, that's Monica. She used to be David."

It was fascinating that this spontaneous lesson I was receiving about trans women was coming from my older brother. He wasn't typically so forthcoming about teaching me anything. Nonetheless, I couldn't help wondering what it must be like to be a different gender. I remember thinking to myself; *Imagine no one knowing what you really are.* While I'm sure Joe didn't want me to go down the path of gender transition, and the little lesson or observation was cautionary in nature, I think he realized that his instincts were correct about how my life was developing.

"Really," I said. "And how did you become such an expert?"

"They all hang out downtown at the Homestead Bar where me and my buddies shoot pool. She gives some of the guys great head."

What he neglected to tell me was that he was part of the group of guys who'd have sex with Monica. Many years later, Monica would boast to me about having sex with all of my brothers at some point. It was almost a rite of passage, and she referred to them as "trade," which I learned early on was a straight guy who didn't mind getting off with a drag queen or a trans woman. You see, even straight guys are not as binary as one would believe. No men were more heterosexual than my majorly macho brothers! Now that I was a teenager myself, it became clearer to them that I was going to be different.

Joe never let up with his constant ribbing and was certain that one day I was going to be trans. How he knew it was beyond me, but he was certainly prophetic. The idea that I could become like Monica or these other trans women terrified me. On several occasions when heading home from school with a group of the neighborhood boys, we bullied the queens, calling them names and even throwing rocks at them in the same way kids would one day do to me. We'd do this until they attempted to give chase and then we'd run.

In my late teens, I came to know all of these "girls" personally. Some would become mentors and lifelong friends. They loved to remind me about being "Cowboy Joe's" little sissy brother. Cowboy Joe was a nickname my brother had because he was trying to be a country western singer, something he had a lot of talent for but, like me, lacked confidence and nurturing to succeed in what he loved to do.

And don't think they forgot about the name-calling and the rock-throwing I did. I was never able to live it down.

• • •

The end of the school year was soon approaching and I had made friends with several girls in my class. It seems that the girls were more accepting of me and less critical than the boys I had tried to befriend. Most were African American, tough girls who didn't put up with any bullshit, and we bonded over our mutual love of Motown and R&B music. They invited me to hang out with them after school and we'd play forty-fives on the porch and dance. I loved music and it became another way to find solace. *American Bandstand* and *Soul Train* were two main staples of my TV diet. The girls loved my dancing. Being a white boy having a real natural rhythm was my saving grace!

One day on the last Friday before graduation, I was standing in line in the cafeteria getting lunch with two of my closest friends Lorna and Sharon, when a kid named Robert Smith came up to me.

"Hey, faggot, hanging with the girls again?" he said. I never found this kid particularly threatening because he was kind of scrawny and weasel-like, but he was always making some smart comment whenever he saw me in the hallways with my female friends.

Lorna turned to me. "Brian, you can't let him talk to you like that!"

Sharon piped in too. "Are you just gonna stand there and let him get away with that?"

Next, Lorna got right up in his face and said, "Leave him alone. He ain't bothering you!"

By this time, I had had it with the little runt, too, and I wasn't going to put up with his bullshit anymore. Soon I'd be off to high school and if I didn't stand up for myself now, I never would. Taking a deep breath, I stepped out of line and took a swing at him. I then grabbed him by the neck and wrestled him to the ground.

Soon a crowd gathered. He got loose and I chased him around a cafeteria table.

I couldn't reach him so I flipped the cafeteria table over onto him and was able to pin him under it.

The girls were so excited and were screaming, "Kick his fucking ass, Brian!"

Soon the principal was yanking me off of him from behind and I was struggling to break free. As I did, I took a wild swing and hit the principal by mistake.

"That's it for you, buddy," the principal said. "You're out of here for good. Get out before I call the police. And don't come back. You are expelled on the spot."

"Wait a minute!" I said. "He started the fight, not me, and he has been harassing me all year long."

"I don't care, Belovitch. Get out now or I am going to call the police!"

Any fool knows that not one but two shout-outs for police means it's time to go. I ran toward the cafeteria exit, happy that I had stood up for myself, but defeated once again since I was being viewed as the trouble-maker. And I knew I was going to be in serious trouble again when I got home.

Later, I was informed that I wouldn't graduate with the rest of my class.

Earlier that year, I had won an award for a drawing I did in art class. It was a beautiful still life in charcoal of a table and chairs on top of a desk and had been on exhibit in the main branch of the downtown library. For the first time ever, I was really proud of one of my accomplishments. When I went to retrieve the drawing and the award from the clerk in the office at Gilbert Stuart, she said, "Oh, that. I threw it out." The one occasion in my short life when I did something estimable and worthwhile, something I could really be proud of, it ended up in the garbage.

After my expulsion, Del felt she was losing more and more control over me and wouldn't let me continue to live with her. She "shipped me off" to live with my father in Fall River, where I would be entering the ninth grade. A new school, a new routine, and a new home environment wouldn't change any confusion about my sexuality or the way I was being perceived by others.

At Henry Lord Junior High School in Fall River, Massachusetts, I made friends with another boy in my homeroom that was just like me. A bit effeminate, Stephen Perry and I were naturally drawn to each other and connected on an unspoken level. The fact that we both knew what we were, although the fact that neither of us ever said we were gay, seemed to be our common bond. We lived close by and did a lot of things together. He was my first friend who didn't judge me on the way I spoke or walked or the things I was interested in. The downside was that other kids in school, mostly the jocks, would see us to together and make the usual homophobic comments. Our hunky, jock math teacher even called us "faggots" in class in front of the other students. Word spread around pretty quick, and after school one day a group of jocks from the soccer team followed me home and began calling me "faggot" and throwing rocks at me. I began walking faster and faster as I felt the rocks whiz by close to my head. I had to get away from them, but I didn't want to run. I was petrified that if they knew where I lived my father might see what was happening. My life was a living hell and I had nowhere to turn. I was in a different city, at a new school, but the same thing was happening all over again.

I took up smoking and even drinking, which provided some relief. There was a liquor store near my house from which it was easy to steal booze. Stephen would go up the counter and distract the clerk while I'd grab whatever was close to the door and run. Boone's Farm Strawberry Wine was a favorite. We'd go off into the field near our house and get really drunk. I loved the feeling immediately; alcohol enabled me to escape the horrors of my already awkward adolescence. When I was younger, my brothers and I would sneak drinks at holiday parties and get a little tipsy. But now that I was older, I drank for comfort. I loved to show off to my friends and I'd get really hammered, so much so that the room would spin and I'd throw up. Unaware of the family history of my grandfather's alcoholism, I nonchalantly viewed it as something everyone needed to go through. At the tender age of fourteen, I was completely unaware that this would begin a lifetime of experimentation with alcohol and drugs that nearly contributed to my early demise.

I remained in Fall River with my father for two years till I was sixteen. By this time, I had already found ways to meet men. Stephen and I cruised the restroom in City Hall where we found glory holes in the bathroom stalls. We had come out to each other and pretended to others we were straight. After school, we'd head downtown and those cruising spots would be our first destination. Both of us told our parents we were going to the library. Not really a lie because we were studying!

Gail Beaudry, who had been a classmate in junior high, had become what I thought was a good friend. She was a big-boned gal, tall and strong with waist-length auburn hair and piercing blue eyes. She was tough, too, and stuck up for me whenever someone bothered me. Her mother took a liking to me and often invited me to have dinner with them at their home on Rodman Street in the Watuppa Heights projects. I think she felt bad for me because my parents were divorced. Gail would sometimes accompany me to Rhode Island on weekends to visit my mother. It was a welcome change for her to get out of Fall River. Ironically, I introduced her to my brother Randy and eventually they dated, fell in love, married, and had two beautiful sons—and I would no longer be included in their newfound happiness.

CHAPTER 5
Runaway

The day finally arrived when I could leave Fall River behind. It wasn't easy convincing my mother but soon I was enrolled in Central High School. Excited to be back in Providence and now in my sophomore year, I was planning to graduate the following year and be done with it, or so I thought. Times were tough at Central High because the climate in Providence was very volatile. It was the early 1970s and there were race riots between the white Italians in Federal Hill and the blacks in South Providence, where we lived. Resentment hung thick. You could feel it as you strolled the hallways of Central High. Everyone was on edge, including me.

By now I was more aware of my sexual impulses and the changes that were taking place within my body. I met another gay boy named Roger Root in a barbering class I was taking. Being openly gay in 1972 was not only dangerous, but also pretty amazing and I admired Roger's courage, which gave me some hope that one day I might be as comfortable in my own skin. Roger was a bit of a rogue and knew all about the gay scene. He had no problem sharing all his knowledge with me. Roger was tall and lean with long shoulder-length hair and had a very sharp wit, which I loved. He was scrappy and wasn't afraid to be confrontational, which I admired. My introduction to the downtown gay scene came courtesy of Mr. Root, as we would frequently skip school and hang out in downtown Providence.

The train station downtown was a notorious gay cruising spot fully equipped with several glory holes in the men's room. Roger was a pothead and introduced me to smoking marijuana. If we needed money for it, he had a way to do that as well. There was a park across from the train station that had become a local cruising area for gay men. Older gay men would drive by in their cars and Roger told me how I could make some extra cash if I wanted to. "The number one rule is to get the money first," he said. "Also make sure you ask them if they're a cop."

Hustling came easy to me. I became good at it. I was honest, cute, young, and eager to please. Besides, when did I ever receive this kind of attention anywhere else? It was encouraging in a bad way. These brief encounters, often in parked cars or in some dark alley, made me feel I was cared for, even if it was temporary. I felt some odd closeness to each of these strangers even though I would rarely see them again.

Roger Root was also a fast-talker and a bit of a con artist. He had quite an assortment of friends, including the other boys who were hustling at the train station and some transvestites. Before long, I would be meeting other boys who had become girls.

One day, Roger convinced me to go with him to some secret place he knew of. He led me down below the train station through a series of stairwells and ladders to a room with cardboard on the floor and the sound of a very large boiler blasting nearby. It looked like this was going to be the first time I would have sex with another boy, rather than a trick. He lit a nearby candle and took a joint out of his pocket. We took a few hits and began having sex. It really wasn't at all what I expected. We didn't even kiss and, again, I was on the bottom and thought this was becoming a habit as he fumbled trying to enter me.

"Ouch!" I yelled. "What the hell are you doing?"

"Shhh. We can't get caught down here," he whispered. "Just relax."

I did relax and in fact it was over quite soon. However, I felt happy that he found me attractive enough and wanted to be with me in this way. Now I was certain that Roger and I would be together—at least for that day anyway. With him you just never knew.

It was getting dark outside and he said he wanted to take me to another secret place. At first I was concerned because with him you never knew what he was up to.

"How would you like to go to the Fife and Drum?"

"The Fife and Drum. Is that a music store?"

He laughed and shook his head. "No, it's a gay bar over on Weybosset and Dorrance Street." So off we went into the heart of downtown Providence.

From the exterior, it resembled any other local bar. Of course, Roger knew the man at the door—heavyset with a dark mustache and a hairy chest, wearing a leather cap, jeans, and a tank top that exposed his muscular tattooed arms. Roger embraced the man and quickly handed him a ten-dollar bill.

The doorman said, "Wait a minute, man, he legal?"

"Oh yeah, for sure, for sure," Roger exclaimed.

The doorman looked at me and said, "You got any ID, kid?"

But before I could answer, Roger called out to a beautiful blond boy who was zipping by with a drink in his hand. "Hey, Paulie, can you help us out here?" Roger pointed with an exasperated expression to the guy at the door. The boy came over and whispered something into the doorman's ear and, like magic, he waved us in.

Inside was overwhelming, with cigarette smoke heavy in the air and the strong odor of spilled beer wafting up my nostrils. Squeezing past the crowded bar, I encountered the intoxicating mix of various men's cologne with beer and smoke. The music was loud and the bar was packed with men of every size, shape, and color. Men were hanging onto one another, some were engaged in conversation, and others were actually making out.

"You can close your mouth now, Brian," Roger said, looking at me sharply.

The boy he had called came over to us. Roger hugged him and gave him a peck on both cheeks.

"I'm Paul Bricker, everyone calls me Paulie," he said. "Pleasure to meet you. Care for a drink?" He was wearing a cool vintage Hawaiian shirt, bunched up and tied at his navel like a woman would do, and cut-off shorts that were so scandalously short that when he turned around parts of his hairy butt cheeks poked out. The shoes he wore added a few extra inches in height from the platform soles, which at the time were all the rage. His hair was close cropped and he had a little dyed orange tail at the nape of his neck.

"Sure, um, I'll have one of those," I said, pointing to his glass. I had no idea what he was drinking but didn't want to appear naive.

Roger wandered off and started talking to some other boy while Paulie fetched me a drink from the bartender. Over the sound system, I heard the first few beats of Diana Ross's hit song "Surrender": *I want the love that you deny me, that I need so desperately, the tenderness you possess, you've deprived me.*

"Oh, my God, I love this song!" I squealed to Paulie as he handed me my drink.

"Well, come on then, let's dance!" Paulie said, grabbing my arm and leading me to the dance floor. Scanning the dance floor, I couldn't believe that men were dancing with other men! At first a familiar feeling of awkwardness tried to trip me up—I had never danced with another guy before—but soon the sweet, comforting sound of my idol Miss Ross singing "Surrender" made everything right in my world.

"By the way," I asked, as we were dancing, "what did you say to the big guy at the door?"

"I told him you were a guest of Bill White," said Paulie.

"Who's that?"

"He's over there," he said, pointing beyond the dance floor to an attractive, older African American man sitting at a piano tinkling the ivories. "He's my lover!"

Pretty cool, I thought. Here it was my first time in a gay bar and already I was meeting the right people. Lucky me. Leave it to Roger, who had drifted off into a corner where he was now making out with someone else. I shrugged it off and thought this was the way boys treated each other. I just kept on dancing, resisting the rejected feeling washing over me and instead enjoyed the moment, the music, and my newfound friend, Paulie, not thinking too much about where I was going or with whom.

Nothing in my sixteen years could have ever prepared me for Paul Evan Bricker. He was by far the most fascinating person I had ever met; he had an amazingly curious mind, was very intelligent, and had a keen sense of humor. A middle-class kid of Russian and Swedish descent, he lived with his mother in a really good part of town on Woodbine Street. (I learned later that his father had committed suicide.) His blond curly hair framed his wholesome face. He had an infectious smile, beautiful full lips, and the bluest twinkling eyes that I swear sparkled when he smiled. His nose was keen, short, and upturned, impish. Never before had I met anyone with so much self-confidence. So sure of himself was he that he too was openly gay and didn't care who knew it.

Good fortune had been in my favor that fateful day that I met Paulie, because from that moment on my life was to change in ways I could never have imagined, with him there for me every step of the way. He would expose me to the better things in life, which, quite possibly, I may never have known had we not met. Fast friends, we became inseparable. Born on May 25, Paulie was a Gemini in every sense of the word and I might have been his long-lost twin. I observed him in action time and time again and I learned a great deal about acceptance from him. Paulie believed in me and saw in me something I had no idea existed.

I soon took Paulie home to meet my family. Del had a million questions about this "Paul kid," so I thought this would be the perfect time for her to meet him. We ambled up the porch steps and entered the kitchen where she was sitting at the table playing solitaire. I heard Jeffery and his friends watching TV in the living room.

"Hey, Ma. This is my friend Paulie, who I told you about," I proudly exclaimed.

The look on Del's face was priceless. She seemed shocked by his obvious gayness but was gracious and didn't let on about her obvious disgust.

"Nice to meet you, Mrs. Belovitch. I've heard so much about you."

"Those are some really high shoes you're wearing," she said, looking down at his red platform shoes and not quite believing he would wear them.

"They're really comfortable. I bought them in New York last time I was there."

Not knowing what to say next, Ma just smiled, rolled her eyes, and went back into the kitchen. Paulie said he'd better be heading home since he had school early in the morning. We stuck our heads into the living room and I introduced him to Jeffrey and his friends. Clearly, they didn't know what to make of any it and looked like they were suppressing adolescent giggles.

"Nice to meet you all. I'll see you soon, Brian," he said, leaving the house.

Once Paulie was gone, Del flew into a rage, calling him a queer and a cocksucker. "Are you taking it up the ass like him, too?" she screamed in fury at me. Her reaction devastated me, so cruel and hateful. I was her son, for God's sake. I heard Jeffery and the Anders brothers laughing their asses off in the living room.

"Since when did you ever know what was good for me?" I screamed at her. I couldn't understand her hatred. Well, if she hated what Paulie was so vehemently, then deep down she must truly hate me, I figured. I stormed upstairs to my bedroom while Del continued to yell and threaten me.

I tried to block it out but finally couldn't take it anymore. Running down the hall, I screamed from the top of the stairs, "Alright, Ma, you're right. You're fucking right about everything and you are right about me, too! I'm a fucking fag, a queer, and a cocksucker. That's right, Ma! That's what I am and I don't even give a fuck who knows it!"

Not the best coming out experience, for sure. It was like pouring gasoline on flames.

Del charged up the stairs, infuriated about the truth I had just let fly from my lips. She held her wooden broomstick fiercely and chased me down the hallway. I tried slamming my door but she burst into my room and broke that broomstick across my back. But that didn't stop her from continuing to beat the shit out of me the same way my father had done after collecting me at the police station when I was ten. In my family, when something terrified or challenged you, you used your fists, scissors, sticks, shoes, hoses, and dishes—whatever was in close proximity. Talking, listening, or trying to reason was never one of the family's strong points. But what she, my father, and others didn't realize was that no amount of physical violence was going to change the path on which I was already set to embark. They couldn't beat the gay out of me. Even though they tried so very hard time and time again to do just that.

After this incident, I knew I had to get away. Although I was sixteen going on thirty, I knew I had to leave. Without knowing where I was going to go, I knew the least I could do was call Paulie. Later that night, when my mother was asleep, I slipped out the second-floor window onto the balcony and shimmied down the drainpipe and ran as fast and as far away as I could, with a little packed bag in hand. Calling Paulie from a telephone booth, I explained everything that had happened and he agreed to meet me downtown at the Fife and Drum.

"Jesus Christ, look at you. Your mother beat you like that?" he asked in disbelief as soon as I arrived at the bar. I broke down and confided in him about some of the other things that happened and he was shocked. He had never had an experience like mine and was incredibly sympathetic. After a few drinks, he assured me I shouldn't worry and invited me to stay at his house for the night.

Paulie's house on Woodbine Street was one of those spacious New England triple-deckers. His brother, Dennis, and Dennis's wife, Bessie, lived on the third floor, Bessie's parents on the second, and his mom, Gloria, on the first floor with her soon-to-be new husband, Stanley Walker. Gloria's apartment was beautifully decorated, with a red, white, and black living room that looked like something from a magazine. She had once worked as an interior decorator and clearly she knew her stuff.

Paulie had spoken highly of his mom, but I had no idea what to expect and was nervous because I was still reeling from my situation. We walked in and Gloria came to greet us. I saw the resemblance immediately. Like

Paulie, she was blonde, blue-eyed, and very beautiful. She wore her hair in a pageboy with bangs, and sitting on her perfect little nose were what would become her signature oversized red-framed glasses.

"This is my good friend Brian Belovitch, and he's going to stay with us," Paulie announced.

Gloria motioned for me to sit on the sofa and was comforting as she listened to me describe my situation. Here I was, in the presence of a mother and her son where there was true admiration, love, respect, and acceptance. It was an honor to be with them as they opened their home to me and made me feel wanted and accepted. It was a hopeful lesson for sure, so much so that I began to cry as I continued to recount the sordid tale of my home life.

Gloria came over and sat by me, hugged me, and told me that everything was going to be all right, that eventually my family would come around. "It may take a while but not to worry, they will." She said I reminded her of a teddy bear, with my big, brown eyes and curly dark hair, and from that day on whenever she asked Paulie about me, she'd say, "How's my little teddy bear?"

Staying with Paulie and Gloria was an act of divine providence, in Providence. There was never any pressure for me to leave; Gloria only asked if I could try to contact my mother. Whenever I did call Del, she'd hang up on me, click, just like that. Nearly sixteen, dropping out of school was inevitable, so I did. It was impossible for me to continue. Having had a brief experience of gay life, knowing there were others just like me, I couldn't bear to go back to high school. Shepard's Department Store downtown was hiring so I got a part-time job in the men's department to make money.

A year older than me, Paulie would soon be graduating from a nearby prep school so we began thinking about getting our own place. We found a small studio sublet in Providence's historic East Side that was walking distance to the Rhode Island School of Design and Brown University and close to downtown, where we spent most of our time. Paulie had enough money from his graduation and I was able to contribute what I made from my job at Shepard's.

My mother and my kid sister Sheila walked into Shepard's one day and I could see they were surprised to find me working there. Del and I still weren't speaking, and I heard her speaking really loudly to my sister.

"Hey, Sheila, look over there at your fag brother. He's dyed his hair, too."

Had she really said something so cutting? To her credit, Paulie and I had been experimenting with bleach so she couldn't help but notice that my hair was now a hideous shade of red. One of the other fun things about Paulie was that he liked to dress up in drag. He had thinned his eyebrows and soon after moving in with him, I did the same, which of course Del couldn't help but notice. "Look, Sheila, he's even plucking his eyebrows!"

From the stares of other customers who could hear her taunts, she was making a bit of a commotion. Before it escalated any further, I ran back into the stockroom and hoped they'd just go away. I slumped down into a pile of boxes of men's shirts and a heavy sadness began to envelop me.

Feeling too ashamed to return to the floor because I was certain my manager had overheard some of the comments, I sat in the dark stockroom devastated and not knowing what to do. Shortly after, I quit the job at Shepard's; I feared a repeat of that day's performance. There were plenty of jobs on the East Side by College Hill. Not long after, I did get another one as a busboy at IHOP on Thayer Street.

I knew of an easier way to make money and, for sure, life was about to take yet another interesting twist, one that not only caught me by surprise but also would forever alter the feelings I had about who and what I was.

CHAPTER 6

Lola

After graduating from his fancy prep school, Paulie had plans to attend beauty school. Inspired by Gloria's work as a makeup artist, he possessed a natural talent for making others look and feel better about themselves. It was a natural fit for him. And the Arthur Angelo School of Hair Design in Providence was the place to go if you were serious about a career in the beauty biz.

Hanging out downtown one day, we bumped into a striking woman with a smooth caramel complexion and a large red Afro. This was Paulie's friend Rusty, and he was asking her for advice on how to sew an outfit he was designing for the opening of a new gay disco called The Gallery. While they spoke, I admired Rusty's appearance. Wearing jeans and a cute camel hair coat, she wore very little makeup, just a touch of mascara, blush, and lipstick. Her glasses were like the type my fifth-grade teacher, Miss Emerjian, wore—cat eye with rhinestones—except on Rusty they made the wearer appear wise and inquisitive.

I overheard Rusty say that she lived in the Lola Apartments. I recognized the name because the apartment building was right across the street from my high school and Roger and I would sometimes sit on a bench and watch the drag queens running in and out of the beauty salon on the building's ground floor. Hearing Rusty speak of the Lola, I now put two and two together and "spooked" or "clocked" her as trans, to utilize language we used back then to determine whether someone was passing as a female or not. The high-pitched nasal tone to Rusty's voice confirmed to me that she was assigned male at birth. Passing was the holy grail for most trans people back in the day, because it meant that you could move through life a little more easily. It was incredibly brave that she was out in broad daylight as if it was the most natural thing for anyone to do. And of course it was!

The next day, Paulie and I made our way to the infamous Lola apartment building to see Rusty, who lived on the third floor. She was an excellent seamstress and did many small jobs for other queens at the Lola, which really came in handy when tricks were slow. The Lola was a well-known destination for men who liked girls of a certain persuasion. Some of the queens had day jobs as men but dressed in drag at night; others weren't as fortunate and had to rely on sex work.

Our visit that day was so she could help Paulie with the outfit he was making for The Gallery opening. I was very excited because this was going to be one of the biggest clubs Providence had ever seen. It would also be my debut of sorts. Paulie and I scored some really cool material at Pilgrim Mills, an old fabric store from the forties that still existed on North Main Street. While the salesman rang up some beautiful baby blue peau de soie satin, I managed to mop an entire bolt of red-and-white polka dot fabric. If I couldn't afford it and it wasn't nailed down, it was mine.

We rang Rusty's doorbell which elicited loud barking from her German Shepherd, Bambi, a beast of a dog who Rusty kept for protection from any shady tricks. Once Bambi let you into the apartment, it was hard to leave without her growling and baring her fangs. Rusty had to put her in the bedroom until we left.

Paulie was unsure on how to work with our new fabric, so he wanted Rusty's opinion before cutting into it. Rusty knew exactly what Paulie needed to do and we left feeling confident that our outfits would turn out just the way we envisioned. The opening was Saturday and we had little time to pull it together. Once back in our apartment, fabric flew everywhere as we started to get to work.

The Lola had made a big impression on me. Like the experience I had when entering the Fife and Drum, I had found another aspect of the gay world, only this time it seemed to be more of what I truly needed. It was the perfect place for me to educate myself on the ways of a new possible life for me as I began considering the idea of changing my gender identity. Rusty soon became an incredible mentor, and I would find my way back to the Lola many times and often got dressed in Rusty's apartment before going out to work the block. There was even a place behind the building where you could pull tricks in and bring them through the back entrance quickly before the cops drove by. I was young, pretty, and made money fairly easily, although it wasn't without its share of dangerous implications.

The first time I turned a trick in drag some guy picked me up on the corner of the Lola. He was handsome, dark, and a bit of a bruiser. I tried to get him to pull into the back of the building where it was more convenient but he resisted and instead drove me over to the Silver Lake section of the city, where there was a wooded area where kids would drink or get stoned. He had agreed to pay me a whopping ten dollars initially. When he turned off the car and started to pull his pants down, I asked, as any good whore would, "Can you pay me first?" He said, "Sure," as he reached down under his seat and whipped out a gun. He made me suck him off for free while holding the gun to my head. It was one of the most terrifying blowjobs I ever gave.

The Gallery opening was a life-changing event for me. It was the first time I was going out in full drag. I had done semi-drag, where I'd dress androgynously by carrying a purse or wearing a little mascara or even an article or two of girl's clothing, but I had never donned full female attire. Paulie and I were a great team when it came to details. He had the ability to turn a bolt of baby blue satin into a halter-top and make pants out of the same fabric in white. The waist was very high and thick, almost like a cummerbund, which accentuated his tiny waist. I wore a red-and-white striped halter with the same high waist red-and-white polka dot pants. I borrowed a pair of awesome five-inch red Goody Two Shoes that Paulie had bought in New York; luckily, we wore the same size. We both wore our own short hair and made jewelry to match. Cleverly, he covered button earrings with scraps of extra fabric.

Living on the East Side put us smack dab in the middle of one of the most creatively vibrant areas of the city. Living near RISD, we made friends with a number of RISD and Brown students. Two particularly fabulous friends lived one building over on our block. Jane, a design student at RISD from Brooklyn, was a zaftig young woman of Russian descent with a knock out style sense. Channeling silent film stars like Gloria Swanson and Theda Bara, she lived for the 1920s and 30s. Her ambition was to become a hat designer. Her current boyfriend was this upper middle-class effete kid with long, curly, frizzy hair that draped well past his shoulders. Steven majored in photography and asked me to model for him, which instilled in me a badly needed boost of confidence. He created some strikingly beautiful images of me that I treasure to this day. Steven later became one of the most accomplished and talented photographers of our time. When I look at those photos, I recall how I had never felt more beautiful than the day I posed for him. On the night of the opening, Jane loaned me a bright, large-brimmed red hat, which completed my outfit.

The four of us headed to the club together, making quite an entrance. Though I was barely seventeen, no one bothered to check for an ID. Breezing through the crowd, we made our way out onto the jam-packed dance floor bogeying to Stevie Wonder's "Superstitious." Feeling free and beautiful for the first time in my very young life, I was overwhelmed by all the attention and compliments. I loved it and was instantly hooked on all the adoration.

At one point in the evening, a very tall black man in a fabulous dashiki came over to me, furiously flapping an intricate lace fan. "Darling," he swooned in a robust James Earl Jones voice, "You look like you stepped right out of some fabulous 1940s movie. Gorgeous! You're just turning it out, girl!"

Turning it out? This was a new phrase for me, but I could easily apply it to him as well. This fellow was none other than André Leon Talley, the long-time arbiter of fashion as a director at *Vogue*. Even back then he had great taste and I knew one day he would go far.

Another frequent Gallery guest was a very tall, slim man with a beautiful and theatrical voice named Jimmy Eichelberger who worked as an actor at Trinity Repertory Company. Running into us at the club, Jimmy recognized our flair for the theatrical and appreciated our youthful style and openness about our sexuality, which in Rhode Island was a radical act. Jimmy would hightail it out of Rhode Island and land in New York as well.

At the dawn of the disco era, in those early days I was beginning to feel a stronger desire to alter my identity. The decision to begin transitioning to the opposite sex was one of great joy, but it also came with an incredible sense of reckless apprehension. The excitement I felt was tempered with a healthy dose of skepticism that I was unable to express to anyone. This was coupled with an unbearable amount of sadness from the rejection that I knew I would ultimately experience. Still, I wasn't able to change the course I had charted for myself. I had this uncontrollable desire to fit in and if it meant changing my gender to do so, then so be it.

As a somewhat effeminate gay boy, my prospects for love were practically non-existent. Gay men of the 1970s were looking to meet other men on the more masculine end of the spectrum. Some guys might have found me attractive as a boy, but it seemed I got way more attention when I dressed in drag. It became a way for me to hide the loneliness I felt as an awkward slightly chubby young man. Sure, I found a way to have sex with other guys, but for the most part it felt that no one was ever going to want to be with me the way I was, which in retrospect was not necessarily true. However, I didn't have the maturity or the self-esteem to see any future in life as a gay man. Dressing as female caused much more of a sensation. There were a whole slew of bisexual or closeted men who preferred me in drag. What started out as a fun expression of creativity became a more serious manifestation of my wanting acceptance and approval outside of myself. I became hooked on the drug of adoration and acceptance of others for how I looked externally, but not for who I was as a person.

Approaching my eighteenth birthday, I would soon be legally able to make my own decisions. Not much could have intervened in my decision-making during this time as my mind was made up. Although I tried, I knew that the path to follow in my heart was not one of being a gay man. Adoring all the attention I was receiving, I blazed forward into a bold adventure as a person who was living at the opposite gender. And I knew just the person to help me along the way. Paulie was supportive and understood my affinity for all things female, but he never desired to change his gender; his dressing in drag was more for theatrics and fun. However, for me it unleashed years of pent-up frustration that I would now be able to release by expressing my gender as female. Becoming my own special creation was exactly what I thought I wanted to do.

Returning to the Lola Apartments provided me with a crash course in everything to do with living life as another gender. There were plenty of willing and a few not-so-willing mentors to me in those early days. Rusty was a tremendous help, freely dispersing expert information whether it was where to get the right hormones or how to pad my hips with a foam girdle. She was street savvy as well. She had quite a few regular tricks that would come visit her. I was young and hardly had regulars myself so my nights were spent tearing up the pavement in and around the Lola Apartments to make ends meet.

Eventually, I decided to join Paulie at the Arthur Angelo School of Hair Design. I wasn't sure if it was something I wanted to do, but I knew that a life of prostitution wasn't going to get me very far. During the day, I attended beauty school as an androgynous boy with eyebrows tweezed within an inch of their life. In the evening, I'd dress up and work the streets to pay my tuition. Indeed, my entire tuition was paid for with money I earned on the streets. Who says sex work is not work? As a baby trans woman, I had already earned the respect of some of the older, more seasoned girls at the Lola. They were quite impressed with my independence.

In many ways, the time I spent hanging out at the Lola was an education at best in how to survive a life that was going to be extremely challenging. There was quite an array of characters in the Lola. One of the most beautiful queens, Rhonda Jewels, was a fine-featured African American who, by day, worked as a hairdresser. In the movie *The Queen*, she's seen in the infamous scene as a contestant who consoles the furious, legendary Crystal LaBeija. She was the envy of many of the girls because of how she looked. Tall, trim, with beautiful shapely legs and exuding class and sophistication, she was the Diana Ross of drag.

Another inhabitant of the Lola was Mona Gomes, a.k.a. Bobby Gomes. She was a wiry, fast-talking hustler always looking for a way to get one over. She had a terrible pockmarked complexion, which she tried to subdue with thick Pan Stik makeup. From far away, she was stunning, but up close, scary. Her wigs were these incredible replicas of Bobbie Gentry or early Dolly Parton and she wore the shortest micro miniskirts on the street and the highest heels. Mona was a speed freak and was always blasted on black beauties, a popular upper that many of the girls used and that she turned me on to. Popping those little dolls gave me incredible stamina and confidence and allowed me to make double the ducats and work until the sun came up.

Mona could be really harsh to any newcomers to the block. She felt particularly threatened by me since I was "a young white queen." Wickedly mean and armed with a razor, she could be a formidable enemy. One night during a fight she sliced my right arm and told me to "stay away or I'll cut off your tits!" But for some reason after that, we got along and I managed to steer clear of her wrath, especially when she was drunk and doing speed, a lethal combination for sure.

There were so many other girls around; Denise, Monique Nicole, Dusty, Dee-Dee, April, Lisa, and Laverne and the gorgeous flame-haired Cuban, Monica, from the Peter Pan Diner. Monica Nunez was hard to clock and, like Rusty, dressed as a woman and had passing privileges twenty-four seven. Being naive to the difference between a transvestite and a transsexual, I would soon come to understand the animosity that developed between these two close but very different groups within our small community.

One Saturday evening, a group of us headed downtown to the Loews Theater to see the film "Cabaret," starring Liza Minnelli. Paulie, Rusty, Monique (a.k.a. Danny Shanley, a feisty, freckle-faced tough Irish queen), Nicole (a.k.a. Kenny who was about six foot two, tall, lean, and was convinced she looked like Naomi Sims, the popular supermodel of the day), and I convened on the corner next to the Lola and began strutting down Broad Street to the movie theater. It was quite a scene to see this gaggle of cross-dressed girls sashaying their way downtown. Cars honked their horns and some nasty boys yelled "faggots," but we loved the attention and blew kisses to fans and offenders alike. I thought of something my mother always said: "You can kill a lot more bees with honey." For once, she was right about something.

Soon we were settled into our seats, the lights dimmed, Joel Grey began singing "Wilkommen," and we were all mesmerized by the wonderful film. In one scene, Marisa Berenson opens the door to Michael York and is introduced to him.

"My name is Natalia." She said and something clicked in me.

"That's it!" I said loudly. "That's going to be my name. Natalia!"

Rusty immediately shushed me, but Nicole stood up and announced, "Ladies and gentlemen, I introduce to you Miss Natalia Darling."

Others in the audience shushed us as well, and Rusty said, "Sit down, Miss Thing, before we're thrown out of here."

Paulie and I laughed hysterically and agreed from here on out that Natalia was going to be my name. Natalia, which eventually was bastardized by Miss Mona to Natisha, which then became Tish, because that was all she could pronounce. Hence, Natalia, a.k.a. Tish, was born!

The movie ended and soon we were strolling back to the Lola. Unbeknownst to me, earlier in the evening when we had been heading down Broad Street to the theater, my mother and brother Joe were in one of the cars that had driven past us. What I never expected was that they would wait patiently for us until we exited the theater, and once again my mother was ready to cause a scene. Since I was still shy of eighteen, she had every legal right. When I saw them coming toward us, I ran around the corner but my brother was fast; he grabbed me and threw me against the side of the theater wall. The girls followed and tried to help.

My mother caught up. "Come over here," she demanded. "You're coming home with us."

The girls stood in silence as my mother grabbed me by the hair and started to drag me away.

"Punch her," Monique screamed. "Don't let her do that to you!" I had never considered hitting my mother before. While I'm sure I could have, I knew I didn't stand a chance with my big brother looking on. With Joey on one side and my mother on the other, I was trapped and they led me to the car on the corner.

Once inside our house, my mother turned to me and said, "I'll lock you up if you pull that runaway shit again. You're ruining our family and are an embarrassment to us all. All the neighbors can see you on the corner of the Lola. What the hell are you doing there?"

I was completely unprepared for what happened at home. Joe ripped off his black leather belt and pummeled me the same way my father had when I had run away at ten. Through it all, though, I thought how stupid they were to think that physical violence was going to make any difference on what had already become my destiny. And, of course, as soon as I could, I took off again, only this time I would not return. Or if I did, it would only be on my terms.

Paulie and I talked incessantly about moving to New York. He had been there many times and entertained me with stories of how wonderful and free it was. If I were going to have any kind of life for myself, I would have to get away from my family for sure. We hadn't finished beauty school, but learned we could complete our hours in New York just as easily. Paulie had some money saved and me, well, I didn't have much but I knew I could work steadily after school at the Lola corner to make as much money as I could to take with me to New York. Once we were there, we could certainly find jobs. Paulie knew of some inexpensive place to live in

Greenwich Village called the Hotel Albert. He had also befriended this other queen named Easha who was headed to New York from Philadelphia, so, in some way, we had a plan.

We had a stoop sale outside of our apartment on Benefit Street. The RISD kids were only too thrilled to buy our stuff, which helped. I wasn't able to make as much money as I had hoped. With just a hundred bucks and a whole lot of chutzpah, I knew I would make my way there. I'm not sure if it was blind faith or perhaps youthful ignorance, but whatever it was took sheer guts. I never once wavered in my decision or thought of not leaving.

Another friend from the Gallery, Miss Claude, called to say he was headed to New York that weekend and offered to give us a ride. He was headed to the infamous Continental Baths for the weekend and wouldn't mind the company. Doubling as an entertainment venue, it jumpstarted some of our most beloved entertainment icons, most notably The Divine Miss M, Bette Midler; and Barry Manilow, who thought nothing of performing for partially clad men in towels. It all sounded too good to be true, and I was content knowing I was finally busting out on my own.

CHAPTER 7
New York Ho!

Miss Claude pulled up in his bright orange Volvo convertible. Eyeing it curiously, I wondered, *How will we ever fit our stuff in there?* The day was sunny and it would be a good day for driving. Claude had just finished his shift at the beauty shop and was ready to hit the road. I was excited, but also a bit scared, as this would be my first trip outside New England. While I knew it was the right thing to do, I would miss everything familiar and certainly would miss my family, although I wasn't sure the feeling was mutual. One might wonder why I would miss my family after they had treated me so badly. But it was in the same way a battered spouse may stay with her husband because it was all she knew or she was too afraid to leave. In my case, my family was all that I had known in my eighteen years. Not all of our time spent together was awful. Yes, they were horrible, but I loved them and hoped they felt the same about me. What's that old saying about picking your friends but not your family? My willingness to forgive could, at times, be to my own detriment.

We crammed our stuffed suitcases into Claude's Volvo and sped onto the entrance ramp, merging onto the highway toward New York City. It was only four hours away, but it seemed like we had been on the road forever when finally, just as sunset fell ahead on the horizon, I saw New York. The buildings shimmered like diamonds in the distance, sparkling up to the sky, reminiscent of the scene in *The Wizard of Oz* when Dorothy and her friends awaken from their sleep and come out of the woods while viewing Oz in the distance. I certainly had the same naïveté as Dorothy, but was growing smarter and savvier by the day. I was about to get an education from New York that I couldn't pay any university to teach me, and this included a master's degree in street survival.

The closer we came, the more I felt the city's magical aura, and I knew I had been right to trust my instincts and my good friend Paulie. We drove through Harlem and then headed south to Greenwich Village. Rows upon rows of buildings were all crammed together into every available space. We weren't in little Rhody anymore. The energy was palpable and the city was bustling with people standing on corners and taxis zigzagging in and out picking up fares. Music emanated from various sources as if a cacophony of voices and sounds were saying welcome, welcome to our home.

After an endless montage of traffic lights, we arrived in the Village, with its tree-lined streets and beautifully maintained brownstones. Claude drove up to the entrance of the Hotel Albert, on the corner of University and East Tenth Street. "Okay, kids, here we are!" he sang out cheerfully.

The hotel lobby looked a bit shabby as we hauled our things up to the front desk, behind which was an older Hispanic man dressed in a T-shirt and khakis. He was bopping along to the beat of salsa music from a nearby radio. Paulie rang the bell three times. The man turned around, snapping off the radio as if we were interrupting his daily salsa lesson.

"*Maricon*, why you ring the bell like that? I can see you are here, you know!"

"Not for salsa lessons, that's for sure," Paulie replied. Paulie took control as always and asked for a room.

"Ha! Okay," the man said, "that will be thirty-five dollars for the week, no guests, and if you lose the key, ju will have to pay extra five dollars! Take the elevator to the tenth floor." He pointed to the right of the desk.

"*Muchas gracias, señor*," Paulie said as the clerk tossed him the key.

Collecting our bags, we moved toward the elevator. The door opened to a heavyset bearded man with tattoos, wearing a motorcycle jacket and jeans with chains hanging from here to there. Carrying a guitar case, he almost knocked us over. The claustrophobic elevator was creaky and cramped, and we exited it into a narrow, windowless hallway with a tattered red carpet runner. Making our way to the room, we passed a small, elderly woman in a housecoat and slippers reeking of cat piss. She shuffled along with her head down and muttered to herself before suddenly letting out a scream. Once we made it to our room, Paulie flicked on the light and immediately we saw a few huge cockroaches scramble out of sight. I screamed my best girly cry. "Ewww!"

The room was tiny, maybe ten by six feet wide. In the corner was a small sink basin with a dripping faucet. The ceiling was high and the walls were a faded, sad bluish hue. To the right of the door was a single bed with a sheet and worn pink blanket and a lonely pillow. The one soot covered window was at the end of the room facing north. If you looked hard enough, you could see the tip of the Empire State Building in the distance. For now, this little rat hole would be our humble home.

Sooner or later, I'd have to find a job. Paulie had the good fortune to secure a sewing job with a designer on Eighth Street. He also started dating someone who lived in the Village so he soon left the Albert to move in with him. Out of drag, Paulie was handsome and never had problems meeting men the way I did. Devastated that he was leaving, I felt lonely being on my own. Still grappling with my gender identity and sexuality, I wasn't having any success in finding a lover.

Having some um, retail skills, I was able to land a job in Hell's Kitchen. I had answered an ad in the *Village Voice* for a stock/sales job at a secondhand shop on Ninth Avenue called Nearly New Thrift Shop. It was here that not only would I become self-supporting, but I'd also make some new friendships and obtain some incredible vintage clothing and other discarded objects, since most of the donations we received were from wealthy New Yorkers on the Upper East Side.

For my interview, the store's manager took me to his tiny cramped office.

"I'm James Aspery," he said, "Jimmy works." He was a slight, congenial man of Irish descent who hailed from Queens, with the accent very much intact. We hit it off and he offered me the job, which I accepted since trying to turn tricks down by the piers on the West Side Highway was getting a bit played out. It was bad enough I spent most of my spare time trolling the piers and prancing up and down Christopher Street looking for love in all the wrong places. After all, I didn't come to New York to continue being a whore, or did I? My starting salary was $150 per week. Jimmy introduced me to the rest of the staff: Christine, a bleached blond curvy cashier, also from Queens, and Mrs. Elizabeth Moore, who was the head of the volunteers who basically priced and moved all the merchandise. She had a high-pitched voice that reminded me of Shirley Booth and was quite energetic and bossy. Lastly, there was the Indian maintenance man, Dita, accent intact. It was his job to move racks, open and close the store, and any heavy lifting, including keeping an eye out for shoplifters.

I loved working at Nearly New. It instilled in me a sense of purpose and kept me busy, but I still wasn't quite settled in my gender confusion. Although Paulie and I had made a pact that we were going to try and live as gay men, I wasn't convinced doing so would work for me. Besides, some of the outfits that came into the store were just too irresistible, let alone for the price. Indeed, one particular black wool, crepe, bugle-beaded, tailored jacket and a fitted slim skirt managed to make their way into my bag and back to my hotel room where I could try them on in private.

So, while my pact was still in effect, I still felt the strong urge to dress as a woman. My boss was a curious and observant guy. Certainly, he knew I was gay and as time went on we became friends and he was very supportive of me, even protective like a father would be. He quizzed me about my eyebrows and why they were tweezed, which eventually led to my life becoming an open book to him. Though he was married with children, he was quite fascinated by me. I believe, although he never expressed it, that he admired my courage at such an early age. In a way, I was out as a gay man even before I began living as a trans person.

In 1974 the New York gay scene was intoxicating. Post-Stonewall, there was a strong sense of freedom of expression and a camaraderie that somehow we were all in this together. The Disco era was in full swing and the Bon Soir on Eighth Street and the original Limelight on Seventh Avenue just below Sheridan Square were some hot spots in the village to go dancing, and also some of the few gay bars that allowed women.

At the Albert, Paulie and I met up with our new trans woman friend from Philadelphia, Easha, and the three of us headed uptown to the notorious Gilded Grape. Still dressed as a boy, I secretly longed to be part of the transgender milieu. It was quite a scene; the Grape was a hodgepodge of every possible gender and sexual identity. While it was predominately transgender women, there was also a heady mix of gay men, lesbian women, bisexual folks, and tranny-chasing tricks. There was also a small group of transvestite men like those portrayed in the book, *Casa Susanna,* who liked to dress as women but were married with wives and families. Coming from such a small city like Providence, I was exposed to the lives of drag queens and trans women; I felt mostly comfortable there. But as I studiously viewed my surroundings, I had so much more to learn about the New York trans experience.

The shows were incredible and some of the trans women were so absolutely stunning. There were so many legendary beauties from that time who hung out there, such as Crystal LaBejia, and International Chrysis who was a star at the Blue Angel Revue, and the infamous Liz Eden, who would be the subject of the Sidney Lumet film *Dog Day Afternoon.* Then there were the local girls, each one as beautiful and as interesting as the next. There were many Latin trans women from all parts of South America and the Caribbean who either lived in the neighborhood or around the corner at the Hildonah Apartments, which wasn't unlike the Lola in Providence.

On occasion celebrities would visit the Gilded Grape, and a frequent visitor was Andy Warhol. It was there where he mined the colorful underbelly of gay subculture for his transvestite portrait series. While I knew some of these ladies from afar later in life, I would get to know some of them on a more personal level. Nevertheless, I was stunned at the size and variety of the community of trans women who were here in New York. I likened it to being in a scene from a Fellini movie every time I went there. There was always something or someone more fascinating to discover.

We also reconnected with Jimmy Eichelberger, who worked at the Candle Shop on Christopher Street, which became a regular stop for us as Paulie and I traipsed up and down the gay ghetto, cruising for boys, looking for weed, or just hanging out with our fellow LGBT folks. Jimmy became a member of the legendary Charles Ludlam's Ridiculous Theatrical Company at One Sheridan Square. It was there that I was introduced to this amazing theatrical genre and attended Jimmy's performance in *Camille*, with Charles in the title role. The night we were going I had an excruciating toothache. I was in agony, not really having the funds or sense then to take care of my teeth. Once inside the theater, I didn't think I was going to make it through the play. Yet, from Charles Ludlam's first entrance, the comedy was so intoxicating it felt like laughing gas and I completely forgot about the pain in my mouth.

Jimmy would later go on to become Ethyl Eichelberger, the groundbreaking and brilliant performance artist. We loved him and everything he did and continued our friendship right up until his death from suicide. The last time I saw Ethyl was when we were both go-go dancing on the bar at the Pyramid Club in the East Village.

"Hey, kid, move over and make some room up there for momma," Ethyl yelled, approaching the edge of the bar. I was thrilled he was climbing up to share the bar with me.

"Can you believe we're here on a bar, after all these years, Ethyl? We're a sight," I said. "I'm trans and you're a queen. We 'trans-queens' are ruling right now."

He laughed. "Trans-queen. I love it!" he exclaimed as we shimmied, shook, bumped, and bounced to the sounds of the B52's "Love Shack," much to the delight of the adoring bar patrons who were getting a real show. He loved my turn of phrase and thought it was a great twist on drag queen. Not only was he a huge talent, he was a great person and friend. Sadly, he was one of the early casualties of AIDS. A very bright light dimmed the day Jimmy died.

One of the other regular characters we would see daily was this African American drag queen that had a reassuring presence. You could count on running into her at any time of day. Marsha P. Johnson was a sight to behold and one of the bravest queens I'd ever met. She was a vision in these incredibly intricate outfits that she must have concocted from bits of fabric feathers and scraps of things she found in the street. I never quite knew anyone as eccentric as her and loved her constant presence in those early days in the Village. I'd often ask, "How are tricks going, Marsha?" To which she would always reply, "Oh, well, you know gurl, it's all good cause Marsha's getting hers."

What I didn't know way back then was that she was also one of the first transgender activists in the movement for equal rights for LGBTQ folks.

My job at Nearly New lasted for about nine months; I couldn't resist the urge to start dressing as a female. Still feeling more and more uncomfortable with myself as an awkward gay nineteen-year-old, the clothing finds were too good to pass up. So, whenever I could, I'd dress at night after work and head uptown to the Gilded Grape.

Also, the idea of actually transitioning was now ever present in my consciousness, and finally having some resources of my own allowed me to take small steps. Many of the girls at club were excellent role models for me on transitioning, and Easha, my neighbor and trans woman friend at the Albert, was particularly helpful. Stunning with a big Cheshire cat grin, Easha was tall and slim and resembled Beverly Johnson, a black supermodel of that era.

One day she took me down to the Lower East Side to a little clinic on Rivington Street to get my first of what would be weekly hormone shots.

"Hey, Mommy, you lookin' good today. You looking for something today?" a banjee boy shouted out to us as we passed on our way to the clinic in the barrio. He grabbed his crotch as an extra incentive to stop. The locals were mostly of Hispanic descent and guys were always hanging out on the street. There was also a lot of drug trafficking taking place, which I was unaware of until Easha pointed it out.

Arriving at the tiny clinic, we ducked inside and I immediately recognized a few other trans women from the club in the waiting room, there for the same thing. We strolled up to the reception desk as a frazzled Latin woman asked for our names, so we could sign in to get our shots. No ID was necessary. I could have been fifteen, for all they knew. The nurse came out and called my name. I went in.

"Hello, sweetie, turn around and drop your pants," the nurse said once we were in the small office. "This will be quick and won't hurt a bit," she said as she jabbed me with the needle full of colorless liquid. Wiping away the blood on my butt with alcohol, she slapped on a Band-Aid and told me, "I'll see you next week."

Leaving the office, I immediately felt a sense of relief that I'd finally rallied the courage to go ahead and begin this part of my journey, though I was unsure as to where it would lead.

CHAPTER 8

Natalia's Dilemma

Hot wax was bubbling up in the little pot on the hotplate in my room at the Hotel Albert. I couldn't afford electrolysis and some of the other girls had told me they used depilatory wax for their facial hair. Applying the wax on my face was tricky because you didn't want to burn your skin—it had to be hot but not scalding. I let it cool down in small patches before ripping it away to leave a softer, more feminine complexion. The problem was that it had to be done frequently and it was wicked painful.

Giving up the gay life was an easy decision. It was too painful for me to continue. Though I gave it a try, I never felt comfortable in the gay scene of the seventies. Traipsing up and down Christopher Street and hanging out on the piers was hardly life affirming. I met men every now and then, but no one was ever interested in me long term. The anonymous sex scene was unfulfilling. Shuffling around in the back rooms of bars or those dank, dark deserted rooms on the piers full of groping and groaning men whose faces you could only glimpse when lit by cigarette lighters or matches left me more depressed and dejected each time I did. Age was a problem, although I didn't realize it at the time. Who in their right mind was going to take seriously an androgynous nineteen-year-old without any sense of self or purpose in life?

One day, on my usual stroll down Christopher Street, a man in tight jean cut-off shorts asked me for a cigarette. I smoked Newports and said,

"If you don't mind menthol." He smiled and said yes and I saw that he was very sexy, with dark wavy hair and a honey caramel complexion. As my eye traveled up and down, I couldn't help noticing the growing bulge in his shorts.

"I'm Ricardo, but call me Ricky," he said as I leaned in to offer him a butt. Within minutes, we were back in my hotel room making mad passionate love. In those days, it wasn't uncommon to go from the street to the sheets.

He told me he recently turned twenty-three and was born in Puerto Rico. We began an intense physical relationship, heavy on the sex and not much else, and he was protective and jealous right from the start. He convinced me to move out of the Albert, where I was now sharing a room with two other trans women, to Jackson Heights, Queens. Going from a cramped, one-room hotel room to a spacious two-bedroom apartment was a great change, except he lived with an older gay man. It never dawned on me that the man was also his sugar daddy.

Things started to get more serious between us and soon I found myself on the 6 train headed uptown to the Bronx to meet his mother and family. The idea that I had a legitimate boyfriend who was great in bed, despite being unemployed and possessive, wasn't enough to convince me to stay in the relationship. I felt trapped, since I wasn't familiar with Queens and didn't like sitting alone in the apartment waiting for him to return. Also, I missed my trans friends back in the village. Ricky didn't approve of me occasionally dressing up as female. He didn't mind my feminine ways, but when it came to presenting as another gender, we clashed.

When I told him I was leaving, he wasn't having any of it and a huge argument ensued. He wouldn't let me leave the apartment and even blocked the door, threatening me if I left. The violence I had witnessed in my own family home came in handy as I spied a huge seashell ornament on the coffee table, picked it up, and threw it at him. It hit him on the head and he fell over and I was able to get out of there. I never went back. Luckily, he didn't come after me and wasn't seriously injured except for a huge bump on his head.

Since Paulie had moved out of the Hotel Albert, I still felt lonely. Constantly feeling insecure about who I was or how I was going to fit in to the world was challenging. Although I was mature beyond my nineteen years, I had very little foundation to stand on. It was hard for me because I was so easily influenced by others. Although I loved the idea of living in New York, it was challenging to be away from my friends and family in Rhode Island. Even though we didn't have the best relationship, my mother, brothers, and sister were still my flesh and blood. I missed what was familiar. While no one would really know it from how I behaved, I was scared most of the time and fearful that something bad might happen to me.

Wilhelmina and Monique would tell me horror stories of tricks not wanting to pay up or getting beaten up and left nearly for dead. Sometimes if you were down on the pier early in the morning, you could catch a gruesome glimpse of the police fishing a dead corpse out of the Hudson. Violence against trans women back then was an even more common occurrence than today.

Since leaving my job at the thrift shop, I was back doing sex work to survive. It was so easy. You could grab a trick most anywhere but it was especially easy down by the piers on West Street, where you could park under the elevated highway or pull into the municipal parking lot to give some quick head.

Dressing as female during the day had me more confident about my gender. I needed very little makeup and, since my beard wasn't heavy, I was able to wax it smooth. The hormones were working and my breasts began to protrude like those of a teenage girl. Not really small in stature, I was always a bit on the curvy side so my shape began to soften as well and passing was becoming much easier.

Paulie was still a huge presence in my life and he had moved uptown after breaking up with his boyfriend and found an apartment in Hell's Kitchen on Forty-Ninth Street, within walking distance of Nearly New thrift shop. He paid one hundred dollars a month for a one-bedroom flat on the third floor. It was one of those classic New York flats, long and narrow with just enough room to make you feel cozy and not cramped.

I was still roughing it out in the Village at the Hotel Albert. Hustling up the thirty-fve dollars a week rent was easy for me to make back then but I still felt restless and unsafe there all by myself. Spending more and more time with my trans women friends that lived upstairs at the Albert temporarily provided a reprise from loneliness and isolation. Wilhelmina Ross was one of them. My new friend took her name Wilhelmina from the modeling agency and Ross for Miss Diana Ross. She was part black and part Cherokee Indian. Tall, kooky, and funny, she was very involved in the burgeoning creative theater scene in the village. It was impressive to me that she was acting in plays. I remember one particularly funny children's play she did in broad daylight at the playground over on Bleecker Street and Hudson. She played the part of the wicked witch. The kids had no idea that the witch was previously a warlock. Her other roommate, Monique, was a beautiful African American trans woman and another older, sage Latina trans woman, Lola, lived nearby. And, yes, Lola was a showgirl. They all lived as female twenty-four seven, much like Rusty and Monica back in Rhode Island.

There was a great sense of community back then. In those early Greenwich Village days, many trans women were generous about teaching me how to survive. Every type of lesson was learned, from where to go to make a few quick bucks to makeup and clothing suggestions and where to get the best hormone shots. It was a feeling that we are all in it together, much like my earlier experience at the Lola with Rusty.

Wilhelmina was also involved with the early Ridiculous Theatrical Company. She was photographed by Andy Warhol in his transvestite series of Polaroid he did in the early seventies. Even though it was tough for trans women to survive back then, these early pioneers knew all the tricks of the trade and I've always been grateful for the care, inspiration, and protection I received from them.

Greenwich Village was such a vibrant and exciting place to live. It was inspiring hanging out at the Bon Soir on Eighth Street and dancing in the same space where Barbra Streisand, Joan Rivers, and Woody Allen began. Whether it was disco dancing at the original Limelight on Seventh

Avenue or dishing and drinking at Peter Rabbit on West Street or catching the latest cabaret show at Trude Heller's, there was always something interesting and fun to do.

However, I still wasn't focused on anything in particular. My days began late and the nights usually ended with the sun coming up after I'd spent time in some dark after-hours club. Another hot spot was the 220 Club on West Houston Street. The 220 was a place filled with trans women, gays, lesbians, drag queens, and transvestites, and of course their admirers. It was a place where you could enter and forget the outside world and be one with your tribe. It became a safe haven where we could come together to be protected and celebrate our differences, while at the same time being allowed to drink, drug, and dance our lives away. The sense of freedom was overpowering at times, but in a good way.

My drug use up until that point was pretty much limited to weed, speed, and booze. But it began to escalate once I was in New York. I occasionally tripped on acid but only with Paulie, whom I trusted with my life. I did love black beauties—amphetamines in black capsules that all the girls would get from their doctors. I loved uppers—they helped me focus in a way that I was never able to do sober. They made it a lot easier to fake light conversation with tricks and quickly get them off so I could move along to the next man, with the task of turning as many tricks as possible before I quit for the night. Also in New York I discovered barbiturates. Tuinal were red and blue capsules that I could take to make me crash after speeding my tits off for days.

• • •

Tired of the constant rat race of New York and unsure about where my life was heading, I decided to return to Rhode Island. Going back to beauty school to finish where I had left off seemed like the best plan. Feeling more confident with my physical changes, it was time for my past to meet my future. Since I had already completed half the requirements for beauty school before I left for New York, it would be easy to do. Returning to my hometown on my terms and with my new female identity confidently in place, I could be my authentic self, or so I thought.

My family situation was the same. My mother never forgave me for the way I came out first as gay and then as trans. Our relationship was strained and several attempts to contact her by phone had been unsuccessful. Every time I called, she'd hang up, which was devastating to me. How could my own mother be so cruel? Wasn't I still her child? My sexuality and gender expression differed from those of her other kids, but did that disqualify me from inclusion in our family? It was so confusing and painful, but somehow I had hope that in time things would change. In fact, I was going to make sure of it. It was time for me to stop living with my head in the sand and make my way back home to confront my family with my newfound female identity. Certainly, if they saw me in person, they would realize that I was serious and this wasn't just some phase I was going through.

My two oldest brothers, Joe and Randy, were both married and living their own lives. Joe was especially shaken up over my coming out and, while he may have felt some responsibility for the trouble in my young life, he was the only one who had some exposure to other trans women. In a strange twist of his thinking, he was most accepting of my situation. He even invited me to his wedding. While I was happy to be included, I remember getting extremely drunk. The pressure of meeting the rest of my extended family at his wedding was more than I could handle. I grew close with his wife and was welcomed to visit them on occasion and to spend time with their two young children, Joey and Jenny. I was their Auntie Tish and, as far as they knew, I always had been.

Randy, on the other hand, showed no compassion at all for my situation and thought nothing of making his disgust for what I had done known. He refused to speak to me whenever I was at my mother's house for Sunday dinner. His wife Gail also turned against me. Their reaction was the most severe of all of my family members.

Perhaps Randy's reaction was triggered by the fact that when we were younger, after my parents' divorce, we would sometimes end up with my Dad on Rodman Street in Fall River. We shared a bedroom with two twin beds. After the lights went out and we were supposed to be asleep, Randy would crawl into my bed. He would climb on top of me face down and proceed to grind his penis on my then ten-year-old buttocks. Did he secretly know what happened to me in the men's room at the movie theater? We never spoke about this. At the time, I thought it was just something that brothers did with each other. Never did I mention it to any of my other siblings or my parents. Perhaps in a house full of boys, this might not have been so unusual, but his assault on me seemed a bit more than horsing around.

Jeffery, two years younger than me, was still living at home when I returned to Providence as transgender. He had a girlfriend from the neighborhood. His reaction was less severe than Randy's and, since he had taken on the role of family clown, most of his comments were comical in nature. Certainly, he might have had some feelings about his brother who was now his sister, but neither he nor any of my siblings were ever good about expressing any type of feeling other than anger. His young girlfriend got pregnant and was kicked out of her parents' house. It was I, the transgender sibling, who took her in and cared for her until she was able to find a place of her own. To this day, I know she was always grateful for the kindness I showed to her in her time of need.

Sheila, the only girl, and her twin, Todd, were just teenagers when I began my transition. While Todd mostly fell into my mother's camp of exile, Sheila was much more sensitive to my situation. She welcomed the idea of having a sister, even if it wasn't from birth. She had someone to confide in and also to look up to. While I became somewhat of a mentor to her, my father had forbidden her to have anything to do with me. He was certain I would corrupt her in every possible moral way. We did get together and I think she got quite an education hanging out at the Lola with me and the other queens who lived there. It certainly wasn't a usual teenage upbringing by any standards. We each had a competitive streak, and thus she would frequently let me know that she was the "real daughter."

• • •

As soon as I decided to move back to Rhode Island, I immediately let Paulie know of my decision. Part of me was torn up about interrupting our friendship this way. Paulie was still working as my replacement at Nearly New, and Jimmy, my former boss, was sad to see me leave New York, too, but wished me well. It was easy to pack up what little belongings I had; everything fit in one suitcase I'd snatched from work. Before leaving the Hotel Albert, I said goodbye to my little band of trans sisters on the tenth floor. They too were sorry to see me go, which made me feel good, as it had always been hard for me to have friends. I was inspired to continue to make more friends, since I had finally gotten the hang of the friendship thing.

"Don't worry, I'll be back," I told my sisters.

Settling into my seat of the New England-bound Amtrak train, my head was swimming with thoughts of what this next phase of my life would be. Rusty had told me of a vacant apartment in the Lola and had put down a deposit for me; the rent was basically the same as my little room at the Albert, but now I'd have my first apartment all to myself. A certain Miss Tony Honolulu had lived there before, but had passed away. Apparently, he had a penchant for sniffing paint thinner, spray paint, and glue, so you had to be careful lighting a cigarette or a joint or the whole place would burst into flames. I never cared for inhalants, but many people were into poppers—amyl nitrates. They were all the rage within the gay community and some of the tricks I turned also liked them.

The train slowly pulled into the station in downtown Providence. Rusty had agreed to meet me. Spotting me as I emerged freshened up from the ladies' restroom, she hurried to greet me.

"Well, girl, New York has done wonders for you!" she said, hugging me. "You're looking very cunty, honey. Those hormones are working you?"

"Yes, can you believe it, girl? Look!"

I lifted up my blouse.

"Oooh, Miss Thing, you're crazy, girl, cover yourself up before they haul us off to jail up in here!" she said patting my blouse down.

Strolling through the cavernous station, we jumped into a waiting cab outside and made our way up Broad Street to the Lola. We paid the driver and made our way up the narrow staircase to the second floor as Rusty got the keys out of her bag. She opened the door into my new apartment and we sauntered in, my suitcase in tow.

"Wow, this is perfect. Thank God, the paint smell is gone," I said as I looked around and realized that I was about to move into a new phase of my life. The walls were freshly painted, the dark blue shag carpeting newly installed, and the place smelled fresh. It was a postage-stamp-sized efficiency apartment similar to Rusty's, but it was mine, all mine. I began to well up with emotion. Rusty gave me a reassuring hug and told me she was happy that I'd come back home and not to worry, things would work out fine. Relieved to be back home where things were easier for me, instinctively I knew that the hardest part of my journey was looming ahead.

After settling into my new place, I called Ma to let her know I was back. The phone rang and rang and no one picked up. It was important for me that I confront my fears about coming out as trans to her and the rest of my family as quickly as possible. I wasn't sure then why it was so important, but in hindsight I guess like any other person in a situation like this, I was only seeking natural comfort from the familiar and hoping for support. Feeling confident that I had made the right decision, it was only normal that I would want to share it with my loved ones.

I woke early the next day, put on a little lipstick, mascara, and light blush and ran a brush through my hair, which by now was loosely falling around my shoulders, like Rita Hayworth in *Gilda*. I slipped into a snug pair of blue jeans along with a soft pastel-colored angora sweater. My small hormone breasts were clearly visible but not quite large enough for me to wear a bra. Grabbing my jacket and shoulder bag off the kitchen counter, I made my way out the door, crossed Broad Street and waited for the Elmwood Avenue bus. It was a short ride to my childhood home.

It was a sunny and cool day as I stepped off the bus and made my way down Stanwood Street. I felt a sense of freedom strolling through my old neighborhood and was comforted by the familiar houses as I passed by. Each one had a story of my youth and many of the neighbors still lived there. Just before I reached my house, Mrs. Manacchio stepped out her door and saw me approach. I waved and said hello but could tell she was startled a bit, recognizing the voice but not the figure. And to think her daughter Cathy had been my childhood friend. Disoriented but friendly, she smiled uncomfortably. Sailing past, she saw me stop at my mother's house and probably figured it out.

My heart pounded as I stepped onto the porch and knocked on the door. No answer. As I turned the knob, the door opened and I heard Portuguese fado music playing on the stereo. The lush velvet sound of Amália Rodrigues's voice singing *"Coimbra"* soothed my nerves as the door opened into our dining room. I felt a breeze brush past me, which meant my mother was at the back door hanging or taking in wash from the clothesline.

Sure enough, Ma entered from the opposite end of the dining room holding a bright plastic basket of laundry. Startled, she dropped the basket at her feet and stared at me from head to toe.

Giving me the once-over, she said, "What are you doing here?" It wasn't the warmest greeting, although my mother wasn't the warm and fuzzy type.

A *hello* or *nice to see* you might have been a more appropriate response, but no. I watched her face twist into annoyance, as she didn't want to see me as I was, but as she wanted me to be.

I felt I should get this over sooner rather than later since I was planning on staying in Rhode Island for a while.

"I got home yesterday. I found a little place on Broad Street."

Without missing a beat, she said, "You mean the place where I saw you hanging out with all those niggers and queers?"

"Yes, the Lola," I said as I removed my jacket. She stared at my chest and saw my breasts, and then flew into a rage.

"Oh my God, what have you done? Are those real?"

"Yes. I've been taking hormone pills and shots." I spoke calmly, trying not to feed into her defensiveness.

"What are you doing? Why are you coming here, bringing this shit into my house? I don't want anything to do with this, you hear me?"

I stared at her in disbelief.

"Get the hell out of here before your brother gets home from school. You're making me sick with this fucking shit, Brian!"

My heart sank as I realized that this had been a bad idea and that she was more concerned about what my brother was going to think about me than the fact that her child had come home.

"Ma, Brian's gone. My name is Natalia now."

She dumped the laundry on the kitchen table and refused to look at me as she began furiously folding an array of sheets, towels, and clothes belonging to my sister and brothers. The Portuguese fado music filled the awkward silence between us.

"Well, I though you should know what I've decided. I was hoping you would at least be happy to see me," I said.

She continued to look down, folding clothes.

"Get out, Brian, and don't ever come around here like that again!" she yelled. "Do you really think I want my neighbors seeing you like this? Get the hell out!"

Holding back tears, I slipped on my little jean jacket, turned, and left before the scene escalated into a shouting match or some other kind of violence. Even though I was no longer a minor, I could still be subjected to her anger and couldn't stop her from losing her temper, throwing something, or even hitting me. Normally, I wouldn't have given up so easily. Instead I would stand my ground and argue my point with true righteous indignation. But I knew I had hit a dead end.

It's as if she perceived that my transition was some purposeful revenge to get back at her or that it was her fault. I understand how difficult it must have been for her, since she surely wasn't able to emotionally process what was happening to me, but for me it was even more devastating because it was important that I keep my family ties. While my familial relationships were never strong, it felt at the time that they were really all I had. I needed them to love me as I was. But how could I achieve that when I had so little love and acceptance for myself? It probably would not happen, not then, perhaps never.

Rejection really did a number on me, especially from my own mother, although I wasn't in touch with just how deeply it hurt me. I just shrugged it off as a temporary thing and looked at it as her problem, not mine.

My siblings were still just as confused, and perhaps as angry, as my mother. If they were going to have to decide on having any type of relationship with me, surely they would not jeopardize their alliance with my mom. Eventually, they would come to accept me in their own ways, but that wouldn't be anytime soon.

It was during this encounter that I realized that my life would never be the same again. The encounter with Del not only added to my confusion, but also made the burden even heavier to bear, piling on the guilt early in my transition and firmly rooting in place the doubt that would nearly cost me my life to erase. I left hoping that pehaps someday perhaps she might come around, but for now, I had to do what I needed to do since my life depended on it.

• • •

I woke the next day feeling more determined than defeated. Once an idea got into my head it was nearly impossible to ignore, so I headed straight to the city clerk's office to file the papers to change my name legally. Going back to hairdressing school as Brian was out of the question. If I was serious about my transition, it had to be done right. From now on, I was going to be known as Natalia Joan Belo. Joan was in homage to Crawford, whom I idolized growing up and whom some people said I resembled. The process was easier than I thought. I presented my birth certificate, filled out the applications, answered a few questions, and received a date to return for probate court.

After I finished, I walked around downtown and stopped in Woolworths to get a few things for my new apartment. Money was scarce and I had to work the corner that night to get some more ducats. Whatever I couldn't afford in the five and dime, I'd steal. Still a practicing shoplifter, I had a rule to always carry a big bag, because, hey, you never know when you're going to need a little extra something.

With very little fanfare I returned to City Hall for my court date. Changed my name and acquired a new ID. Looking at it for the first time, I saw my sex was listed: F for female! Next on the list was to get back into beauty school. Some staff already knew of my changes. Still, I think they were a little bit startled by the new me when I returned to classes.

Hairdressing wasn't something I felt passionate about. Back then the options for legitimate work for trans women were limited. Figuring I probably could make a living and get myself off the streets, I continued with school. I did it, but once I graduated no one would hire me. It was back to sex work to survive, which in a way was easier as the rejection was less hard to handle. Still being young and desirable made working the streets easier, but no less dangerous. Most of the time guys wanted oral sex. Most of it took place right in their car. There were a few spots around town that were not far off the main drag. It was rare that I brought them up to my apartment. That would cost them more money. Maybe if they were cute they might get a better rate but I still charged extra for the room. Tricks would usually go for the younger girls first, as they knew they might have a better chance at taking advantage of their youthful inexperience. But I was already quite adept at navigating the pitfalls of sex work.

After some time had passed, I found a nicer, more spacious apartment up Broad Street on Parkis Avenue. There was less heat, less street competition. The Lola was a great place to live, but the competition was fierce and I felt it was time to move on to greener turf. More confident in my outward appearance, I started dating and got involved with a guy I met one night at the disco. Bobby Petisi was Italian, sexy, and swarthy. He grew up in Federal Hill, a section of Providence (the same one as Lou, my mom's boyfriend). At last someone found me attractive enough that he wanted to be with me. I was blindly in love with the idea of newfound romance. Living every day as a female gave me a newfound confidence. My electrolysis treatments were working and my hair was longer. The hormones were doing wonders for my skin and my breasts were a full cup size bigger. There was only one problem: Bobby was a heroin addict. Too young and naive was I to even absorb the enormity of what that problem entailed.

Marijuana was one of the drugs that I used most consistently. Heroin was something I only knew about from movies or television. I had no idea the amount of lying and deceit that addicts were able to conjure up. Bobby was always hitting me up for money; not that I was rich, and what little money I had didn't go far. It never occurred to me he was using smack.

Money would also go missing from my friend Monica's purse. We would often do things together with her and her boyfriend at the time. Unbeknownst to me, Bobby was stealing her money too. The final straw was when he stole quite a bit of money she had been saving to pay the rent. He had broken my golden rule of never stealing from friends. We had a tremendous fight and falling out over it.

Eventually, Bobby got busted for robbery, and he ended up in prison. And like a fool, I would spend my Saturday afternoons riding the bus up to see him. As I played the dutiful girlfriend, it was always a bit of a shit show when I arrived to visit. He had begged me to smuggle in drugs for him since he was detoxing from heroin really badly. Other inmates would get their girlfriends to get five milligrams of Valium, stack them up, and place them in the cut-off end of a balloon. They would keep them in their mouth and either kiss their boyfriends or slip them across the table when the guards weren't looking. Without even considering the consequences, I did what he asked and, luckily, I never got caught. Little did I know I wasn't the only one who was visiting Bobby doing this.

One of the guards had become flirtatious and smitten with me. His name was Al and he became one of my regular tricks. He would tell me things I didn't know about Bobby, such as the fact that another woman was visiting him as well. Al also let me know what day the woman was visiting so I could see for myself. Of course, being a graduate of the life school of drama, I did just that. Devastated that I had been used, I felt rejected by Bobby and more incomplete because of my gender confusion. Del was still struggling with my transition and my siblings were also very confused. They had distanced themselves from me. I felt so alone in a place that I had returned to home. With those ongoing family problems and the pressure of trying to make a life for myself, not to mention my ongoing untreated depression and anxiety, I did what anyone else in that position might do.

Later that afternoon, I went to the liquor store and bought a cheap bottle of vodka. Back home alone, I started taking swigs form the bottle while listening to Billie Holiday serenade my sorrows with "Ain't Nobody's Business if I Do" on my stereo. Slowly, I took one Valium, and then another (I had quite a stash from my new career as a drug mule for Bobby). Before long, the whole bottle of pills was gone, as was most of the vodka. I drunk-drug dialed a few friends and one of them was Paulie's mom Gloria. She got along with everyone and really liked my brother Joe. She had his phone number and was smart enough to call him. She let him know she thought the situation was serious. I wasn't religious, but her calling Joe was really one of those Higher Purpose moments in my life when outside forces intervened. Little did I know I was being looked after even then.

Miraculously, I wandered out of the building and teetered onto busy Elmwood Avenue weaving and bobbing through the honking traffic on my way to Rusty's apartment. Later I learned I had collapsed and was taken out by ambulance to St. Joseph's Hospital. My stomach was pumped and I was in a coma for forty-eight hours before I regained consciousness.

When I finally did wake up groggy from all the drugs, I saw my father, my mother, and my two older brothers in the room.

"What the hell were you thinking?" my father said, tears streaming down his face. It was the only time in my entire life that I had ever seen my father cry.

"Do you know you almost died? You've been comatose for two days, Brian!"

At the moment, despite the grogginess from the drugs that remained in my system, I realized something sharp and profound: I had to try to kill myself for my father and the rest of my family to take me seriously. *Really?* This revelation both stunned me and gave me a determined surge of adrenaline.

"Get the fuck out of my room!" I screamed at all of them. "I don't need your sympathy. If this is what I have to do to get your attention, I don't need it. Get out, all of you, now!"

By this point, I had become so excitable that I accidentally pulled the IV out of my arm. A nurse came running in and asked them to leave as she attended to my arm.

While I was grateful that I hadn't died, what had taken place depressed me greatly. The guilt my family felt about not accepting me was as painful to me as the fact that I had almost killed myself because of it. There was a temporary shift in my family's attitude that signaled to me that there was some remorse on their part for treating me so badly. My suicide attempt was never addressed openly, but I felt a tiny shift in how they were treating me. While our interactions felt different, it didn't last. It only softened the blow I had been struck by my own attempt at self-destruction.

I was forced into therapy before I could be released from the hospital, which I resented because, again, I saw all of this as someone else's problem, not mine. I hated the judgmental attitude of the therapists and the psychiatrists that I was mandated to see and really fought them every step of the way. At one point, I was subjected to extensive psychological testing, some of which was standard. But the weirdest was when they attached wires from a machine to my penis to measure how I responded to pornography shown on a small monitor. The whole thing was very *Clockwork Orange* and, because I was so young, I had no idea that I could have refused to participate. As it turns out, the final determination of this exhaustive psychiatric evaluation was that, in their professional opinion, I was not considered a candidate for gender reassignment surgery. Seriously? I had already come this far in my transition and now they were suggesting I had made a mistake. Surely, they had to be wrong. I interpreted it as some sort of prejudicial judgment to deny medical options to those who were truly transgender. Upon my release, I resumed my transition with a vengeance.

CHAPTER 9

Antonio's Girl

Regaining my footing, I came to the realization that Providence wasn't the place for me after all. Folding my tent like a thief in the night, I headed back to New York City, trash bags and all.

Paulie was overjoyed to have me back with him in the city.

"I can keep a better eye on your crazy ass," he said.

His one-bedroom railroad flat in Hell's Kitchen oozed New York City charm and I was grateful for the futon in the living room. He liked my old job at Nearly New but was antsy to do something more, and soon got his perfect job working in a fast-paced environment with a celebrity clientele at the Make Up Center on East Fifty-Fifth Street. He put his hair and makeup talents to good use and started to build a reputation as one of the best makeup artists on staff. Soon, he would be teaching makeup and serving private clients.

I was still reeling from my traumatic experience in Rhode Island and trying to make sense of the harsh reception and rejection I'd been subjected to back home. Luckily, Paulie instilled in me his belief that I could succeed at whatever I chose to do. Hairdressing was definitely out, though, even though I had a license. I just wasn't feeling it.

The only thing I was passionate about was continuing my transition. Above all else, I was intent on being consistent with estrogen injections once a week. I also kept my regular electrolysis appointments to get rid of any unwanted facial hair. My sole objective became to achieve an awesome sense of "realness," or what the transgender community today calls "the passing privilege," meaning that you can get further in life if no one really knows you're trans, but assumes you are the gender you're presenting. During this time, I worked extra hard on the street making some extra cash to have my nose fixed at a swanky Park Avenue surgeon. It completely transformed my face by smoothing out the bump where my father had hit me in the nose when I was a kid, and it softened my facial appearance even more. If people did "spook" you, that is, figure out that you're not the gender you're presenting yourself as, then your challenges were greater. Being trans was still considered far outside of the normal spectrum of gender and it could be very dangerous if you weren't careful.

Frequently in my case, men wouldn't know my gender was different from my birth assignment. This could lead to all kinds of awkward situations and sometimes they would be very unpleasant and downright mean. When and if I did tell them, shouts of "You're a guy!" would often be the ultimate insult, especially after I'd worked so hard to not be considered male.

• • •

It was an exciting time to be back in New York. I had just turned twenty-one in 1977 and the Disco Era was in full swing. Paulie and I had plenty of energy to get out to all the latest clubs and we were in close contact with our friends from Rhode Island, Steven and Jane, who lived in the Village.

For our first foray into fabulousness, I wore a beautiful dress that Paulie had created, inspired by Yves Saint Laurent's fantasy collection. The top was slate gray velvet with huge mutton sleeves. A tightly fitted bodice held together with metal eyelets and a silk cord jacked up my cleavage amply. Paulie snatched my hair back into a tight chignon and stuck pheasant feathers in one side. I wore long dangling gypsy type earrings to complete the look. Taking our fashion very seriously, we never left the house without looking like there wasn't some epic planning involved. After all, you never knew whom you might meet.

We arrived at Hurrah, a hot new club on Sixty-Second Street, where a huge line snaked down the block. Unbothered, we strolled right up to the front of the line and the doorman took one look at us and swept us in. Choruses of Thelma Houston's "Don't Leave Me This Way" filled the stairwell as we made our way closer and closer to the dance floor. To my right, perfectly perched in a banquette where you couldn't miss them, sat Andy Warhol, Truman Capote, Margaux Hemingway, and the fashion designer Halston chatting away.

"Put your eyes back into their sockets," Paulie said as we passed by. "It's rude to stare."

The throbbing disco beat beckoned us out onto the packed dance floor. I knew how to clear some space for me to flaunt some of my favorite moves. One trick I learned was a dizzying disco spin that usually sent anyone nearby running for cover. Paulie stuck a bottle of poppers up my nose. Hiking my skirt and revealing the pastel petticoats, I lifted one leg and swung it cancan girl style as I blasted off into disco infinity.

Spinning and spinning, I caught a glimpse of Steven and Jane chatting up two very handsome Latino men. At that moment, no matter my sorrow at again leaving home, everything was right with the world and with me.

"Natalia, I want you to meet an artist friend of mine," Steven said, after I had stopped dancing and joined him and Jane. "This is Antonio Lopez."

"Hello," the handsome man said as I put out my hand that he kissed in a gentlemanly manner. "My dear, you look fantastic. I loved watching you dance. You're a wild woman out there. I'd love you to come to my studio so I can draw you." He handed me his card. "This is my partner, Juan," Antonio said, turning to the other handsome fellow standing next to him.

"Such a pleasure," I said, flabbergasted. "Thanks so much. It's very sweet of you to say."

The music seemed to get louder as the DJ spun into "Midnight Love Affair," with Carol Douglas singing, *Midnight love affair, how can I make you stay?*

Paulie was soon dragging me back onto the dance floor, though I heard Antonio shout over the music, "Call me! I look forward to hearing from you."

"Oh my God!" Paulie shouted over the music. "Do you know who he is? He's one of the top fashion illustrators right now!"

Steven and Jane were excited for me, too, impressed that Antonio had singled me out of the crowd.

Not wanting to waste any time, I connected with Antonio right away. We set a date for me to come by his studio. Later, he called me back and suggested that I go over to Studio 54 to meet his friend, Carmen D'Alessio, who was still looking for more models for the club's opening night. Maybe they'd want me to join their act of descending from ceiling swings like an old Ziegfeld Girls revue? What an incredible opportunity and how thoughtful it was for Antonio to remember me.

Putting on fresh lipstick and a little mascara, I traipsed right over there. Studio 54 was only a stone's throw from our apartment on West Forty-Ninth Street. Ringing the bell at the back entrance, I managed to get into the club by saying, "I'm here to meet with Carmen."

An incredibly chaotic scene ensued inside with the loud sounds of drills and hammers and people shouting filling the cavernous space. Off to one side, people in suits were huddled in an intense meeting, and over by the stage some dancers rehearsed a number. A bit bewildered, I just sat on the silver banquette watching all these people running around doing all kinds of last-minute detail work.

Finally, I asked someone who looked important whizzing by, "Have you seen Carmen?"

"No!" the person said, clearly annoyed. After sitting around for a couple of hours waiting for this Carmen person, still, no one acknowledged me. With this front row seat to New York nightlife, I felt I was more in the way than anything else.

Just before I was up and so out of there, Carmen appeared, clipboard in hand, amongst a loud cacophony of sighs, questions, answers, and a whole lot of drama in tow. She was flanked with an entourage of gay men on each side.

I quickly rose up from the banquette. "Ms. D'Alessio, I'm Natalia, one of Antonio's girls. He sent me here for a showgirl number."

She scanned me up and down like some street market vendor, and shook her head. "No, no, we were seeing girls yesterday, not today. It's too late. We don't need any more girls." She spoke angrily and walked away.

Feeling flustered, foolish, and incredibly frustrated, I went home and began preparing for the opening night's festivities.

• • •

When Paulie and I arrived at Studio 54 later that evening, the crowd on the street was so massive that it was next to impossible to get in through the main entrance, so we made our way to the less-crowded back entrance, on Fifty-Third Street. There, every time the doorman opened the door, the crowd lurched forward like a human wave, each time inching closer and closer.

As Paulie and I became swept up in the crowd as doors opened and people kept pushing their way in, I just happened to catch a glimpse of a familiar face. Wearing a straw hat—which did little to hide her famous mug—a henley T-shirt, and suspenders snapped to skintight bell-bottom faded jeans that flopped over snakeskin cowboy boots, was one of my early idols, Cher. Amazing that even a superstar like Cher had to push her way into this joint. I knew it was going to be a good night.

Making our way out onto the dance floor, I saw that the place was packed like sardines as people twirled and danced themselves into frenzy. Over by the stage, the iconic moon was gliding up and down with the infamous coke spoon up its nose. Celebrities were everywhere, mingling within the crowd or languishing in the silver leather banquettes that encircled the dance floor. Photographers were snapping away and I was posing much more than dancing and loving every minute.

Soon I noticed a commotion in the middle of the dance floor. Then I saw a large bunch of swirling balloons, which could mean only one thing: the entrance of the reigning pre-op trans superstar of the era, Potassa de la Fayette. Sought after by the fashion elite, photographed by Andy Warhol, and intimate friend of Salvador Dalí, she traveled with an entourage of younger Latin and butch queens. Potassa had shocked everyone by posing for Warhol completely nude and revealing her larger than average penis. It was known within our circle that she preferred an active role in between the sheets. I found it fascinating that she could be so open about her naked body when I felt so ashamed most of the time about my own genitalia. She was a notorious thief as well; my shoplifting paled in comparison. Indeed, Paulie told me that she wore off-the-rack couture that was often mopped right from under the nose of distracted Saks sales clerks or plucked from a smashed window at Henri Bendel or Bergdorf Goodman.

Seeing her now at the center of the Studio 54 dance floor, I, too, was transfixed by her mesmerizing antics and made mental notes for myself that someday I might be as audacious and thrilling as she.

Studio 54 was all over the press the next day. One headline read "Day of the Locusts" and featured the story of how guests impatient with waiting to get into the pleasure palace had forced their way in through the VIP side entrance. Steven called later in the day to tell me there were photos of me on the cover of *Men's Wear Daily*, the male version of *Women's Wear Daily*. After feeling so disappointed about the Carmen fiasco, I felt vindicated and buoyed by my ability to make a splash on my own. So, in my own small way I made it into the show despite the forces that were preventing me otherwise.

Another chance to make my mark would come soon enough. Jumping out of a taxi, I made my way up the stairs to Antonio's Union Square studio. Everything was happening so fast for me since returning to New York. Antonio wanted to do a few sketches of me and then include me in a full photo shoot with his usual bevy of beautiful models for an article on him in *Oui* magazine titled "Antonio's Girls." When I got to the studio, I had no idea what to expect since my only experience modeling was for Steven at RISD. But I felt confident that I could pull it off, given my devotion to fashion, style, and anything dramatic. Paulie came along to do my makeup and hair and I was comforted by his presence. All the other girls were cisgendered and none of them cared either way about my gender, though a few of the butch queens on the set were quite fixated on me. Another legendary illustrator, Joe Eula, was there as well.

Antonio asked me if I was comfortable modeling nude. *Well*, I thought, *as long as I could stay tucked*, I had figured as much since it was *Oui* magazine—not *Elle*—and was fine with it. At a recent visit to Dr. David Messier's office, I had had another session of silicone injections to increase the size of my breasts. Silicone was the Juvéderm of its day. In the seventies, everyone was running to Park Avenue plastic surgeons like Dr. Messier to inject it into their faces, chins, breasts, buttocks, and hips. Even some men were injecting it into their calves. All the trans women began to look alike, similar to the over use of Botox and face fillers today. The look was to get a tiny upturned nose and puff up your cheeks and chin with silicone. Some girls went over the top, injecting it into their breasts, buttocks, and hips. Apparently, and unbeknownst to me, it was in an experimental stage and would soon be banned. While I was satisfied after getting a reasonable amount into my cheeks, hips, and breasts, I was unable to escape the hideous side effects.

At the onset of these outbreaks I'd start to feel a burning, itching sensation within my breast. This was a clear indication I was in for another episode of soreness and hardening. The silicone injections would begin to clump together. A tiny lump would form and begin to expand, gaining width like a snowball rolling downhill. My skin would become hot, hard to the touch, and inflamed. At the time the only remedy was to go back to Dr. Messier and have him inject cortisone directly into the hardened area and prescribe prednisone pills. Eventually this would soften the silicone and eliminate the inflammation that occurred. The same thing would happen to the area around my hips. Using humor to alleviate the fear and mask my pain, I often joked that I felt like a human lava lamp. Sadly, even today some have died from overdoing these illegal procedures. It was no joke.

During that time, Antonio Lopez was doing a series of photo shoots of models popping out of candy bars. Most of his models were not the traditional classic beauties you would see in *Vogue*. Most of them shared an interesting exotic quality. He loved women and especially strong ones at that. As Paulie was preparing my makeup, the elevator door opened into his loft and I heard this cackling laughter fill the room. I turned to see who it was. The reigning disco queen herself, Grace Jones, slithered in like a panther unleashed. She couldn't have been more charming and down to earth. Paulie squealed, "It's fucking Grace Jones," as she slipped into the empty seat by me. When Paulie was finished we immediately got on the subject of astrology, which she loved and had a lively chat about her Taurean ways and her current boyfriend at the time, Jean-Paul Goude, a Sagittarius—an impossible match.

Antonio was ready and about to create one of his most iconic photos of Grace Jones climbing out of an oversized Almond Joy bar. I could barely contain my excitement as I watched her twist and writhe in the oversize candy bar with her recent hit "I Need a Man" blasting from the speakers. I took notes for when it was my turn. Later that day he shot me coming out of a Bazooka Bubble Gum wrapper. Some time later when I looked closely at the photos, I could see red inflammation already starting to appear on my breasts. Eventually this caused me an incredible amount of pain and suffering later on in my life, although not nearly frequently or as painful thanks to mega powerful antibiotic treatment.

But at that moment, life was serving me a delicious dish of adventurous freedom and I was too busy devouring as much of it as I could. Besides, I was having way too much fun. Throwing caution to the wind, I never once considered the consequences of my impulsive need to alter my appearance. The cost would come at a much higher expense than a few sessions of silicone. It was much more than the consciousness of an impetuous twenty-one-year-old. Pity the poor soul who would try to talk me out of it.

Another fabulous outing with Antonio was when he invited Paulie and me to attend a Fiorucci fashion show at Enchanted Gardens, the club owned by Steve Rubell and Ian Schrager before their mega success with Studio 54. Antonio had done a recent installation for Fiorucci, the au current retail shop on East Fifty-Ninth Street, where windows displayed huge cardboard cutouts of models wearing Fiorucci—including me!

The club was located in an abandoned country club on a city golf course in Queens, and the party was in full swing when we arrived. The special guest performer was Grace Jones, whose new single, "I Need a Man," was rocketing up the disco music charts. Grace suddenly appeared to entertain the crowd with a manic, mad lip-synch dressed in head to toe Fiorucci. Paulie and I had popped quaaludes before leaving and were feeling no pain now that we had arrived. Steven and Jane came along too. We were all dancing up a storm during a frenzy of disco when one of my stiletto heels snapped, and for the rest of the evening I hobbled around like Lucy or Ethel would do in *I Love Lucy*. I was high as a kite and, all the while, acting like an imaginary heel was holding up my shoe. Never did I feel more out of place than in this super well-heeled crowd.

CHAPTER 10

Club Crawl

While Studio 54 was the crème de la crème of New York City nightclubs, it spawned a succession of other great clubs, like Xenon, New York, New York, and Starship Discovery. Studio could be such a hassle, but these other clubs took less effort to get into and, besides, all I really wanted to do was go out, drink, drug, dance, and try to look fabulously fashionable doing it.

Although I felt comfortable in the predominantly trans atmosphere at the Gilded Grape on Eighth Avenue in Hell's Kitchen, which was a short walk from our apartment, I was often anxious and fearful there. Instead of punching a time clock at some job, I went to the Grape to earn my keep. It was safer than working on the stroll in Times Square and the guys knew what they were getting, looking only for those "girls with something extra" like myself. Being a younger trans woman might have made it easier for me to find tricks, but it also created tension with some of the heavily-seasoned regular girls who frequented the bar. I mean, it sure wasn't *Cheers*!

Go-Go boy nights were especially popular at the Gilded Grape because all the hot boys from the notorious Haymarket hustler bar up the street would come and try to make some extra cash by stuffing their huge packages into tiny, tight speedos as they danced for dollars.

If you arrived before six o'clock, there was no cover charge. This was a high-traffic time to catch a few tricks before the night's festivities began. Some girls worked nonstop at the Grape and could be fierce competitors for any guy that walked in the joint. Me, I was lazy and often made only enough money to pay my rent, and keep me in food, hormones, and other necessities. Usually, I would turn two or three tricks a day if I could. Sometimes, I wouldn't even make it halfway down Eighth Avenue before picking up a trick. If you were hungry, there was a free meal from the open buffet at the Grape. Ideally, it was best to score some cash early before the evening crowd strolled in and then have the rest of the night for fun and frolicking.

Diagonally across from the club was a short-term hotel where you could get your tricks to rent a cheap room. Or I would just drag them back to our apartment. If Paulie was out, this was even better. Some of the trans girls lived above the Gilded Grape in the Camelot Apartments, so if you gave them a few bucks they'd let you use their room. Down the block on West Forty-Fifth Street there was another apartment building called the Hildonah Court that housed a lot of the trans women.

Some of the men who came to the Gilded Grape were looking for more than a one-time fling and there were plenty of trans women to choose from. There were many Latino guys from the Bronx who were into trans women, a.k.a. banjee boys. Today we refer to these men as trans amorous. Back then we called them tranny chasers. Some of these guys hustled the older gay men who came to the club. There was a tight sense of community, mostly because of the frequency at which we went there. I had never experienced this in any other nightclub or bar that I hung out at. If you left with a trick, someone was watching and it felt less dangerous than jumping in and out of cars on Ninth Avenue. I became friendly with a lot of the other trans women there and the doormen were especially flirtatious if you looked good and didn't cause trouble.

One of the more infamous people who did a short stint as a bouncer at the Gilded Grape was a scrappy, rough-looking Irish guy named Mickey. He was very sexy in a beat-up kind of Marlon Brando way. A huge flirt, too, and the girls loved it. *Rough trade* is how people would describe him. If a trick was being annoying or if you were having any kind of hassle, he had your back for sure. Many years later, this same scrappy but sexy guy would go on to become an A-list movie star with some incredible acting chops. Mickey Rourke has spoken publicly about his lean and mean salad days in Hell's Kitchen.

If you were lucky enough to have passing privilege, your chances of finding a steady guy were much higher than if you were a little less soft in the looks department. The problem was that everyone was eager to hook up. God forbid if you had the misfortune of sleeping with another trans woman's "husband," a term used to define the relationship status. If a guy was known as so-and-so's husband, it meant he was more serious than a one-night stand and you'd better be careful. I witnessed more than one screaming, bitch slapping, and knockdown, drag-out fight over somebody else's "husband" in the club.

One night I met Sonny Fox, who was tall and trim with dark eyes and hair. He had a bushy mustache that hung over his thin lips like that of the seventies porn star Harry Reems. I hadn't seen him before and, as he followed me from the bar to the back of the club, I could tell he was trying to chat me up. Since my near fatal overdose in Providence, I hadn't been in a relationship. At twenty-one, I was still very gullible and I learned later that I wasn't the only one he was chatting up.

I was flattered that Sonny was laying such a heavy rap, especially since he was sexy in a Guido kind of way. He was charming and had a killer smile. When he told me he was from Queens, I replied, "Well, I'm from normal parents," which he found really funny. He had grown up in a practicing Jewish middle-class community in Forest Hills and worked for a telemarketing company.

Ending up at my apartment, we made love; the sex was okay but not the fireworks I had expected. Sonny had also bragged that his ex-girlfriend was Cory Daye, the lead singer of Dr. Buzzard's Original Savannah Band. I was impressed because I was a huge fan of their music, but to this day, I'm not sure how true it was.

Quickly we became a couple and he got a job as a bouncer at the 220 Club, an after-hours club in the Village, after losing his alleged job as a telemarketer. I'm naturally suspicious. Mistrust of others was bred into me at a very early age so it wasn't surprising when I became suspicious of Sonny.

He'd disappear for endless periods of time, telling me he was "running out for cigarettes" or "going to the deli for beer." Hours later he'd come back seeming very different from before. I couldn't figure out why.

The 220 Club opened at 4:00 a.m. and had a nondescript entrance on Houston Street. You had to ring the bell a few times before gaining entrance. It was Sonny's job to frisk all the patrons for weapons and to keep a general sense of peace within the club.

On ground level, the club had a long bar, dark-paneled walls, and dim lights, and in the back was coat check, run by an extremely handsome woman. "They call me Stormé," the woman said, in a slightly honeyed southern drawl.

She was of mixed race and her salt-and-pepper hair was short but picked out into a mini Afro. She wore a leather vest and Levi jeans neatly tucked into heavy black motorcycle boots, giving her a scary biker look.

"If anyone fucks with you, make sure you let me know right away."

Stormé would always call me "darling." She called everyone darling, though surely I thought it was just for me. She loved to regale me with stories of her time as a male MC for the Jewel Box Revue, the legendary female impersonator show in the East Village where Judy Garland and Frank Sinatra were frequent guests. I never knew until many years later that Stormé allegedly was the woman whose scuffle with the police set off the now historic gay civil rights movement at the Stonewall bar in 1969. Not surprisingly, she was as humble as anyone I had ever known. I maintained a friendship with her until very late in her life, feeling grateful that not only had I been touched by her kindness, but also inspired by her ferocious activism to this day.

Several months later, I entered—and won—a beauty contest at the club. The title of "Miss 220, 1977" brought some clout and soon I was always given free entrance to 220 and other Mafia-run clubs in the city. To be honest, being named Miss 220 elevated my status within the trans community and gave me a little local celebrity status—and, of course, it also incited jealousy and competition from some of the other girls. For the first time, I felt seen in the world and this definitely didn't hurt my ego.

I wanted to share my good fortune with my mother, so I had to run down to the corner phone booth on west Forty-Ninth and Ninth Avenue. Fumbling for the correct amount of change, I dialed Ma's number.

"That will be seventy cents please," the operator said as I dumped the coins into the slot. The phone rang several times before my mother answered.

"Hello," she said.

"Hi, Ma, it's me, calling from New York," I said.

She hung up.

Standing at the phone booth for a minute I tried to decide if I should call back or not. Dejected, I left the booth and headed back up the street to my apartment. I felt so sad that my decision to try and be who I was caused so much unhappiness for my family and me.

• • •

What also hurt was my escalating use of drugs and alcohol. My newfound status as the reigning Miss 220 brought with it the responsibility to represent the club at other bar events. Another Village haunt was a dim bar called Kelly's Village West. Its owner, Kelly Dunkle, was another no-nonsense, tough lady who was cut from the same cloth as Stormé; although smaller in stature, she was no less fierce. Her fine Irish features were framed by bleached blond hair, slicked back into a fifties pompadour. Kelly was the overseer for both the 220 Club and Kelly's. Her work at the 220 seemed more of a favor that she owed to some unknown entity. It was never clearly spelled out, but inferred that she was working for some big family.

I was obligated to attend any event they might be having or even any cabaret or drag show that was going on there. Even if I didn't want to go, it was hard to resist the underlying sense of duty. During these events, there was always free blow and plenty of booze. It wasn't unusual to spend quite a bit of time in the office at Kelly's doing lines of blow and sipping on champagne. I had a really low tolerance to alcohol and honestly it wasn't my favorite thing but as usual I went along to get along. By the time I was ready to hit the 220 Club, I was already in a sorry state.

There was less time to attend some of the bigger discos like Xenon, housed in the Henry Miller Theater on West Forty-Third Street. Xenon was the latest club. John F. Kennedy Jr. was a frequent guest and an unknown DJ named Jellybean Benitez got his start there. He would go on to romance and collaborate with us to one of our most iconic pop stars, Madonna. It soon became an alternative and hipper club to be seen at than Studio 54.

The Gilded Grape closed and reopened as the new GG's Barnum Room. It was still transgender central, occupying the old Diplomat Hotel. Someone had the brilliant idea to include a trapeze and a net above the old lobby entrance. Every night there were shows including scantily clad flying go-go boys and trans women in bikinis. It was a huge hit with the bridge and tunnel crowd and the New York nightlife crowd. While I imagined myself trying to join in on the circus atmosphere, my heels were happily planted on the disco floor. It didn't stop some of the other trans girls flying on the trapeze above the dance floor like some crazy disco bats.

GG's Barnum Room wasn't exempt from providing us girls with the opportunity to make some extra cash. The clientele from the old Gilded Grape soon discovered this new location and men were continuously on the prowl for some action. Another way you could make some money there was by doing some lip-synching performances. As the reigning Miss 220, I got to perform there and was paid a hundred bucks a night. It was easy money. While I wasn't comfortable with lip-synching, I rose to the challenge.

For one of my first gigs as Miss 220, I chose to lip-synch to Donna Summer's "I Remember Yesterday." Donna was a surefire crowd pleaser and, since my hair was wild and curly, I could easily pull off her look. The audience sauntered up and stuffed dollar bills in my dress or hand as I wildly interpreted Ms. Summer's popular song. It was a lot of fun and a welcome alternative to sex work to earn some extra coins.

CHAPTER 11

Lush Life

What Sonny had failed to tell me in those early days of our burgeoning relationship was that he was a heroin addict. It was always one more made-up story after the next. Sadly, I felt sorry for him, especially when he came clean to me about his struggle with addiction. For me, it provided the opportunity to try and rescue him from his misery. Little did I know of the cunning, baffling power of addiction and how it was a much bigger dragon to slay. Never did I imagine the invaluable lesson I was about to learn, which nearly cost me my life.

One day I begged Sonny Fox to let me try heroin.

"Come on, Sonny, hit me up. I want to see what the big deal is." I couldn't for the life of me understand what it was that made him so completely obsessed with using this drug.

Reluctantly, he honored my request. Cooking up a little of the brown powder, he filled the syringe and popped it into my upper arm.

"I don't feel anything," I said. "That's it? Put it in my arm the way you do it." I insisted.

What the fuck? Is this really all there is to heroin? I thought. He cooked up some more of the brown powder. Wrapping a belt around my arm, he asked me to clench my fist until he put the needle in. Within seconds, I felt a ringing in my ears and a numbness came over me that made me understand why people went crazy for heroin. Instantly, I was hooked. But not before I felt a churning in my stomach sending me running to the bathroom to throw up.

I also realized, through shooting heroin for the first time, that all my problems and anxieties would vanish. It quickly became apparent that the only problem I had now was how and where do I get more.

Our arguments were vicious. I grew hysterical when he would disappear and come back nicely buzzed and nod off at home. Even worse was our sex life, because heroin really is a hard-on killer. Why have a dick if you can't use it? By now my own drug use had escalated to frequent use of Tuinal and speed, booze, and occasional weed. Not innocent by any means. But when it came to my own substance abuse I was in denial because I wasn't a full-fledged junkie.

By this time, I was deeply enmeshed in the New York nightclub culture and my days often started in the afternoon around two or three. Sonny and I were now living together in the Forty-Ninth Street apartment, since Paulie had moved back down to the Village to be with his new lover, Stanley.

Marrying into Sonny's world of heroin addiction took me to some of the lowest depths of my drug use. We would cop at any given time of day or night. Now, just like my old flame Bobby, I was hooked. I had no problem heading out to the street to make money to get more. In fact, it was convenient where we lived because you could catch a trick on Eighth Avenue any time, day or night, and one spot that was especially active was at Forty-Fifth and Ninth Avenue.

One night when a car pulled around the corner, I strolled up to the window and said hello. No sooner did I bend down to the driver, another car pulled up behind me with blaring sirens. Next, I was hauled up to 100 Centre Street in Harlem. The cop strip-searched me and placed me in a cell by myself for the night.

The cop on duty was a greasy, heavyset guy whose acne clearly suggested way too many visits to the local donut shop. He led me down to the holding area and put me into the last cell. I had no money, no cigarettes, and no heroin. It was going to be a long night. Since it was 1977 BC (before cellphones), I also had no way to get in touch with Sonny. Surely, he was thinking I'd run off again with somebody for fun.

The big cop was extra nice and brought me a candy bar and some Cheetos. I asked him for a smoke. He said he'd give me five bucks and a pack of Newports if I took care of him, his eyes widening as he looked down to his crotch. It was late. Soon, I'd be heading downtown to court and would need money to get back home if they let me go. Without any consideration, I agreed and he unbuckled his pants and pushed his junk through the cell bars for me to get him off. Physically, he was quite disgusting, but the fact that he would abuse his power and take advantage of me was what really pissed me off. This was only the beginning of years of humiliation related to my drug use.

Another time, Sonny and I entered an abandoned building on Eldridge Street in the Lower East Side to buy a set of works so we could shoot up. Right there, with other addicts lit by dim candlelight, he hit me up first so I could revive that illusive feeling of nothingness that comes with a heroin rush. Getting arrested or dying in that burned-out building hadn't occurred to me. Living fully as a trans woman, I found it harder and harder to face the daily struggles of my life. Drugs became a substitute for purpose in my life. The great thing I discovered was that all my problems, and there were many, all became one. Chasing numb was all that mattered.

Our addiction escalated and our screaming fights played in and out of public. I was now working as a barmaid at the 220 Club and liked to take Tuinal to take the edge off, but if I took too many I could be especially belligerent, especially to Sonny. One night I was tending bar on the second floor and taunted Sonny from the top of the staircase, provoking him to grab me by the hair and drag me down the concrete steps to the club's door and onto the street, which was glared in sunlight so bright it hurt my skin. One might think I'd be sore from having my ass dragged down concrete stairs, but no, the sun hurt more, brightly focused as it was on the mess I had made of my life.

Stormé DeLarverie, hearing all the commotion, rushed to my rescue.

"All right, you two. This doesn't look like loving to me. You're going to bring the cops down here if you don't cut this crap. Sonny," she yelled, "get the hell back up those stairs now!"

She turned to me. "Now, darling, come with me so we can get you cleaned up." My pantyhose were torn up and blood was running down one leg, but I felt no pain because I was so blasted.

· · ·

Fighting at the club cost both Sonny and me our jobs and, with our addiction to heroin spiraling out of control, soon our place to live too. Sadly, the only option was to head back to Rhode Island with my tuck between my legs. But was I taking my problems with me? Sonny wasn't going to let me go that easy. He agreed to score some street methadone for us to take the edge off while traveling, and promised me he would stop using once we got out of New York.

Del finally was taking my phone calls, and had eventually warmed up to the idea of my transition. She had started to realize it was more than just a phase. Now, I was faced with the ultimate test. We needed to get out of the city fast and I was nervous about how she would react, but made the call anyway.

"Hello, Ma, it's me."

"Well hello, Tishy, what's up?"

"I was wondering if you could do me a big favor. We're having trouble finding work here and thought it might be better to be back in Rhode Island."

"Oh really?" she said in a suspicious tone.

"Do you think we could come and stay with you for a bit till we get on our feet?"

There was silence and then, "I work every day and go to bed early. If you come here, you have to promise not to be a bother. No running around in the clubs until all hours. I need my rest."

"Thanks, Ma. It means the world to me."

My plea to her worked and she agreed to put us up for a little while. Unfortunately, she didn't know there was a third guest coming along, our little friend addiction. Del had been living pretty much by herself in our childhood home. On some level, I'm sure she was happy to have me back in Providence. She was even generous enough to get Sonny a job with her at Rhode Imports driving new cars off the freighters in the shipyard. Her position as a manager conferred a certain amount of clout. But gambling was the glue that Del and Sonny bonded over.

The little apartment we found a block over from my Ma's house was sufficient, though moving locations wouldn't remedy the seriousness of our addiction. In fact, it only escalated it further.

I worked the streets of Providence while Sonny worked with my mom. One night I was venturing downtown to try and make some money, but found myself feeling incredibly depressed, so depressed in fact that I ended up on the steps of Grace Church in downtown Providence. It was here where I had attempted to be in the boys' choir years before until my Jewish father found out and forbade me to continue.

It was dusk and the thought of moving from this special, solemn place to try to suck some dick to make a few bucks made me feel even lower. And the incredible dysfunction of my relationship and where I was at age twenty-two was overwhelming. The seriousness of my addiction and my inability to find peace within my gender identity and a place in the world was finally taking its toll. I wanted to die. I remained glued to the church steps. Unable to move, I tasted the warm salty tears trickling down my cheeks and falling across my painted red lips.

I don't know why but I was moved to look up and, in the distance, I saw a figure approach. His hair was long and flowing like a holdover from the sixties and he wore drawstring cotton pants and a loose shirt opened at the neck that revealed a soft tuft of chest hair. Clearly, it was a man and I couldn't help noticing the Jesus vibe he was giving off. I looked down at his feet and saw that he was wearing sandals.

"Hello," he said. "Are you okay?"

Wiping away tears, I said, "Yes, I'm fine. Do you want to go out?"

"You seem a little upset, my friend."

"I'm okay. I just need to make a few coins, that's all."

Something about this man seemed very different. I couldn't put my finger on it, but somehow he could see me as I really was. He could tell that there was heaviness and darkness in my heart. I can't remember his name, but I can see his smiling, open face and his long flowing blond hair falling around his shoulders. What happened next was what I can only describe as some sort of divine intervention. He sat down next to me and told me that whatever I was going through was okay and that he was happy to listen to whatever it was that was bothering me.

Before long we were walking and found ourselves at some park in Federal Hill by the Armory. Hours had now passed and I hadn't turned one trick or made any money. But I felt I was in the care of someone special that wanted nothing from me other than to see me safe from harm. Lying in the moist grass, we watched the sun begin to rise. Both of us just lay there quietly taking in the brilliant spectacle of a new day. It hadn't even occurred to me that I had been out all night long talking and walking with this man.

"I have to go," I said. "My boyfriend is going to kill me."

"Okay. Why don't I walk you home?"

I agreed and before long I was at my front door. I felt so close to this odd fellow and hated to see him go.

"If you want to wait for my boyfriend to leave for work, you could come up for a little while longer." Pointing up to my window, I told him that I'd wave when the coast was clear.

Hoping the scene wouldn't turn ugly, I told Sonny that I had been out all night but couldn't make a dime. Begrudgingly, he believed me and left for work. From the window, I watched him walk away from our apartment building to the nearby bus stop. When he was far enough away, I waved for my friend to come up. While I had no particular agenda, my new friend was very handsome though sex wasn't something I had even considered. He could tell my anxiety was welling up and suggested I lie down on the bed to relax.

I did so because I had such great trust in him.

"Why don't you close your eyes and try to get some rest," he said. "It's been a very long night for you."

I lay back and closed my eyes. He began to gently rub my forehead and slowly massage my face, before moving down to my neck and the front of my shoulders. I remained quiet. His touch was soft and soothing and never before had I been handled so lovingly by anyone, not even as a child. My skin tingled with his touch. He slowly removed my blouse and massaged my breasts. He was making his way down to my jeans.

Quickly, my mind went to the fearful place it always did whenever someone reached below my waist. Tensing up, I panicked and felt ashamed, imagining how he would react to what was between my legs. While I knew of other trans women friends who were quite proud of using their penis in sexual situations, for me it felt wrong. It was incongruous with the fact that I was presenting myself as female, in sexual situations as well as in the world at large, and so I should also only remain passive sexually.

The truth is it felt shameful using my penis in any way. It was something with which I was never comfortable. Even if a trick paid me, revealing my penis always created a moment of terror. It would take years of therapy before I could be at peace with my body as a complete and functioning entity.

My breathing became shorter as I felt my friend unbutton and tug on my bell-bottom jeans as he slid them off. Slowly, he began massaging my legs and thighs. All the while, he asked that I keep my eyes closed. It felt incredible. Then, without hesitation, he reached for my penis and performed oral sex on me until I reached the most amazing climax I have ever had. He still wanted me to keep my eyes closed, which was no problem due to the level of release and relaxation I had just experienced. What was more amazing was that I didn't feel shame about the sex we had. It felt loving and caring, something I wasn't at all used to.

Finally, when I did open my eyes, he was gone. Feeling lightheaded, I rose up and went to the window and looked out. He was walking away, but then turned, looked up, saw me, and waved as he disappeared around the corner.

What had just happened? Suddenly, it felt as though I knew what I had to do with my life. Somehow this stranger had instilled a sense of faith in me that I had never had before that day. Intuitively, I knew I had to end my relationship with Sonny. Something told me that when he came home I would do just that. Feeling a sense of peace, I drifted off to sleep and didn't wake up until I heard a key jiggling in the lock.

• • •

Immediately, Sonny began to grill me about the night before and he eventually let on that he had seen the stranger who had kept me safe all night come into the apartment. We had a knockdown drag-out fight, with fists flying and things getting smashed. I told him to get out and that I was through with his abuse and his drug habit and that I wanted no more of it. He lunged at me and placed his hands around my neck, squeezing and squeezing until I began to feel faint. I kicked him hard in the balls just in time and gasped for air. I began screaming so loudly that he eventually panicked and took one more swing at me as he headed for the door.

"Get out! Get out before I call the police!" I yelled as he scrambled down the hallway stairs.

Finally, he was gone. I collapsed into a pile of anguish over the enormity of what had just occurred. He might have strangled me to death had I not kicked him. If I called the cops now, surely they would want me to go down to the police station to make a statement. Knowing too well from experience that they would mock me, I decided not to put myself through that.

Paulie was so grateful that I was okay after I frantically dialed his number in New York and explained the events of the past twenty-four hours. Throughout our friendship, he was always fearful that I would meet the wrong person or meet some horrible fate because of my identity. When you are living as a trans woman with passing privilege, it's very easy to get men really pissed off at you. If you don't tell them right off the bat that you are trans, it can—and often does—turn out badly. Murder isn't an uncommon response from these guys. Their masculinity is so threatened. It's extremely confusing why they would be turned on or sexually attracted to a woman who wasn't assigned female at birth. Many times, men didn't know when they met me. Predicting their reaction became a science all its own. I just knew I had to be very careful. You could never tell what reaction some men would have. To this day, many trans women are still murdered. Paulie's fears were not unfounded. I did take incredible risks. How I didn't meet a worse fate than nearly being strangled to death by Sonny was nothing short of a miracle.

I told Paulie how my encounter with the longhaired stranger had made me realize that I must make changes in my life. He reminded me of my dream to become an actress and suggested that I might think about getting back on track with that goal.

"You have a right to happiness just like anyone else, Tish," he said. "That guy was sent to you as sign that there's a better life for you than the one you have with Sonny."

I was comforted hearing him call me by my nickname. I felt so loved by him whenever he called me Tish, a pet name that was mostly used by Paulie and my family members.

I next called my mother and explained what happened with Sonny, altering some of the facts, of course, but telling her just enough of the details to get him fired from his job. Eventually he took up with another trans women, Dusty, a former friend from my coming-out years at the Gallery Disco who had also transitioned. Rumor had it that she had a lot more to tuck than most girls and that Sonny was on the receiving end of it. While I had once considered her a friend, I wasn't the least bit concerned that they both continued to use heroin. They deserved each other's misery.

CHAPTER 12

Drama Major

On my way out of City Hall, after dropping off some paperwork, I bumped into a well-dressed, good looking guy. Excusing my clumsy self, I stopped at the bottom of the steps. I freed a Newport cigarette from my purse and the man asked if I needed a light. We struck up a conversation and he told me he worked at the State House as a Rhode Island state representative.

Immediately, I thought, *Well, I could use a few extra bucks.* Although I was trying to change my life, I still couldn't resist making some desperately needed money.

Exchanging pleasantries he handed me his card and asked for my number. Having developed a sixth sense about these things, it was obvious to me that he hadn't spooked me as trans but pegged me for a cis woman. Playing it cool, I scribbled my number on a book of matches and handed it to him.

His name was Vincent, Vinnie for short. He called me the next day and it felt safe for me to invite him over. He arrived at my apartment with flowers and a bottle of wine, which I thought was pretty classy. After a few glasses, it wasn't long before the topic of sex came up. He was going on and on about Marlon Brando and how *The Last Tango in Paris* was one of his favorite movies. He said he especially liked the sex scene when Marlon butters up Maria Schneider for anal sex.

I took this as my cue to negotiate some business. Walking over to the fridge, I pulled out a stick of Land O' Lakes butter and waving it in my hand, asked, "Is this what you had in mind?"

Since I hadn't told him I wasn't female at birth, I orchestrated the whole scene by bending over and instructing him to keep his hands on my breasts as I played the Maria Schneider role. He never knew I didn't have a vagina because I kept my free hand over my crotch as if I was stimulating myself. It was an old trick that one of my trans girlfriends had taught me. I continued to schedule his visits and played out this little scenario for a number of months, until a chance encounter would lead my life into an entirely new direction.

Now twenty-three, I was so thankful for Paulie's caring and sound advice. It was a welcome change. He was always there, gently nudging or guiding me in the right direction; he possessed the well-oiled morals I sorely lacked. I desperately needed to find something that brought me some joy, and acting soon became everything for me.

Step one was to get my GED and then apply to Rhode Island College. Education took money and while I paid my way through beauty school by working on street corners at night, I was trying really hard not to rely on sex work as a way of life. Getting some financial assistance was the first order of business. Besides, the daily grind of sex work played heavily on what little self-esteem I had. After my last escapade into heroin addiction, let alone the inherent legal and physical danger involved, I had to make a change. Since some of my other trans friends had applied and received welfare and food stamps because of their gender identity, I would too.

Being a high school dropout, I knew if I was going to make an attempt at a better life the first thing I had to do was get my GED. Having obtained some support for my basic needs—food, rent, and utilities from Public Assistance—this would be a little more bearable. If I did make some cash on the side, I could use it for hormones, electrolysis, and anything else I might need. I studied to get my GED and managed to pass. I was eligible for financial assistance for college and, before I knew it, I had my books and classes were set to begin.

I had met another trans woman through Paulie on one of my last visits to New York. Dana Brough's waspy uptight parents in New Britain, Connecticut, were so unhappy about her desire to transition to female that they had all but disowned her. She was working at an office job, which Paulie thought was impressive, as did I. Trans or gender nonconforming folks rarely worked in such places back then. Dana became Dayna. Blonde, blue-eyed, and highly educated, she was like no one I knew except Paulie. He thought she might be a positive influence on me now that I was trying to set my life on a better course. Soon she left New York and came to Providence and we would become roommates. I became Dayna's drag-mother in the same way Rusty was mine. We used the term *drag-mother*, as there wasn't a rigid distinction of LGBTQ terminology like there is today. If you called someone *tranny*, it was considered a real compliment to that person, not an insult like so many trans women find it to be today.

My brother Jeffery found me a great two-bedroom apartment. He lived on the third floor with his girlfriend and their two small children. While I don't think Jeffery ever really got over the changes I made, he did accept me to the best of his ability and I was able to have a relationship with him and his family. Unlike my older brother Randy who had rejected me and kept his kids from me, Jeffery let me babysit on occasion for him, which was a huge change in our relationship. I especially enjoyed being Auntie Tish to my young niece and nephew.

During this time, I was far along in my transition and was enjoying my passing privilege. Most of the time I wasn't being recognized as a trans woman because I'd become so convincing in my female identity. I wore very little makeup and was so proud that my complexion was soft and creamy. The extensive electrolysis and hormones had done wonders for my transformation. In fact, no one in college suspected I was trans—or if they did, I wasn't aware of it. Today it wouldn't be that big a deal to see a trans person in college, but in 1979 it was a very rare occurrence.

Through the CETA program, (Comprehensive Employment and Training Act) I applied and was accepted to work at the Rhode Island Housing Authority to provide arts and crafts projects to the residents. The clients and staff could never pronounce *Natalia* so instead they called me "Miss Natalie." It made me sound like some *Romper Room* hostess but it always gave me chuckle.

Before I knew it, my first day of classes at Rhode Island College arrived. I managed to give myself plenty of time to get there, as I didn't want to be late on my first day. I pulled my hair up into a classic French twist and fluffed some curls to frame my face. I headed outside to catch the bus up to school. My excitement grew as the college campus appeared in the distance. The reality that I had managed to pull myself up and get back on course with my life felt great. It was evident I was on a new journey. At that moment, I decided not to let anything interfere with my plans for my education. Being the first in my family to attend college, I felt proud.

Walking onto campus, I was filled with a heady mix of fear, joy, and skepticism. Well aware of the obstacles I might face as a trans woman, I didn't let them stop me. Walking down the hall of the campus building, I found the classroom for Introduction to Theater History. I took a seat by the window in the back.

Professor Joseph D. Graham entered. Resembling the actor Tony Randall, he began his lecture by speaking about the origins of Greek theater. While I felt like a fish out of water—since my theatrical knowledge consisted of two plays, *Inherit the Wind* and *The Crucible*, from high school—I was riveted by his talk and was able to relax and get away from my own concerns. I felt equally relaxed in my three other courses—English 101, Dance and Movement, and Acting 101—and found it easy to make friends. One day a burly gay guy with a mass of wild wavy brown curls and a snaggletooth grin, walked into my theater history class. He made a beeline to sit next to me.

"Excuse me, hon, is this seat free? I'm John and who might this vision of loveliness before my eyes be?" He slid into the empty desk beside me, dumping his books on top.

A bit startled by his obvious gayness, I said, "I'm Natalia. Nice to meet you." I spoke in the breathiest tone I could muster.

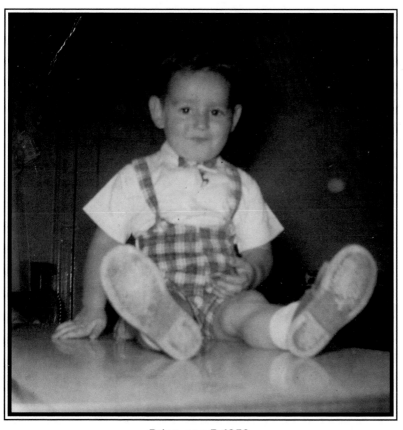

Brian, age 3, 1959.
(Courtesy of the Belovitch Archive)

Brian (age 5), Del, and
Itsy Newport.
(Courtesy of the
Belovitch Archive)

Joseph, Randall, Brian, and Jeffery.
(Courtesy of the Belovitch Archive)

Brian, age 11, and Shelia in 1967 in Stanwood.
(Courtesy of the Belovitch Archive)

Brian, age 14, in junior high in Fall River.
(Courtesy of the Belovitch Archive)

Natalia in 1972 in Rusty's Lola apartment.
(Courtesy of the Belovitch Archive)

Natalia, age 17, and Paul
Bricker, age 18, in 1973.
(Courtesy of the
Belovitch Archive)

Natalia as Miss 220.
(Courtesy of the
Belovitch Archive)

Natalia springing out of a Bazooka Bubble Gum wrapper
as one of Antonio's girls in 1977.
(Courtesy of the Estate of Antonio Lopez and Juan Ramos)

Antonio's girls in 1977.
(Courtesy of The Estate of Antonio Lopez and Juan Ramos)

Natalia and Denny's wedding in Rhode Island in 1980. (Courtesy of the Belovitch Archive)

Natalia and Denny in Germany in 1981. (Courtesy of the Belovitch Archive)

While he was a bit overwhelming at first—think big queen on campus—John and I became fast friends and confidants. He worked at the campus cafeteria so we'd always hang out there during lunchtime. He was fascinated with me because he had never met a trans woman who actually looked like and presented as a woman. Most of his experiences were with overly made-up drag queens. My friendship with John proved to be invaluable, with him guiding me through the somewhat baffling procedures of college life. I didn't have the luxury of attending orientation or coming straight from high school with some expectations having already been understood. In a way, I was ignorant to campus life and how things worked in higher education. Remember, my education was mostly in the streets. John knew everyone and was well liked. But I did worry that his being so openly gay on campus might bring more scrutiny to me.

Weeks into the first semester, auditions were happening for the spring 1980 production. Professor Graham was directing the next production and invited me to audition for the part of Vanessa in Woody Allen's *Play It Again, Sam*. She's one of the male lead's fantasy women and appears in a dream sequence. Professor Graham offered me the role and soon rehearsals were under way.

If you had told me then that I would be making my stage debut on April 24, 1980, after all that had transpired with Sonny, I would have thought you were insane. The debut would indeed happen, but not without a few bumps along the way. For one thing, the costume designer, Eva, had a very different idea than I did on what Vanessa should look like. When Eva enthusiastically showed me a sketch for my costume, I couldn't help but laugh out loud at how ridiculous it was. Eva had my character in a short harlequin printed minidress that reeked of clown couture rather than sexy, while Vanessa was a total sex bombshell who made her reputation taking on the entire football team at Yale. I needed to be more siren than loon.

My opinion did not go well with Eva, who dug in her high heels and was appalled that I would even question her design. I explained the situation to the director, Professor Graham, who clearly understood and advocated for me to the designer, which I thought would be the end of it. But it wasn't. In the meantime, Rusty had designed me a full-length black satin charmeuse gown, a knock-off of Rita Hayworth's dress in *Gilda*. After all, I took this very seriously. If I was going to be making my stage debut, it had to be perfect. My perfectionism was about to rear its ugly little head in a way that would persist to this day.

No student had ever challenged a designer in the theater department this way so it became a big deal. I was asked to model both costumes in front of the head of the theater department, Professor David Burn, who also taught my acting class and, of course, didn't like me. He never called on me in class to do any scenes and would instead only use the same three pretty college girls and two handsome men. This really pissed me off, which didn't go unnoticed by John who was also in the class. Professor Burn also loved to drink. He could always be found drinking after class in the college pub, holding court with the same group of favorite actors.

The day had come and I wasn't happy that I had to model both out-fits. As I modeled the ugly clown couture mini, I couldn't help but make a comment about how awful it looked.

"This is really more for a skit on *Laugh-In*," I blurted out.

Professor Burn seized the opportunity to act out his trans phobia and said, "Just shut up and show us the costume. If I need your opinion, I'll ask for it."

"Well, we already know what that is," I said. "Isn't that why we're here?"

"Didn't I tell you to keep your mouth shut?"

"Listen, I'm not going to take any bullshit from a drunk like you!" I blurted out.

What followed was a nasty exchange between us with me calling him out on his prejudice and how he couldn't talk to me that way. I don't know what got into me, but standing up for myself was new and I kind of liked how it made me feel. Burn had contempt for everything I stood for. But I wasn't going to allow him or anyone else to bully me or abuse me in the way I had let Sonny do in the past.

In the end, Professor Graham made the final decision and I wore Rusty's satin gown and made quite a splash in my scene in the play. After I entered in a puff of smoke, my first line was, "I've had many men, my first at twelve, and once I took on the entire Delta Kappa Phi fraternity at Yale. It's still a record in New Haven!" The audience howled with laughter at my acting, but not at me. I hit every beat and nailed the monologue every time. This made me a bit of an overnight sensation on campus and the whole theater department was buzzing about the big costume drama that had unfolded behind the curtain. Overall, the experience ratcheted up my confidence and not once did anyone ever make any reference to my gender identity or question my talent ever again. Paulie came all the way from New York to see me. His mom Gloria came along too.

"Oh boy, you were outta this world," Gloria exclaimed, giving me a hug. "You belong on the stage, Tishy! Just startling! Could you hear the response from the audience?"

Paulie piped in, too. "All those guys were howling and whistling. Imagine if they ever knew!"

I had invited Del and her friend Helen but they never showed up. My siblings, on the other hand, were not interested in theater, let alone trying to do anything outside of their comfort zone.

As I basked in the excitement of my achievement that night I couldn't help feeling overwhelmed at how my life was changing. Going from an ex-heroin addict, street prostitute, and survivor of domestic violence with a junkie boyfriend to a college student majoring in theater and working part-time at a legitimate job as an arts and crafts instructor with inner city residents and seniors was beyond my comprehension. Imagine my surprise at this seismic shift in lifestyle. As I headed back to my dressing room to change I caught a glimpse in the mirror. I began to weep tears of gratitude, wondering what other challenges were ahead in my twenty-two-year-old life.

CHAPTER 13

Love Connection

Paulie was making a toast. "Here's to Tish, a true star with a heart as big as her reputation at Yale and the best friend anyone could have."

After the play, Paulie and I had headed downtown to celebrate my stage success at a popular little gay bar called the Mira Bar. It had a real seventies modern look, with a black shiny interior, low lighting, and a curved sleek black Formica bar with high stools. Behind the bar a mirror wrapped around the length of the wall so that anywhere you looked you could easily see others' reflections. It was great for flirting and a good way to keep your eye on what was happening around you.

Happy for the first time, I was truly overwhelmed by all the good that was happening in my life, despite the daily struggle to find my place in the world.

Paulie leaned over and asked, "Is it still cool to smoke weed in here?"

I nodded as we dashed over to the ladies' room.

Once inside, Paulie fired up a joint and took the first long hit. He passed it to me and I pulled it deep into my lungs and, just as I was about to exhale, the door burst open.

It was the handsome doorman I had noticed earlier when he had held the door for me as we entered the bar. He was a bit taller than me with dreamy sea green eyes and dirty blond hair that just brushed his shirt collar.

He was shaking his head with a disapproving look, one a parent might give a naughty child. "Sorry, but the boss doesn't want this going on in here. You're going to have to take it outside."

"No problem, handsome," I said, looking at Paulie and flashing my eyes for him to leave. I got a really good look at him now, as I finally let the smoke escape my lips. Our eyes met and he blushed. Now that we were alone, he leaned in and asked me my name.

"I'm Tish," I said.

"Tish?" he repeated.

"Yes, Tish. It rhymes with fish." I said, giggling like a geisha.

"I'm Denny, short for Dennis."

The weed was good and I was buzzed. "You want a hit?" I passed him the joint and he took a little pull on it and then leaned close to my face, our lips almost touching. He blew the smoke into my mouth, shotgun style, as the sound of Joni Mitchell's voice singing the first chorus of "Help Me" emanated from the bar outside. *Help me. I think I'm falling in love again. When I get that crazy feeling, I know I'm in trouble again.*

Denny pulled back for me to exhale and then leaned in and began kissing me. This was the time when my initial anxiety about being trans would typically rocket through the roof. If it hadn't been for the hazy buzz, I would have pulled away and played my usual coy, *What kind of girl do you take me for?* routine. But it was too late. His kiss was soft, sweet, and gentle. I had a sixth sense about men and somehow knew when they were going to be cool or not cool with my gender identity. But we were in a gay bar, after all, and he worked here.

We ended up back at my apartment on Goddard Street and made love all night long. He never asked me about my gender so my hunch that he might have had figured it out had been right. The next morning, I explained to Denny how Tish came to be. I expressed what I hoped would happen in the future. This wasn't the first time I had recalled my story to a potential partner but this time it did feel different. There was an acceptance I hadn't felt with any other man before. Could this be the real thing?

Like me, Denny was from a broken home and a large family. Like mine, his mother was a single mom who raised a bunch of kids on her own. Denny had a past, too, which involved legal problems and ending up in a home for boys at one point in his early life. At nineteen years old, he was a bit young for me, but then I was barely twenty-three. His father was Italian and his mom was French, which provided him with his classic good looks. What I liked most about him immediately was his cool composure and steady manner. Nothing really seemed to bother him, which made sense because he was born under the sign of Capricorn, a very stable and grounded earth sign, in sharp contrast to my triple fire sign status.

Things moved fast. Before long, I moved my man in and I was strategizing on how to get rid of Dayna. She was well on her way in her transition. I was tired of her being the third wheel in our relationship. She was needy and having to include her everywhere we went was an imposition.

Eventually, Dayna and I had a huge falling out. She was moving in with her boyfriend and tried to skip out without paying her share of the rent. After all I had done for her, this wasn't a good way to treat a friend. She was ungrateful for all the guidance and care I had shown her and I really resented it. Sometime later she made some half-assed apology and we restarted our friendship. As fate would have it, our paths would cross again later in New York at a moment when my life would take yet another unforeseen direction.

Denny found a job and we were bringing in a little more money so we found another apartment within walking distance of my job. But I soon discovered that Denny truly had a bad temper and had trouble keeping jobs because his anger would get the best of him.

While I was content with the state of my physical being, I wasn't ever happy with the size of my breasts. Being a big-boned gal with broad shoulders, I knew a fuller bust line would detract from that and feminize my appearance even more. Luckily, I was receiving health benefits from my job. Knowing it would be challenging to get it done in Rhode Island, I went to New York and consulted with Dr. David Messier, who had already plied my hips and breasts with silicone. The doctor somehow finagled a way to get my insurance to pay for my hospital stay and the procedure itself. Messier was one of the shadiest and most unethical plastic surgeons on Park Avenue. He would write prescriptions for anything I wanted on more than one occasion. His waiting room could be a real horror show. Often, I would see someone who resembled Jocelyn Wildenstein, the current New York socialite who overdosed on plastic surgery. She clearly had no idea when to stop. She's known as the lion woman of New York as her face ended up resembling a lion. If he were at all ethical, he would refuse to do more work on patients like that.

The day arrived when I was scheduled to be in Yonkers for my procedure. Paulie escorted me on the trip and did his best to calm me on the train. I settled in and was prepped for the surgery; I was stripped to the waist and felt the nurse strap my arms out from my sides like some crucified Jesus. Slowly, they administered the anesthesia and I felt a little loopy, sensing the wheels under the gurney rolling down the hall to the operating room. Once we were inside, Dr. Messier came in and asked me if I was okay. I said, "Whatever you do, just make them big and bouncy," right as I lost consciousness.

Awaking in my room and still feeling no pain, I was wrapped in gauze around my torso. Reaching down and feeling my chest, I could tell there was a big improvement in size.

More confident in my physical appearance, it was time to meet Denny's entire family in Woonsocket, Rhode Island. His mother, an ex-nurse who had been born in Wyoming, adored me and loved that I was in college studying theater and English. I really hit it off with his sister and half-siblings as well. They never knew my gender was ever something other than what I presented.

One day I was home alone sitting at the kitchen table in front of a pile of Popsicle sticks trying to come up with ideas for my arts and crafts class when Denny came through the door. He had a look on his face suggesting he had a secret he couldn't wait to tell me. He told me he had gone downtown to the recruitment office and joined the Army. My whole life flashed before my eyes, as I was certain this was his way of ending our relationship, for there was no way I could see myself fitting into this plan at all. "Don't ask, don't tell" wasn't even on the radar yet and if you were gay you kept it a secret and certainly never let on to anyone; otherwise, you could be thrown out.

"Are you out of your fucking mind?" I said. "There's no way in hell we can be together if you join the Army."

"Well, there is one way," he said.

"And what's that?"

"We can get married and you can come overseas with me."

"Married?" I said. "Honey, are you stoned?"

Sometimes being a little naive can be an advantage. Never once did I think about the legality of what I was about to attempt. The wheels in my mind began to spin. I thought, *Well, I do have identification that states my gender as female.* All I needed to do was show a driver's license at the City Hall clerk's office; then I guess it wouldn't be too difficult. Getting the license was easy but when I went to take the required blood test, I sat there sweating the whole time, worrying that you might be able to tell a person's sex by their blood. Luckily, you can't. The whole process was a lot easier than we expected. We even decided to have a small ceremony with Denny's Catholic priest friend/trick on the side performing the ceremony. Was this really happening, I thought to myself, as I imagined my future as the wife of a handsome Army GI?

My current boss at the Housing Authority, Ann, let us use her lovely home on the East Side of Providence for the wedding. We invited Denny's entire immediate family and a few close friends from school and work. Paulie would be the best man and my friend Lori Freeman agreed to be my maid of honor. I invited Del and my Aunt Connie, who really was the only supportive member of my extended family.

Unlike my mother, Aunt Connie had always really appreciated my sensitivity. I felt that she might have known all along that I was going to be different from the rest of my siblings. Her two children, Debbie and Guy, were also fun to be around. If I felt love from any family member, it was from my aunt, who never shamed me or made me feel badly.

I decided that it was too risky to invite any of my siblings, although my youngest brother, David, did attend with my mother. He was barely a teenager and didn't pose as much of a threat as my other siblings. Joe, Randy, Jeffery, and the twins Todd and Sheila were persona non grata. I couldn't risk any scene with my family of origin. Since Denny's family knew nothing of my gender, I swore my mother and Aunt Connie to secrecy.

Paulie made my gown out of beautiful inexpensive ivory-colored lace, with layers of ruffles that cascaded full length to the floor. Gloria, Paulie's mom, made her Swedish meatballs and one of my coworkers brought lasagna. Gloria later told me she talked to Del while Denny and I were together standing before the priest.

"Del, isn't Denny so handsome? They look so beautiful together."

"Well you know he doesn't have a pot to piss in, not a nickel to his name."

All through the party, I was paranoid whenever I saw anyone talking to my new husband's family. I hated that, even at that joyous occasion, I had to worry about hiding the fact that I was transgender. Fortunately, the champagne that was flowing freed me of this guilt.

At one point, I glanced over at my mother, who had a look of utter bewilderment. Her face displayed not only her surprise at how smoothly things were going, but also how clearly perplexed she was by the actual reality that her son who was now her daughter had married a man under illegal conditions who was enlisted in the US Army and would soon take her far away from home. While she never expressed it to me in this way, I'm sure she was terrified for my safety.

Denny was assigned to an Army base in Schweinfurt, West Germany. The plan was that he would go first to settle into his deployment duties and find an apartment where we could live, and I would join him later. I sent in a request for a passport, but it was rejected because I hadn't provided proof that I was living as a female. Although I had changed my name legally and had a female driver's license, the passport office must have noticed that my social security card didn't match my new name. There was no way I could go to Germany with a passport that stated my gender as male while my appearance was female.

If anyone could help me, I thought perhaps the doctor I saw for my hormone treatments could. He understood my dilemma and wrote a letter stating that I was living my life as a female and that he was treating me for gender reassignment, which I included with my second passport application. Anxiously checking the mailbox every day, I breathed a huge sigh of relief when I finally retrieved the envelope with my name neatly spelled out: Mrs. Natalia Gervais. Inside was my new passport. Quickly flipping through, I found my name and near the box for gender was a check mark that read *female*. Now all I had to do was get to West Germany in one piece.

After my dramatic fiasco with Professor Burn in the theater department, and because my marijuana use had now escalated to the point where it affected my motivation, it was inevitable that I lost interest in continuing my studies at Rhode Island College. My grades suffered as a result. I quit school believing the lie I would tell myself that one day perhaps I would get back to it. I was much more wrapped up in the coming reality of being an Army wife. I felt that I had reached a pinnacle in my young life. My transition was nearly finished; not only did I have passing privilege, but my legal female identity was complete. And soon I would have the means and support of my husband should I want to start planning for the final phase of transition, gender reassignment surgery.

CHAPTER 14

Army Hausfrau

After five months of sheer agony, I finally got the go ahead from Denny to depart for West Germany. I had convinced myself that the only reason he married me was to get extra money in his paycheck and that he had no intention of having me join him. Jealousy fueled my insecurity as I imagined he was involved with someone else, perhaps a woman assigned female at birth.

Paranoia proved to be unfounded as the day arrived and my mother and Aunt Connie escorted me to Logan Airport. The drive from Providence with my mother to Boston had proved especially uncomfortable because I had to listen to her constant criticism and complaints the entire way. While things had improved in our relationship, she could still be negative and critical, often letting fear overtake her. She continued to go on about how something terrible might happen and questioned my decision to go to Germany right up until the very last minute. I believe in her early life she had been so disappointed in her own marriage to my father that deep down she didn't have much belief that things would work out for me. She often clung to a victim/martyr mentality about things. Even something as simple as getting somewhere on time could be filled with fraught and anxiety. At one point, I wanted to scream, "Shut the fuck up already!" But I didn't. I kept my head in the clouds.

At the gate, we awkwardly hugged. Tears trickled down my mom's face as I made my way into the line to the terminal for departure. I couldn't help thinking how far we'd come in our relationship. I knew her tears were genuine and coming from a place of true concern for her child as she embarked on this new chapter of her young life.

Settling into my seat, it finally hit me that this was really happening and I began to feel overwhelmed and excited about this new phase of my life. The plane began to taxi to the runway and before I knew it we were lifting up into the air.

The stewardess offered drinks and snacks. I opted for a glass of white wine to take the edge off my anxiety. Opening my purse, I pulled out a little bottle of Valium, which I saved for the trip. I'd flown before but never this far, so it would be ideal if I could sleep most of the way. Asking the stewardess to bring me a blanket, I wrapped myself up and swallowed the pills with the remainder of wine and slowly dozed off.

Over the loudspeaker, I heard the captain saying that we would be touching down in Frankfurt soon. Making my way to the restroom, I freshened up a bit. The plum-colored sweater and skirt ensemble I was wearing held up well. Smoothing out my skirt, I pulled it up, reached into my panties to adjust my tuck, which had come loose during the flight. While I was used to it, tucking away my penis was such an unpleasant feeling and, if on a long trip like this where you are sitting most of the time, it can be especially painful, so I made sure to give myself a little extra room between my legs.

Exiting the plane, my anxiety rose like mercury in a thermometer. The sign for customs loomed ahead and, while I was confident I looked okay, I never knew how anyone was going to react at first glance. Moving up in the line, a very handsome customs agent asked for my passport, looked at it, handed it back, and pointed me toward the military area where dependents were to be processed. Soon I saw the Army men dressed in their uniforms and armed with weapons. There was no turning back now. This would be the ultimate test of my passing privilege. If I made it through here, I was golden.

Another guard reviewed my passport and asked me where I was going. He sized me up like a hungry wolf ready to dine on a fine meal, obviously pleased with the way I looked in my snug sweater suit.

"You can head right over there through that door, miss. That's where the family waiting area is." He smiled and inside I felt a deep sense of relief and thanked him in the softest and sexiest voice I could muster.

Making my way through the swinging doors, I looked around and saw other wives being greeted by their husbands. At first I didn't see Denny so I headed toward a bench to wait for him.

"Psssst, looking for me?"

There he was looking as handsome as ever, dressed casually in a pull-over sweater and jeans. The sweater clung to his arms showing off his hugely expanded biceps. He had been working out and his body looked solid and strong as ever. I felt a little tinge of weakness in my knees knowing soon we would be together again sexually as we had been so often before. He held me close and kissed me perfectly. It was as if we were never apart. We both chuckled like excited teenagers on their first date. My heart felt full knowing that we were together again at last.

We collected my suitcases and headed toward a shuttle that would take us to the station to get a train to our little town outside of Frankfurt. The enormous Frankfurt train station with its high ceilings and imposing steel structures made me feel like I was entering a scene from *Casablanca* with me as Ingrid Bergman and Denny as Humphrey Bogart. Enhancing my fantasy, it couldn't have been more romantic.

Arriving at the Schweinfurt station stop, Denny hailed a taxi. "Am Bergl' Nummer 19 in Schweinfurt bitte," he said to the driver as we sped off to our new home.

We traveled on a winding road not far from what was the center of town. I couldn't help but notice how clean everything was; the streets gleamed in the sun without litter, a leaf, or stray branch in sight. Our apartment building was a large mustard-colored stucco structure with a roof draped in brick-colored clay tiles and smoke escaping from a few of the stacks above it. It housed six apartments total with our flat on the top floor. It was ideal because I hated anyone above me and we had a pleasant view of the town.

The apartment itself was a good sized one-bedroom, which was perfect for us. The funny thing about German houses is that they don't have closets. Instead, they have freestanding cabinets called *Wandschrank*, or *Schranks*. The apartment was sparsely furnished in a sleek, somewhat utilitarian, style.

The apartment tour ended in the bedroom where we made love until we both passed out. I felt safe being held in my man's arms. The morning brought many things to attend to. What was most pressing was getting me acclimated to the base on Fort Ledward. Denny informed me of the procedures for new dependents arriving from the states. I'd have to get a military ID that allowed me access to all the family services on the base.

Going through customs was nothing compared to the fear I had approaching the gatehouse to the barracks. The guard asked me for my passport. I handed it over and smiled as he glanced at it and waved us on through. Denny gave me a tour of the base as we walked toward the operations office to get my new photo ID. Confident of my passing privilege, I was always on guard when it came to every aspect of my female identity. I had rehearsed answers for any questions that might arise related to any suspicious aspect of my appearance. For example, if someone commented on the size of my hands or feet I would gleefully respond, "Oh that's nothing. You should see my brothers, they're gigantic!" I was relieved when the photo was taken and I was presented with my US Military ID that allowed me access to services provided for family members. Shopping at the PX was a surreal experience for me knowing my situation and having a first-rate view of military family life. The wives and family members all looked the same to me. I felt self-conscious as I knew I didn't.

Settling into German life became a bit easier once I started to find my way around and learn a bit of the language. But married life quickly became routine and it wasn't long before I became bored with my short-lived domestic bliss. On days when Denny was at work or away for long periods at a time, I found it hard to fill my day. There was only so much shopping, cleaning, and cooking a girl could do. I was too fearful of making any friends because the stakes were high if someone found out my not-so-little secret.

Improvement arrived in the form of my friendly downstairs neighbor, Berta Korhonen. "Call me Betty for short," she said. Her husband has been an American GI and she spoke perfect English. Taller and broader than me, her body was strong and full figured. At sixty, she was active and had only a slight limp. And she had a hollow leg allowing her to drink most men under the table. She released me from the burden of loneliness as I spent hours in her home listening to her regale me of stories from days gone by and tales from her time in the states.

She adored me and treated me like a long-lost daughter. My beauty school training finally came in handy as I ended up doing her hair. She would insist on paying me. Our excursions into downtown Schweinfurt to have lunch and some beer at one of her favorite guesthouses were frequent and fun. She had a son who lived in East Berlin and they didn't have the best relationship.

Once a month on payday, Denny would invite a couple of his closest friends over for dinner and I'd prepare some good old-fashioned American cuisine. My meatloaf and mashed potatoes were killer and the guys loved my cooking. One of his friends, an Italian guy from Brooklyn, was a bit of a flirt with me behind Denny's back. While I enjoyed the attention, I knew I had to be careful.

Whenever I went onto the base, I made sure I was dressed impeccably and looked my best. Men responded to my natural sensuality wherever I went. One sunny day I was exiting the library with some books. A huge group of GIs had gathered across the road. That day I was wearing the same outfit I had worn on the plane, the one that hugged and accentuated my every curve. My neatly-set hair fell just below my shoulders and framed my face nicely. I wasn't heavy into makeup and wore only the basics, a little blush, mascara, and my favorite fire-engine-red lipstick.

Unprepared was I for the sea of green military fatigues of sexy GIs before me as I stepped out into the sunlight. A cacophony of complimentary catcalls and whistles ensued. Straightening up my shoulders with a confidence that wasn't hard to muster, I strolled past them with a stride reminiscent of Marilyn Monroe in *Niagara*. The guys couldn't stand that I was unfazed by their lascivious attention. I couldn't help thinking to myself that they would probably beat me to death if they knew, reminding me of the dangerous life I had chosen to live.

I had a close call with one of the other wives. I befriended this Puerto Rican girl from the Bronx; she was sassy and fun to hang out with and at least she had a little style, unlike so many of the girls who dressed in KMart couture. Our husbands were away on maneuvers and she invited me to stay overnight at her house. I welcomed her company because I was growing depressed in my Army wife role. She lived a short cab ride away, further away from town in the German countryside.

Zulima had a neighbor downstairs who was from Texas with a five-year-old girl who I swear was Patty McCormack from *The Bad Seed* reincarnated. Millie, the girl's mom, was one of those born-again Christian types, plain in appearance and grossly obese. She just couldn't quite figure out what was different about me, but she sensed the devil I'm sure. Zulima and I had a quite a few laughs at her expense and her ignorance of life in general. Together we all played Spades with our husbands. One night, Millie's husband was playing footsie with me under the table. Being the mischievous type that I am, I relished the thought of his Jesus-loving wife finding out about what was going on down under.

Some nights I stayed over at Zulima's. I had to be very careful about changing in the bathroom. While most women are comfortable naked around each other, it wasn't the same for me. Before bedtime, I locked the bathroom door to shower and slip into my nighties. I would emerge in a cute little cotton baby doll top with matching panties to bed.

I climbed into Zulima's bed and we talked a bit before dozing off. I couldn't help but think what a comical moment it was. At that moment, it felt like a scene from *Some Like It Hot* minus the sexual tension. Here I was a married transgender woman in bed with a cisgender married woman who didn't know my assigned birth gender. I imagined the scenarios that most people would think of as I rolled over, smiling to myself about the absurdity of it all.

• • •

The military includes all dependents and family on evacuation maneuvers. This happens a couple of times per year. I was unlucky that it happened soon after I arrived. Denny was away but I was still required to attend. His friend Billy gladly drove me to the base. A corn-fed Midwestern boy, Billy was friendly, polite, and wholesomely good-looking. His wife was a petite, nondescript blonde who was very pregnant with their first child. Billy was nice enough to escort me to the evacuation exercise site at a large bunker on base. His wife had already completed it and was exempt.

The bunker was a hubbub of activity with all types of family members, children, and soldiers milling about. After we were processed, we were instructed to get into our cars and exit the base as if it were a real event. At that moment, the sky opened up and it began to pour rain. It seemed like an eternity as a line of cars snaked all the way out of Fort Ledward. Billy reached over me and opened the glove compartment, brushing ever so gently against me. He retrieved a hefty bag of hash.

"Looks like we're going to be here a while," he said, grinning. "Want to smoke a bit?" Naturally, I agreed and soon the car was filled with smoke. Cracking a window to let some of the smoke escape, he suggested moving to the back since we hadn't moved an inch in what seemed like an eternity. Immediately, I knew where this was going. Although I was nervous, I thought, *What could really happen surrounded by cars queued up to exit the base?* We hopped into the back seat and within minutes the rap began.

"You know Denny is lucky to have such a beautiful gal like you," he said.

"Your wife is very pretty, as well," I said, trying to remind him of her.

"Well, thank you, ma'am, she is, but if you don't mind me saying so, you're sexy."

I ate it up like candy. Who doesn't like a stream of compliments, especially from a sexy GI? While getting hit on wasn't a rare occurrence, I'd been faithful to Denny while there. It was much too dangerous to fool around with anyone.

Billy moved closer as we continued to smoke. He leaned over and placed his hand on my thigh. *Uh-oh*, I thought. Gently, I moved his hand away and played the married woman card and said it wouldn't be right. Persisting, as all men do, he landed his hand on my breast and tried to slip it under my sweater. It was as if we were teenagers on a first date at the drive-in movie, the horny boy trying to hit as many bases as he could. Virtue was never my strong point. I couldn't help but be seduced by his sexy advances. I let him caress my breasts. He made a beeline for my crotch with his other hand but I slapped it away forcefully. Pouting, he complied with my request.

"We can't do that. I told you, that's only for my husband." Imagine how badly this might have gone if he'd persisted. He was hard and unbuckling his fatigues, proudly displaying his more than average equipment. Like I said, virtue wasn't ever my strong point. Stoned and turned on, I made him promise to keep it a secret as I proceeded to take one for the team. The poor guy's wife was knocked up so I felt it was my duty to provide service for our boys. Happily, he finished, and soon the whole maneuver exercise was complete. I guess it was just a coincidence they called it maneuvers.

• • •

Soon all of the secrecy, the boredom, and the feelings of isolation would take their toll as my drinking and drug use escalated. I missed my friends the most and there wasn't anyone I could really be myself with. The other Army wives and I smoked copious amounts of weed or hash almost every day while in Germany. It really began to affect my mood and it made my depression bubble to the surface. I tried journaling to help me understand the complicated emotions I was experiencing. Temporarily it aided me but it didn't alleviate the struggle I was experiencing with trying to find some balance in the world. Playing house was fun for a while. Fully aware that I was getting older and the idea that I had to come to some decision about my gender identify was growing ever more persistent. It was a nagging uncertainty that no amount of writing, hash smoking, and sexual activity would take away, as was evident from my diary.

June 4, 1981

As I lie here listening to something I don't understand, I become suddenly aware of the uselessness of my existence. It shocks me into a trancelike state of reality. I'm boldly confronted with my present life situation in a manner that utterly distorts and diffuses my thoughts! Do I exist for any special or meaningful reason? Or am I only a means to an end? Do I find myself giving and receiving nothing in return? Only time can answer as only the future holds the answers. Why one bothers to rise from sleep at all only to be faced with the same boring existence is beyond me! But, to continue to do so is pure insanity. I feel I have failed. Anyone else would consider me a success. But it doesn't matter what anyone else thinks, simply being that I'm an individualist. My happiness can in no way compare to another's. Every human has different tastes and desires. Although I'm deeply loved by some, I feel that has little validity. In many ways it may have more but when one is feeling so empty how can such love be regulated in return? The answers seem so far away. I wonder if there is any sense in it all, this madness called life?

Out of the blue I received a phone call that my mother had taken ill. Sadly, Del's heavy smoking and poor diet had finally caught up to her. She was fifty-two when she had a series of heart attacks, which eventually led to a stroke. Suddenly I was faced with an opportunity to cut and run. After less than a year, my trip overseas came to an abrupt end as I went home to care for my mother. Certainly, Denny would understand. On some level he would even be glad to be rid of me because I had grown increasingly more difficult, constantly complaining. Quite frankly I couldn't wait to leave Germany, as lovely as it was.

We started having terrible arguments about petty things, such as how much makeup I was wearing. Denny became controlling about where I could go and what I could do. But mostly it was due to my insecurity and the uncertainty of where my life was heading. My increasingly uncomfortable feelings about my gender reassignment dilemma added to my stress. Existing in between genders was taxing. My body didn't match my outward presentation and while I never really would truly know what a woman felt like, I resented other women and men for being complete in their physical bodies. The physical act of tucking my penis between my legs had become a regular routine. But, every day it was a constant reminder that physically I was different from everyone else. The true and often painful realization of where my life was at that moment and the physical and emotional turmoil I felt became increasingly more difficult to accept. It was now manifesting itself into high anxiety, and was highlighted by the fear of discovery that I was not assigned female at birth and the constant pressure of having to make some decision soon.

Denny would have been happier if I had undergone gender reassignment surgery, but I wasn't convinced that was the solution. Having been witness to so many of my trans friends who did have surgery ending up either crazily addicted to drugs or dead from suicide left me with a healthy dose of skepticism to go that route. I was searching for a solution, not more strife. While trans women present as women, sometimes men's attraction to us was more about what we'd been born with between our legs. I've always believed men loved us for that difference. On some level I wasn't prepared to accept that reality; however I wasn't really clear of what my own desire for happiness was at that point because so much of what I felt was really dependent on the reaction of others. I didn't really have a very strong sense of identity and my low self-esteem was deeply masked by drugs, alcohol, and unrealistic expectations of myself. Perhaps on some deep unconscious level, I knew enough not to make any irreversible decisions.

At the airport on my way back to the United States, I had a sinking feeling that Denny and I wouldn't last. My hopes of a happy marriage and a thriving relationship were dashed by the banality of everyday domestic life. It wasn't in my nature to play such a passive role, even if it was as the wife of a handsome GI.

Back in Providence, I moved back in with my mother. She was recovering from her heart attack, still smoking, and really resented my being there. Not long after I arrived, we had another epic fight. She kicked me out yet again. With nowhere to go, I reunited with my estranged friend Dayna who was living in Meriden, Connecticut. Dayna needed a roommate and it was a safe transition place for me until my husband returned from Germany.

Dayna worked at a mall nearby, and with her help I easily got a job at a women's clothing store, Ups & Downs. As far as the management knew, I was an Army wife who needed a job until my husband finished his tour of duty and rarely anyone spooked me. Dayna, on the other hand, wasn't as convincing in her transition. She had been on hormones for a while, and looked much better, but her voice and Adam's apple were dead giveaways and it was so painful to watch when kids would come by the store after school and gawk at her.

Denny informed me that his last year of tour duty would be at Fort Lewis in Tacoma, Washington. I looked forward to being reunited with my husband, but I remained skeptical of our relationship. Growing a bit more mature, my youth was a commodity with a fast expiration date. Time waits for no one. If I didn't start to pursue my own dreams, I'd end up frustrated and bitter. The acting bug had never left and I wanted more than anything to continue my pursuit of a theatrical career. Anyone else might have shied away from the impracticality of my choice, but Paulie always instilled in me a sense that anything was possible. If I really felt passionately about something, the challenge for me was to do it.

CHAPTER 15

Footlights

"You'll be reading the part of Carla in *Kennedy's Children*. It's going to be the first section here." The artistic director of the Freighthouse Theater pointed to the monologue on the page showing me where to end. "Take a moment to look it over. You can start whenever you're ready."

Inhaling deeply, I channeled my best breathy version of Marilyn Monroe and began. "I'm not interested in the sixties. I'm not interested in any of these nostalgic eras they're reviving, to tell you the truth. I mean, what are they really all about? I keep hearing the faggots I know saying, 'Oh, but New York now is really Berlin in the thirties again,' or 'Carla, darling, buy some ballerina pumps; if the market takes an upward swing we're going to be back in the fifties!' But we're not, you know. That's just people trying, so desperately, to find some—meaning for their own time."

"That was great Natalia, thanks for coming in and reading for us. We'll be in touch soon. Do you have any questions?"

"Will you begin rehearsals very soon?" I asked as I gathered my things. I thought, *I should at least ask something.* Out into the parking lot, I felt my audition went well but sometimes you just never can tell. There are so many things to take into consideration when auditioning for a role.

• • •

Exiting the plane at Seattle–Tacoma International Airport, I was relieved I didn't have to go through any military clearance or customs that might refuse my entrance. Denny had flown ahead and found us a small efficiency apartment not far from Fort Lewis. Happily, I still had my military ID from Germany that allowed me access to the base, so I didn't have to go through that fear-inducing registration process again. It was easy just to pick up where we left off and, though I felt less pressure about being discovered as transgender, I still needed to remain very guarded about it.

Washington state was famous for its persistent, pale gray overcast sky. At times, it felt the weather was reflecting the heaviness I was carrying around in my heart. My daily struggles as a trans person had not subsided even with the geographic change. Soon I found another job, except this time it was a sales position at an organization notorious for its right wing and strict religious views. When I arrived at the office for the interview and saw the red-and-white iconic sign of the Salvation Army, I stopped, shook my head, and thought, *They will never hire me in a million years.* Wrong! In fact, they were impressed with my slight resume and offered me the position on the spot.

Though my passing privilege gained me access into some strange situations, I have to say that this one was high on the list. The store was housed in an old cavernous car dealership and it was my job to stock the racks and keep things neat for the customers. Occasionally, I'd work the register when the manager Ida, a tough-talking Northwestern woman, went out to lunch. Most of the other workers were from the Salvation Army residence and worked for their keep. They tiptoed around Miss Ida and were afraid to piss her off because she had a real nasty side.

After work one day, I grabbed the local newspaper and read an ad for a new theater company in Tacoma. They were holding auditions for their first season. The Freighthouse Theater was housed in an old freight house downtown by the train tracks on the outskirts of Tacoma. Scribbling down the date, address, and phone number, I couldn't wait to tell the hubby the good news. At first, he was disapproving and not very supportive. However, I wasn't going to let that deter me. Here I was in a new place and no one knew me. This was a great opportunity not only to get back onto the stage where I rightly belonged, but also to meet some new and interesting people.

Soon the time approached for my evening appointment to meet with the artistic director. Dressing conservatively, I found a beautiful white, long-sleeved chiffon blouse at the Salvation Army. It had a thin black velvet pussy bow at the neck and I paired it with my black jersey pencil skirt. A low-heeled kitten pump in black patent leather completed the look. Feeling energized and confident, I whipped the rollers out of my hair and furiously tamed my mane into place.

I kissed the hubby goodbye and he wished me well, knowing anything else on his part would be a mistake. I jumped into our 1980 coppertone Camaro and sped to downtown Tacoma. Pulling up outside the Freight-house Theater, my nerves started to get the best of me. I recognized these old familiar feelings of self-hatred and doubt that were trying to undermine my newfound confidence. Just as I had done so many times before, I shook it off and paid it no mind.

The artistic director, Gary, greeted me at the entrance and welcomed me into the space. He was an imposing, tall, dark-haired, swarthy fellow. His speech was soft with a soothing quality. However, I could tell some fierce, quiet intensity simmered under his calm exterior.

"Hello, you must be Natalia," he said, extending his hand. "I'm Gary."

"So very nice to meet you. Wow, what a great building this is." I spoke like a starstruck fan.

"Yes, we lucked out with the location. Come on in, let me show you around." As he motioned for me to follow him, my nervousness dissipated. The theater was enclosed in the abandoned freight house, a funky old building by the train tracks. On the side near the tracks there were large, heavy sliding doors. A few other people were in the theater busily preparing set pieces. It was impressive that this group had gutted and converted it into an intimate theater space. The seats on risers framed the space in three sections.

We sat in a row of the risers and Gary asked me about my previous experience at Rhode Island College. And to my surprise, he asked if I was up for the challenge of joining a fledging new company. Without hesitation, I said, "Of course," infusing my best "let's put on a show!" enthusiasm. He asked me to read for the part of Carla in *Kennedy's Children*, a well-known drama by Robert Patrick. Carla was the bombshell role based on Marilyn Monroe who exposes all her insecurities pertaining to her sex appeal and treatment as a sex object. Typecasting, I thought? It could have been a role written for me. Those who are perceived only as sexual objects for the pleasure of others can have devastating lives.

While inside I felt like a shattered nervous wreck, somehow I managed to give a good audition for the part. Gary thanked me for coming in and I left feeling upbeat about the audition. The next day I received a phone call and he thought I would be a welcome addition to the company and would love me to do the part of Carla. Hanging up the phone, I squealed with delight.

"Denny, I got the part. I got the part!" As I danced around our efficiency apartment, I felt so proud that I had actually retained enough of my training as an actor to secure a role.

"That's great, honey. I'm so proud of you," he said sheepishly, which was a lot for him.

Rehearsals started immediately and soon I was immersed in the world where I finally felt like I belonged. There were some great folks in our company and a few of the women and I would become very close friends. One in particular was a lady named Carolyn Jones, a divorced single mom with acting aspirations and a full-time job of her own. We hit it off right away and went out for drinks after rehearsals. Together, we discovered our affinity for marijuana and she had a great source, too. She was one of the very few people who came right out and asked me about my gender orientation, although I wasn't entirely honest because I led her to believe I had gender confirmation surgery. Her questioning of me really put me off a bit at first, but I respected that she had the nerve to ask me for such personal information. Because of her candor, we bonded. She became my confidante and the keeper of my secrets.

Kennedy's Children was a huge hit and the reviews were all positive. Prior to the reviews coming out, most people were concerned about whether they were good or bad, but for me the anxiety that someone would out me as trans was palpable. It never happened. Except for Carolyn, no one ever questioned my gender. Being a member of the Freighthouse Theater was an incredible experience that gave me a great boost of confidence. It made me confident that I could actually make acting work.

Socializing and drinking after rehearsals and openings was a big part of theater life, as it still is today. Alcohol was never really my thing but when I did drink, I drank to get drunk not just to unwind. I preferred unfurling. Somehow my nasty side came out when I was drinking and it escalated during the time we spent in Tacoma, and my daily use of weed didn't help.

There were always lots of parties. One couple had a big Victorian house up from the city and hosted the company fairly often. The husband, a handsome, preppy English professor, was especially smitten with me. His wife was a waspy, slim, petite ingenue type and not a really good actress at all, so it wasn't surprising that Mr. Preppy was fascinated with my sultry looks and hourglass figure.

One night, after another successful opening night of our next production, *Who's Afraid of Virginia Woolf?*, we all headed to their home after the show. Spirits were especially high and the booze and drugs were flowing. Their house was lavish, with three floors with many rooms to get away from the parlor floor where most of the party was taking place. Somehow, I ended up on the third floor alone with the professor. I had had quite a few drinks, as did he, and I knew his reputation as a womanizer from Carolyn, who was a magnet when it came to everyone else's secrets. He rolled up a joint and we smoked. It was good and I was quickly stoned. In fact, the weed made me even a little more so. Without any overtures from me, he grabbed me and stuck his tongue down my throat. I secretly enjoyed that he was trying this, knowing his wife would freak out for sure if she knew.

Before I had a chance to push him away, his hands were fumbling with the belt of my jeans. He was trying to shove his hands down into my crotch. He was physically much bigger and stronger than I and when I tried to counter my weight against him, he wouldn't budge. All the while, he kept telling me how hot he was for me and how good he was going to give it to me. It was then that I realized that this guy was really drunk and was serious about trying to get a piece of me. And he didn't know that the piece he'd get would be what I jokingly called "a pussy on a stick!"

Unable to move, I ordered him to stop but he still tried to pull down my jeans. Finally, I gave him the strongest shove I could muster, sprang up, and refastened my belt. Had he raped me, who knows what would have happened? Composing myself, I made my way back downstairs, pulled Carolyn aside, told her what happened, and left the party. Next time I saw him, he acted as if nothing had ever happened.

• • •

Not long before we left Washington to move back East, I had an epic meltdown in our apartment one day. The clock was ticking and I felt that soon I would have to make some decision about gender confirmation surgery. In my mind, I was convinced it was the only thing that would keep my marriage together, as my biggest fear was that Denny would leave me for a biological woman. Our downstairs neighbor was a knockout redhead. I sensed a certain excitement in Denny whenever she was around. Even though I became good friends with this woman, she triggered a deep sense of inadequacy in me that once again shook me to my core. It was at that precise moment in 1983 that I realized I could never really measure up to a cisgendered woman like her, in spite of all the surgical and cosmetic interventions I had undergone.

One morning after a heavy night of drinking, I awoke in a panic, suspicious that Denny was fucking our neighbor. With zero facts and no tangible evidence, this outright hallucination on my part contributed to my insecurity about where we were headed in our relationship. I began to cry and rant and rave about how I would never be at peace. Tears streamed down my face in buckets and eventually I took to my bed and curled up in a ball, sobbing as if I had received the most awful news of my life.

Denny had no idea how to handle the situation and all he could do was just sit with me till it passed. I didn't possess the ability to express to him in a mature and sensible way just what was going on with me. We never spoke of it again. During a recent phone conversation, he reminded me that we never really talked much about anything of importance and that our relationship went on like that for many years. It was easily the first indicator that something was terribly wrong with the decisions I had made earlier in my young life, although at the time I was unable to process the regretful and remorseful feelings that were surfacing.

One year had passed. It was time to leave Washington. We decided to move to New York City. I wanted to be close to my Paulie, who had been busy building his successful career as a makeup artist. Continuing my acting career was important to me. The time I spent with the Freighthouse Theater was valuable and placed me in a good position to carry the momentum forward to New York where it really mattered.

We packed up our little powder blue Datsun to capacity with our clothes and things we'd need for our cross-country road trip. The Army had paid to ship some of our larger possessions to New York. Unfortunately, it was the middle of winter and not the ideal time to be driving across the Rocky Mountains. It was a typical gray Washington day when we departed. Never did I think I would be longing for it as I did once we drove straight into a snowstorm over the mountains.

The snow was so thick we could barely see a few feet ahead of us as we drove up and up the slippery highway. Trailer trucks were slipping backwards and for the first time I believed I wouldn't make it out of this situation alive. It was foolish to make a trip like this during this time of year, but neither Denny nor I had had the foresight to think it through.

Nevertheless, somehow very, very, slowly we made it over the dangerous mountain pass. It wasn't without a great deal of hysteria and screaming on my part. As I freaked out over the situation, Denny basically ignored me in true Capricorn style and proceeded ahead, never looking back with his goal clearly in sight.

By the time we reached the Midwest, I was sufficiently insufferable with my constant whining and complaining that Denny had finally had enough and so had I. At one point, it got so bad that I made him stop the car. In the middle of Nebraska, I got out and refused to get back in. The bickering and arguing had finally pushed me over the edge and all I wanted to do was flee. Eventually, he calmed me down and we finally made it to New York.

The plan once we arrived was that we were going to stay with my sister Sheila and her boyfriend who was a Dominican drug dealer. She had a son with him and they lived in Grand Concourse in the Bronx. It was temporary until we found a place of our own. My sister and I have a complicated relationship. Since I was a brother who became a gorgeous sister, there was always some underlying tension that we never discussed. It just kind of lay thick in the air like smog. We quickly found a place of our own, a top floor studio in the Park Slope section of Brooklyn. Settling into Brooklyn, I started looking for auditions in *Backstage*, the show business bible for actors. In the meantime, through the *Village Voice*, I found a job as a salesgirl at the Third Avenue Bazaar, a family-owned home furnishing store.

The owner was an affable Jewish native New Yorker. He was such a lovely man and I think he always had a crush on me. No one in the store knew I was trans. All they knew was that I was a decent, married girl from Brooklyn looking for my big acting break. Denny used to pick me up after work every day after his shift at a parking garage in the Village on Greenwich Street.

Boredom within my marriage started to wear me down. I'd grown impatient with Denny's career choice. After spending three years in the US Army, his work in a parking garage was hardly upwardly mobile.

June 4, 1981

As I lie here listening to something I don't understand, I become suddenly aware of the uselessness of my existence. It shocks me into a trancelike state of reality. I am boldly confronted with my present life situation in a manner that utterly distorts and diffuses my thoughts!

Am I existing for any special or meaningful reason? Or am I only a means to an end. Do I find myself giving and recieving nothing in return? Only time can answer these questions as only the future holds the answers. Why one bother to rise at all from sleep only to be faced with the same boring existence is beyond me! But, to continue to do it is pure insanity.

I feel I have fayled. Anyone else would consider me a success. But it doesn't matter what anyone else thinks, simply being that I am an individualist! My happiness can in no way compare to anothers. Every human has different taste and desires.

Although I am deeply loved by some, I feel it has little validity. In many ways it may have more, but when one is feeling so empty, how can such love be regulated in return. The answers seem so far away. I wonder if there is any sense in it all, this madness called life!!
..

Natalia's diary entry from June 4, 1981.
(Courtesy of the Belovitch Archive)

Natalia modeling in NYC in 1983.
(Courtesy of the Belovitch Archive)

Natalia as Lucy in *You're a Good Man, Charlie Brown* in 1984.
(Courtesy of the Belovitch Archive)

Natalia performing at the Limelight.
(Courtesy of James Mulqueen)

Natalia performing at Danceteria.
(Courtesy of James Mulqueen)

Natalia performing at Danceteria
with Michael Musto.
(Courtesy of James Mulqueen)

Natalia with Dolph Lundgren and Antonio in 1985.
(Courtesy of James Mulqueen)

Natalia with Edith O'Hara at the 13th Street Theatre.
(Courtesy of the Belovitch Archive)

Brian in Miami after
re-transitioning.
(Courtesy of the
Belovitch Archive)

Brian outside the theater
running his Off-Broadway play,
Boys Don't Wear Lipstick.
(Courtesy of the
Belovitch Archive)

Brian with Stanley, Gloria's husband, and Gloria, Paulie's mom, in 1996.
(Courtesy of the Belovitch Archive)

Brian and Jim.
(Courtesy of Michael David Lambdin)

Brian and Jim on their wedding day.
(Courtesy of the Belovitch Archive)

Distractions found their way to me easily in Manhattan. Men were always stalking me at work and I loved the attention.

One day a tall, handsome man came into the store at closing time. As it turned out, Denny wasn't picking me up after work and this guy was especially persistent, so I agreed to meet him for a drink. He lived right across the street in a doorman building. He was an actor on Broadway understudying Sergio Franchi in the musical *Nine* based on Fellini's film *8½*. I was super excited to hear this because I naively believed such a chance encounter could lead to some kind of break for me in the theater. Think Lana Turner in Schwab's drugstore on Sunset and Crescent.

The short version is we met for a drink and he invited me to the show that night. He had to be in the audience as an understudy. Starstruck, I agreed and ended up seeing the entire show. After the show, he invited me back to his place for a nightcap. My husband was at work so he wouldn't know where I was. After a few drinks, things got a little out of hand. He was making serious moves on me. So intense were his advances that I had to spill the beans and hope his macho demeanor would subside. Needless to say, he was completely freaked out, but that didn't stop him from going all the way with me. Anxious to get out of there before Denny got home, he slipped me his number, albeit a wrong one and said *arrivederci*, and I made my way back to Brooklyn.

The inauspicious start of my theatrical career didn't deter me. Paulie had a friend who knew a Broadway producer. He was casting a show based on an older film set in Greece. Paulie's friend, Louise, an upscale business-woman, took an interest in me and thought I might be able to get a small part in the show based on my exotic Mediterranean looks. I was excited when Paulie told me, even more so when I got an actual interview with this Broadway legend.

I dressed in a simple pink wrap dress and my flat Capezio shoes the day of my meeting with the producer. Denny insisted on going with me and drove me up to the East Fifties to my appointment and waited in the car while I went in. In true theatrical fashion, Mr. Broadway took his seat behind his big desk and proceeded to ask me a few perfunctory questions about my acting. He reminded me of one of my older Jewish uncles I had met as a child. He was undressing me with his eyes the entire time. Clearly, he had this routine down.

"Well, Natalia," he said, "there might be something for you in the show after all." Dumb me didn't ask what, where, or when. I only heard that he had a part for me!

"Come on over here for a minute so I can tell you a little about it." He moved from behind the desk to a couch in the corner of his office. I remember a sinking, sad feeling that, yes, I really was being propositioned with the proverbial casting couch routine.

He stretched out in front of me and proceeded to unbuckle his belt and slip his boxer shorts down. "Why don't you take care of me, sweetheart, and I'll take care of you."

This was where my acting really came in handy. I acted as if something like this had never happened before and how I was doing him a huge favor as I reached down pulling a Monica Lewinsky on Mr. Broadway. As this was happening, I couldn't help but think of my poor husband waiting in the car while his wife was upstairs on her knees.

I never got the call for that show, and was happy when it was a big fat flop. All in a day's work, I supposed.

Dialing the phone, I couldn't wait to tell Paulie how it went.

"Did you get the part?" he asked.

"Well, let's just say I did him a favor. Let's see if he returns it." As I filled him in on the details, Paulie screamed with horror when I told him, but we did have a great laugh over it. Truly disheartened, I didn't let it dampen my theatrical ambitions. He invited me to the movies the next day to cheer me up. There was a great film at the Quad he wanted me to see.

Everything stopped when I spent time with my best friend and I agreed to meet him at his place on Cornelia Street in the Village, a cozy fifth-floor walk-up that he shared with his current lover, Stanley. Even better, Stanley would be at work so I would have Paulie all to myself.

The sun was high and bright as I bounded up the steps to the vestibule. When I rang Paulie's bell, the buzzer was out of service. I went back out into the street and called up to him to come to the window to toss down the keys. Once inside his apartment, I slipped out of my Keds sneakers, Paulie fired up a joint, and we got into a hysterical fit of the giggles over Mr. Broadway. The irony that the producer thought he was getting head from a sexy showgirl, when in fact she was a former show boy, struck us as divine retribution for the fact that he'd taken advantage of me that way. If that happened today, I'd be a millionaire suing for sexual harassment.

Checking the time, Paulie finished dressing and I grabbed my sneakers. He stood over me as I tied my Keds and then he asked, "Tish, what are you doing?"

"What does it look like?" I said. "I'm tying my sneakers."

"But that's not how you tie your shoes."

"Well, that's how I tie my shoes," I said, getting defensive. "Look," I said, "I make two little bows like this and then loop them over each other," as I demonstrated for him. "Now, come on. Let's go."

He leaned over, put his hand on my shoulder, and looked me in the eye. "Tish, were you abused? That's not how you tie your shoes. No one bothered to take the time to teach you," he said calmly.

What Paulie said rang absolutely true. His razor-sharp assessment shook me to my very core. Although I tried to resist, I could feel tears forming in the corners of my eyes.

Without warning, I started to sob violently. My whole body shook as I realized I never considered this truth about myself. Paulie cried too. He hugged me so tight and although it was a comfort I couldn't stop sobbing. My body went limp and while it felt good to cry I was embarrassed about how deeply my loving friend's observation affected me. I didn't need to describe to him in detail the amount of abuse I had suffered as a child. He knew the stories. Coming to terms with the sheer neglect that had occurred and how painful it was to accept—that was what really hit home. Perhaps things might have been so different if only someone paid attention to me.

The sad reality that there hadn't been anyone to keep me safe the way children should be kept safe was devastating.

When I finally stopped crying, he sat me down and said, "Here, look at this." He actually showed me how to tie my shoes. After a few attempts on my own, I eventually figured it out. To this very day, whenever I reach down to tie my shoes it's Paulie I think of smiling down on me, keeping me together and grounded as the well-tied laces of any pair of shoes I'm walking in.

Washing my face, I reapplied some mascara and a fresh coat of lipstick and a little powder. We left the apartment and headed to see *Amadeus* at the Quad, lighting up another joint on the way.

On West Thirteenth Street, we came upon a bright chartreuse-colored townhouse with a frayed awning that read "13TH STREET REPERTORY THEATER COMPANY." I noticed a billboard listing its current offerings as well as an ad for actors to join the company.

The next day, I called the theater.

"Hello, 13th Street Theater, how may I help you?" the woman on the phone said pleasantly. She introduced herself as the artistic director of the company, asked me a few questions, and gave me an appointment for the next day. The following day, I stepped down the stone slab stairs leading into the entrance of the theater lobby. A silver-haired woman was scurrying about beyond the lobby window. There was a cozy, rustic feel to the place. One wall was plastered with black and white headshots of the actors in the company. On other walls were posters of the company's previous productions, including *The Indian Wants the Bronx*, starring a then-unknown Al Pacino and John Cazale. I played the same part the vicious teaser Murphy had played at the Freighthouse, a switch on the original part played by a man. This was a promising sign, or at least a good icebreaker.

"You must be Natalia," the woman said, extending her hand. "I'm Eva. We spoke on the phone." She was a large woman with her silver shoulder-length hair cut into a sensible bob. She had incredibly blue eyes and an air of calm about her. She asked the girl in the box office to answer the phone while she interviewed me.

"Come sit by the window here so we can have a little chat," she said. We sat down on the overstuffed window seat. With a smile and a twinkle in her eye, she said, "Tell me a little about yourself."

I launched into my recent ex-military wife exposé and told her about Tacoma and the theater there. She was from Coeur d'Alene, Idaho, and was very familiar with the Pacific Northwest. I mentioned that I had played the role in *The Indian Wants the Bronx*. She was impressed that I knew the play and that our little company had bravely cast a female in the role.

Eva and I got on like a house on fire. Perhaps it was fate that we met. Later, she would become the good parent I never had. She welcomed me—as well as hundreds if not thousands of other young actors with stars in their eyes—to a chance and a place to hone their craft. Being a company member meant paying ten dollars a month in dues and volunteering three hours per week. Agreeing to those terms allowed you to audition for roles in the plays she produced. The only catch with Eva was that you had to keep up your part of the bargain. Which meant that if you took on a responsibility, you'd better follow through. My hunch about her steely determination was on the money—she didn't suffer fools lightly.

There isn't enough space in this memoir to tell you how many valuable lessons I learned from Eva. Some were harder than others but each experience was learned through love, tolerance, and forgiveness. Like learning a foreign language, it took practice and perseverance but the work was worth it.

I was cast to play the mother of four kids in foster care in a new play, *In the Waiting Place*, directed by Kent Green, a handsome fellow also from Massachusetts whom I had met earlier through Dayna. He was so surprised to see me when I walked into the audition, and soon we had a fast friendship.

Generally, the reviews of the play were positive, but one review was from a gay guy who clearly was transphobic. "Mommy resembled Divine on a bad day," he wrote. It was his way of outing me as trans, which had nothing to do with the play or my character. Given the opportunity, some gay men could be vicious about exposing my identity as a trans woman. It didn't deter me, however, and the Divine comparison went over many people's heads.

I went on to do quite a bit of work at the 13th Street Theater, and Denny became increasingly irritated with me being away so much. But I wasn't surprised, as I knew we were coming to the end of the road. After months of shouting matches, in and out of public, I packed my bags and moved into the theater with Eva. It was the right thing to do, although I was devastated and felt like a failure. It had been the longest relationship I had up until that point in my life and Denny had provided me with an amazing amount of stability. Soon I would realize just how much I would miss that security as I threw myself head first into the theater company.

Eva gave me a job right away, as a manager, which gave me a daily routine and allowed me to earn a small salary. My passing privilege remained intact and, for the most part, most of the other actors didn't know my story, which was fine with me. Most importantly, my confidence as an actor grew and days turned into months and soon I'd been there a while.

Paulie had become so successful in his career as a makeup artist that he was constantly traveling all over the world. He was spending a lot of time in Milan, where he met an adorable Italian guy named Paolo. Paulie fell in love with Paolo and was naturally conflicted about his relationship with Stanley Obey, his lover in New York, which put him under a great deal of stress. He began complaining about excruciating headaches. His doctor told him that they had discovered a tiny aneurysm in his brain, which, if he wasn't careful, could erupt and cause a seizure or a stroke.

Several months had passed since Paulie had told me of his diagnosis and one day in March 1984, I was up in the second-floor rehearsal space when Kent knocked on the door to let me know I had a phone call. It was Gloria, Paulie's mother.

"Tish, "she said, "I have some bad news. Paulie collapsed while at work in Milan. He had an aneurysm. He's in a coma and the doctors don't think he'll live."

I dropped the phone and screamed. I became hysterical, crying in long jags. Eventually, I calmed down a bit and got back on the phone with Gloria, who was trying to speak through her own grief. She had booked a flight to Milan with her husband and Stanley to bring Paulie home.

Paulie didn't make it and I had never felt so alone in my entire life. Not only had I lost my husband of five years, but I had also lost the best friend anyone could ever have.

Arrangements were made quickly and a service was planned in Rhode Island. I had to get up and speak in public—as myself—for the first time. Somehow, I got through it, reading a poem we both liked.

• • •

Back in New York, I was grateful that Eva was leasing a theater in Thomaston, Connecticut, for the summer, since I needed to get out of New York. Eva appointed Kent and I general managers. We would also act and direct. There was so much work to do that it helped to bury the grief I felt over Paulie and the ending of my marriage. It also provided ample opportunity to drink. My drinking began to escalate. We drank before and after everything we did. Drugs were scarce, but Kent and I managed to furrow them out in Waterbury, Connecticut, a short drive away where some of the actors were housed.

The season was packed with fun plays and musicals. I got cast as Lucy Van Pelt in *You're a Good Man, Charlie Brown!* or what could have been more aptly titled as *You're Really a Good Man, Lucy Van Pelt!* During the run, we had great audiences and terrific reviews. Some family and friends came from New York. My mother, still frail from yet another a heart attack, did manage to come from Rhode Island. Our relationship had mellowed, but there was an underlying anger I could always sense between us. Her narcissistic streak allowed her to feel my transition was something I was doing to make her life miserable. Nevertheless, I was grateful she made the effort. I was now realizing you had to take your victories wherever they came from.

After the last performance, one of the actors introduced me to her parents and a friend of theirs. Johnny R. was a burly, successful Italian

American businessman from Staten Island. Later, I found out he was in the middle of a divorce. He clearly flirted with me when we met, as most men did, but I didn't think much of it. Once our summer season ended and we returned to New York, I received a lovely note from "Mr. Johnny R." saying how impressed he was with my "talents" along with an invitation to dinner, which fed into my old Hollywood glamour style of thinking. I loved the sense of respectability it presented, even though this was just another clear fantasy on my part. As my mother would say, "Nothing is for nothing, kid." She was right about that.

Johnny R. was looking for more than dinner. We carried on a long courtship until eventually he professed his love for me. Knowing full well what I was doing, I never told him I was trans. When I did, he was of course gobsmacked, but it didn't deter the persistent overtures of his love for me. In fact, he now had even more of a reason to be with me. He even offered to pay for my surgery and proposed marriage once his divorce was final. Being the second wife of a Staten Island businessman just wasn't in the cards for me, not even the built-in pool would seal the deal.

Sex with Johnny was complicated. He was large, hairy, and his hygiene left room for improvement. His breath was bad as well. There were times when I cringed knowing I would have to have sex with him, always trying to put it off for as long as I could. Eventually, I had to give in if I wanted to continue with our financial arrangement.

Another Capricorn, like Sonny and my ex, he too was possessive and controlling. The last thing I needed was a repeat of my prior relationship. In retrospect, I guess there was something I badly needed to learn from my relationships. If it weren't for the fact that he was bankrolling my stage shows and was so supportive of my career, I would have never been with him. This seems particularly callous and shallow on my part, but sadly it was all I knew back then. It piqued my interest if I knew you could do something for me. If you couldn't, I wouldn't be bothered. Youthful ignorance let me believe everyone operated the same way and learning how to survive in a world where no one looked out for me made justification easier. Of course, I had taken it to the extreme.

Johnny would give me anything I asked for. I had always wanted to do a musical revue of sixties pop songs. Johnny bankrolled the entire production, paying for the band, costumes, rehearsals, publicity, and anything else I needed. He was so generous and really believed I was headed for the big time. He wasn't the only one in my corner. Eva had graciously given me the late Friday and Saturday time slots. Dubbing myself the downtown party girl I came up with a concept for the revue. It was called *It's My Party*, complete with male back-up singers, a three-piece band, and silly patter about parties I had attended. The revue premiered at the 13th Street Theater in December 1984. As a trans woman singing with my own husky contralto voice, I'd created something that was a bit daring for its time. Perhaps punk rock legend Jayne County was the only other trans woman singing with her voice back then. One particular reviewer liked my voice, calling it "a good voice but untrained," which was accurate since I was mostly self-taught except for a few vocal lessons in college.

This little music revue became the catalyst that introduced me to New York nightlife at a much bigger and higher professional level than ever before. During the run of the show, one of my back-up singers, Bobby, a terrific singer on his own with extensive experience with live music shows, invited a friend to our show. I had met Bobby during a showcase we did for a potential Broadway show based on the Jewel Box Revue and we had become fast friends. His friend had just become a writer for the nightlife column in the *Village Voice*, taking the place of the legendary Arthur Bell who had recently passed away.

Bobby's friend had thick, dark, curly hair like mine and wore really dark sunglasses, adding an additional air of mystery. Michael Musto had grown up in Bensonhurst and reminded me of many of the Italian American kids I went to school with back in Providence. Close in age, we shared many of the same pop cultural touchstones, and as we chatted about the show he revealed his idolization for anything Motown in particular. We bonded over our slavish devotion to Diana Ross and anything Supremes-related.

Not long after, I ran into Michael again at Studio 54 while doing a show with Bobby called *Surf's Up*. It was my delightful task to come out in the tiniest bikini possible holding two huge beach balls in front of my breasts like an early Divine Miss M. while the group sang "Itsy Bitsy Teenie Weenie Yellow Polka Dot Bikini." Cheesy but, hey, that's showbiz and I was so grateful for the opportunity and the, um . . . exposure.

Surprisingly, Michael was a fantastic singer; his sound was truly soulful and I could hear the Motown inspiration in his phrasing. He was a guest with the band and we hung out after the show in the basement of Studio 54 where many years earlier I had roamed around looking for the party—now I was the party! Our friendship blossomed and soon he was inviting me to some of the most fun and exciting entertainment venues in the city. Everyone wanted to meet Michael. Not only was he a brilliant writer, he was just a lovely, down-to-earth guy once you got to know him. Unlike me, most people were more interested in getting a mention in his column than actually knowing him. Many decades later, we are still the best of friends.

Because I spent so much time with him, I often found myself in situations that made great copy for his column. One memorable event was the Academy of Motion Picture Arts and Sciences tribute to the smart, sophisticated screen style of Myrna Loy. It was all Hollywood glamour! I sat in the middle of Hollywood royalty like Lauren Bacall, Lena Horne, Lillian Gish, and Joe Mankiewicz, to name a few of those paying homage to Miss Loy.

Sitting to my right was film director Miloš Forman, with Michael on my left. My sapphire blue and silver sequined dress sparkled appropriately in a sea of black-tie formal attire. But the longer I sat, the more I felt numbness and burning in my crotch. It seems the seam of my pantyhose was cutting across the base of my penis, which was safely stuffed and tucked between my legs.

I turned to Michael and said, "If this doesn't end anytime soon, I'm going to have my sex change right here in Carnegie Hall."

Michael covered his face with his hand, trying to stifle his laughter. To my surprise, next week at the very top of his column was my exact quote as he recounted the event for all his loyal readers. As thrilling as it was to open the *Village Voice* and see my name in print, it was an inadvertent coming out for me as a trans person. There I was, un-tucked for the world to see.

In retrospect, Michael certainly wasn't being malicious. It felt strange that I had no say in such a personal matter. But then again, I felt it didn't matter what I had to say for so much of my life, so why start now? Johnny R. was jealous of my friendship with Michael and accused me of having an affair with him. Little did he know that Michael and I would never end up in bed together, unless it was a G-rated slumber party.

As my popularity rose in the New York Club scene, I expanded my show to include a full band. One night I attended a party in the Village at the home of nightlife videographer Nelson Sullivan, who would go on to become a legend in the nightclub scene as someone way ahead of his time for being the selfie-king of his day with a video camera instead of a cell phone. He documented and meticulously archived one of the most creative and vibrant times in New York artistic history. Sadly, his life was cut short before he was able to appreciate the full respect he deserved for his artistic contribution to New York City creative history. It was sheer genius what he did. For preservation, his entire collection has been donated to the New York University Fales Library.

At Nelson's party, I met another person who would be instrumental in raising my entertainment profile. Gabriel Rotello was a talented musician and party promoter, and he had already established a credible and exciting presence on the New York music scene. Later in life, he would be one of the founding editors of *Out Week* magazine and an accomplished, bestselling author and producer in his own right. And like Michael, another very good friend still. At Nelson's party, people were gushing about my show to him when he flat-out said, "Well, since everyone is saying how fabulous you are, I think you need to be in the next Downtown Dukes and Divas show."

Just like that, I was plucked from relative obscurity and thrust onto the New York club scene in a very big way. Before I knew it, I was in Gabriel's loft in midtown rehearsing for the next big show, which included so many other amazingly talented singers.

Unbeknownst to me, my ascent as one of the so-called downtown dar-lings at the height of the pre–Giuliani nightclub scene was both a blessing and a curse, a wacky, wonderful whirlwind of wild escapades from the heights of New York City glamour to the depths of a despair I had no idea I would ever know again. I was finally being recognized for my obvious talent as an actress and a singer, but it felt like I was under the curse of a trans woman. Only recently have I realized that it was the wrong time in history for me. I was always ahead of my time, and it was this painful and self-destructive truth that nearly dimmed the bright light I so desperately was trying to step into.

CHAPTER 16

Hell's Kitchen Consequential

By 1985, Johnny R. was campaigning for me to leave Eva and move from the theater out on my own. His motives for getting me out of the theater were selfish because he wanted me solely dependent on him and living alone so that he could have regular access to me whenever he liked.

He found me an affordable, small studio apartment in Hell's Kitchen on West Forty-Fifth Street. Ironically, it was in the Hildonah Apartments where I had been a frequent visitor so many years ago as a young trans woman in training. In five minutes, he could walk to me from his office on Fifth Avenue. The problem was that he was becoming just as possessive and jealous as my ex-husband Denny. He wanted to take our relationship to the next level and I was completely uninterested in that. I could barely stand to kiss him let alone think there was any chance to further our relationship. Out of desperation and a need to further my career I kept Johnny around. I'm not proud about how I treated someone who was so crazy in love with me, but back then survival was more on my mind than any idea of ethics. Eventually, I had to end my relationship with him because not only was it so unbearable to me on a physical level, but I began to also feel even worse about myself for stringing him along. I basically came clean with him and forced myself to admit the awful truth that I wasn't in love with him and couldn't see it happening. He was devastated and it was a painful detachment for him. For me I just left more afraid.

However, the invitations continued to pour in and I was in demand as a coveted guest at many different events in the city. There were so many openings, parties, and shows. Some are more memorable than others but only a handful stand out. I loved the nightlife; something about it was so seductive and decadent. Waking up late in the day to start planning for the evening ahead became a regular way of life. I had all the time in the world to do whatever I pleased. I didn't realize the price I was going to pay for this lavish luxury.

Living smack dab in the middle of Hell's Kitchen was both an advantage and a detriment. I was close to the pulse of the creativity of Broadway and the thousands of aspiring artists who had come to New York to make their dreams come true. On the other hand, I was a stone's throw from Times Square, which had not yet been given the whitewash of the upcoming Giuliani era. There was still a seedy underbelly that you didn't have to look very far to find. In fact, I could walk out my door and up the block to Eighth Avenue and grab a trick any time of day. Sidewalks in the neighborhood simmered with the energy of earlier days gone by when it had been primarily hooker heaven.

Add into the mix the arrival of crack cocaine in the mid-eighties and it became a heady mix of debauched drama and drudgery prime for that location. I was first introduced to freebase cocaine in 1985 on Christmas Eve, when my old friend Monica from Rhode Island was visiting. She was staying with of all people, Dayna Brough at her East Seventh Street apartment where she had started her own business as a madam providing trans women for a select and exclusive clientele. Dayna and I didn't see much of each other, but occasionally enjoyed celebrating the holiday together. For trans outcasts, Christmas was especially difficult. Like a family of choice, we'd often come together as we had in the past. But this particular night is one scorched into my memory, much like the rock of crackling cocaine I was about to inhale from the pipe in my hand.

Like a tiger springing from captivity, my addiction was unleashed and ratcheted up to take me down the horrible path it does for most addicts. Nothing could contain the overwhelming urge to use this drug. Once I took the first hit, all bets were off that I'd be able to stop. Addicts are just wired that way. For some reason, though, when it comes to coke, it happens much quicker.

Cocaine wasn't the sole focus of my life just yet; it was more a guest star. Cocaine had been readily accessible to me for years. It certainly wasn't a new drug to me, but smoking it was an entirely different experience. It would be well over a year before I would be at the mercy of crack, crackpots, crackheads, and a whole lot of crazy.

Life felt split. It was as if someone took a pencil and divided parts of me into different versions of myself. Here I was in my late twenties, rapidly approaching thirty, still trying to carve out a career as an actress and singer, attending sporadic auditions when I could get up the nerve, and taking classes at H. B. Studio in Greenwich Village. Living as a trans woman still created a great deal of confusion in my mind as I constantly questioned which state of gender I was going to occupy. Another role I played was that of a high-priced escort catering to a fairly decent clientele of men who had an appetite for pre-operation girls like me—a girl with something extra. These so-called gentlemen were also holed up in some of the city's swankiest hotels. One of my favorites was the Waldorf Astoria. And, lastly, my new identity as a burgeoning crack addict.

It was a similar feeling to the one I had when I did heroin for the first time. Except this was a different sensation: it felt sexier and more stimulating to me than heroin. Dope just numbed me to everything, whereas after I took my first hit of freebase, I was doomed. It was the perfect combination of numbness and stimulation I had been looking for my entire life. That night on Christmas Eve 1985, I was the recipient of one of the worse presents ever given to me.

Dayna had already honed the art of cooking up freebase. And she wasn't shy about sharing her culinary knowledge with me. In fact, it came in very handy because most of the tricks we saw back then loved how crazily horny freebase made them. They could stay hard and have sex for hours. Shortly after, I traveled well stocked with my own little pipe, baking soda, and glass bottles.

The effects of living the life of an active addict don't always happen right away, but in my case the signs were becoming obvious to some of my friends. One in particular noticed I was borrowing money on a more frequent basis. Another took into account that I was later and later for appointments and rehearsals. I would disappear for days and no one would know my where- abouts. Usually I was holed up in my tiny studio apartment with a trick or other trans woman from the neighborhood on a smoking binge.

My last job on the nightclub circuit was at the legendary Saint in the Lower East Side, housed in the same building as the Fillmore East. I worked as a doorperson, so it was left to my discretion whether you got in or not. It was a highly coveted spot in the nightlife world, but the pay was shit. The exposure was more valued than the salary. It was also here at the Saint that I would host my last public event, having that brief but memo- rable phone call with Andy Warhol, whom I knew from various events. But by the end of that gig, I was sneaking off to the bathroom every five minutes to take or scrape off another hit of crack using the stem and torch that became a well-worn accessory in my purse. One night I just walked off the job to cop more crack and never returned.

Sadly, even for my live shows I wasn't able to stop long enough to make it to the stage. One night at the Limelight, I was scheduled to appear in a duet with Michael Musto. Instead of being in the wings getting ready for my performance, I was holed up in a bathroom stall. I could barely hear the emcee introducing me as I was firing up a rock and taking one last hit before going onstage. Poor Michael was basically left standing there, befuddled by my absence. For what must have seemed like an eter- nity to him, I made a frantic stumbling, Judy Garland entrance. He was furious and rightfully so, though at the time I didn't care. Hitting the pipe took priority over everything else, including long and good friendships.

In the middle of all this insanity, I still had to show up for the calls I booked through the escort service. One night my madam sent me to the

Upper West Side home of a regular client of the agency. The apartment was well appointed and immediately my eye was drawn to the mantel where I spotted a glistening Academy Award in all its glorious gold. Peeking at the photographs scattered about the living room, I recognized that this guy was the husband of a famous Oscar-winning Hollywood actress. He also was really kinky. It turned out Oscars weren't the only thing he liked golden. Fulfilling these guys' fantasies was something I was used to, but this was taking it a bit far, even for me. On his impeccably-tiled bathroom floor, I let go a stream covering him while he gleefully masturbated. Finishing, he stuffed several extra hundred-dollar bills into my hand as he ushered me out of his tony abode. The tip was all mine; the agency would only get their cut.

Another time, in a moment of sheer personal pleasure, I allowed myself to have a little fun, too. After another Limelight event, I was hosting one of the sexy and handsome bouncers of the club had been extra flirtatious with me.

We were both exiting the club at the same time when he called out to me, "Where you headed, sexy?"

"Uptown, Hell's Kitchen. Going my way?"

"Sure, hop in. I'll give you a lift."

I waved to the other doorman, Willy, as I entered my escort's car. He would see that I was leaving with the bouncer and I knew it would be common knowledge the next day at the club. But then it was always a good idea to have someone see you leave a club in case of any trouble.

On the way, we chatted and stopped for a drink at the Film Center Café on Ninth Avenue, near my place. After drinks, it became obvious he was up for a little more fun so I asked him up to my apartment. Within minutes, he was kissing me deeply and passionately. I'd forgotten how wonderful it was just to be kissed for kissing's sake. Usually there was an awkward moment when I had to explain to the guy that I was a bit different than most girls. When they'd ask how, I'd go on to say, "Well, my mother lives upstairs," pointing to my breasts and "my father lives downstairs," pointing between my legs. Sometimes they'd get it right away and other times not at all, like the guy in my earlier transition who pulled a gun on me and made me go down on him before kicking me out of the car telling me, "If you weren't so pretty I'd blow your fucking brains out!"

There was no need for explanation now because after some hot and heavy above the waist kissing and caressing, I ended up kneeling before him. I was so turned on that I had an orgasm in my pink, cotton panties I never removed. I don't know if he ever knew the deal about me or not but since so many other coworkers did I would be surprised if he didn't. Several years later he became a successful Academy Award–nominated actor who today has quite an extensive film career. Sadly, my fantasy that our rendezvous was something more than a one-night stand ended just as quickly as it began. While I had no idea he would be so successful, it is funny how Oscar and I kept running into each other.

It wasn't unusual that the famous, infamous, and not so famous would rub shoulders in the clubs. There was a regular bunch of celebrity frequent flyers. One of the most notable was Sylvia Miles, who was often ridiculed for attending every event including envelope openings. Andy Warhol, Keith Haring, and Jean-Michel Basquiat often could be found at the hottest clubs in the city. Actors like Matt Dillon, Robert Downey, Jr., and Judd Nelson were also regular nightclub crawlers. Nightlife was so vibrant and creative in New York City then. There was an incredible surge of creativity that was coming out of the club scene. Little did I know I strutted my stuff on the same stage that launched Madonna's career at Danceteria. She famously bounced around the East Village club scene before hitting the big time. Authors like Tama Janowitz, Jay McInerny, Bret Easton Ellis, and Dominick Dunne added extra oomph to the cultural milieu.

There, too, was the whole East Village performance art scene with Karen Finley, Tim Miller, Penny Arcade, and Eric Bogosian. The Pyramid Club was a major incubator and instigator for many of those in today's current pool of talent. Tabboo!, Hapi Phace, Ethyl Eichelberger, Lypsinka, Joey Arias, Olympia, and Hattie Hathaway raised the bar of drag extravagance nightly. The legendary Lady Bunny and the whole Atlanta migration of queens the nightlife brought to New York (Lahoma Van Zandt, Floyd, Larry Tee, and the Now Explosion) were all major contributors to the vibrant and burgeoning eighties drag scene. My friend Nelson Sullivan knew a lot of these queens and it was always fun to run around with him and his ubiquitous video camera documenting all these shenanigans.

One day he invited me over to his house in the Meatpacking District for some lunch. After, we headed over to the Jane West Hotel to meet the latest Atlanta arrivals. He filled me in on the way that his friends were part of a funky new band called Star Booty. One of the leaders of this kooky crew was an extra tall, lean, pretty black fellow sporting a multi-colored Mohawk, trimmed with colorful feathers. His friends were holed up in the Jane West Hotel for the time being. The queen with the Mohawk was sweetly intense and my first thought upon meeting him was that there was something very special about him. His upbeat energy and innate drive reminded me of an idling car motor. I remember thinking to myself, *This kid is really going places.* That kid was RuPaul Charles and today he's gone on to become the phenomenally successful drag impresario of *RuPaul's Drag Race.*

If one club wasn't having a good night, all you had to do was jump in a cab or take a short walk somewhere else. Clubs like Danceteria, Lime-light, Palladium, Area, and Pyramid were all operating about the same time. Michael Musto referred to our group as the "Celebutants," a coined phrase for someone who is famous for nothing. The core group included Dianne Brill, James St. James, Lisa Edelstein, Anita Sarko, and me.

On the horizon was the premiere of Federico Fellini's *Ginger & Fred* at the Museum of Modern Art on March 26, 1986. Never was I so excited to attend any other event. This was one of the most highly anticipated films of his career and sure to be epic. It was the culmination of everything I had been striving for. You see, in my mind I truly believed I was destined to be a film star like Sophia Loren or Anita Ekberg, another exquisite Fellini creation.

Dressing the part of an Italian cinema film goddess wasn't especially challenging for me, but doing so on limited resources was proving to be tricky. My wardrobe was in dire need of an upgrade, and since Johnny R. was completely out of the picture, I had to be more resourceful when it came to finding new outfits to dazzle my admirers, or at least the ones I imagined I had.

Meticulously dolled up wearing a skintight gold lamé cocktail dress that had been handed down to me from my mother, I exited my tiny Hell's Kitchen studio with every bit of confidence I could possibly muster. Several cabs veered toward the corner of Ninth and Forty-Fifth to pick me up. Jumping into the first one I could, I told the driver, "Museum of Modern Art at Fifty-Third and Sixth Avenue, please."

Once there, the street was lined with limos and taxis patiently idling in place waiting to drop off their patrons at the front entrance of the museum. Paying my fare, I slowly spilled out of my taxi like Cinderella on the night of the ball and I stepped onto the red carpet, which was lined with photographers hoping to catch that ever-elusive photo that would make their time here worthwhile. Immediately, the cameras flashed as I strolled into the screening tightly clutching the coveted invitation in my hand. The paparazzi were firing away at Isabella Rossellini and one of the stars of the film, Marcello Mastroianni.

Once inside, I made my way to the middle of the theater and strategically placed myself in the center of the audience. Soon the lights went down and the film credits began to roll. I could barely contain the excitement surging through my body. The buzzed feeling was a palpable part of this auspicious event. For some people, it was pretty routine and probably even boring, but for me it was the culmination of much of what I was trying to achieve as an actress and a performer. This is where I felt I truly belonged.

Fine, the end in Italian, flickered across the screen as the last credit rolled. The audience leapt to its feet with uproarious applause. The lights rose slowly as the director of MoMA took the podium to introduce the maestro himself, who was sitting in the front row with his beautiful wife, Giulietta Masina. "Ladies and gentlemen," he began, "please give a warm New York welcome to perhaps one of the greatest treasures of filmmaking,

Federico Fellini." Again, the audience went wild and the love and adoration for this cinematic genius was clearly obvious. After expressing a few brief words and gratitude for his lovely wife, he exited.

Filing out of the theater I squeezed my way through the crowded exit. I was seeing spots from all the cameras taking photos. The after reception was a short block down at Trump Tower. I caused quite a commotion in my golden dress as cars were beeping their horns and cabbies were shouting out to me. Approaching the entrance I saw flashbulbs exploding like fireworks in the lobby. As I entered, I saw Federico Fellini up ahead where he had graciously stopped to pose for the press photographers. Quickly, I stepped up my pace and made a mad dash to where he was, noticing that Diane Brill, Anita Sarko, James St. James, and Lisa Edelstein were also angling for a spot as well. All seasoned press whores from way back when, we knew a great photo opportunity when we saw one. They were a few steps ahead of me, with each one perfectly bookending Fellini so that when I arrived there was only one place for me to go. I slipped in front and knelt down before him as if I were about to receive Holy Communion from the film gods.

The paparazzi went wild.

"Mr. Fellini, look here," one cried.

"Over here sir, please look up," said another.

"Look up? I prefer to look down!" he replied, his gaze training like a laser on my ever-expanding ample bosom dangling in his direct line of vision.

I nearly died when I heard what he said. As all the photographers laughed, I looked over my shoulder to see Stephen Sabin, the nightlife editor of *Details* magazine. He was scribbling in vivid detail the exchange that just took place, which would later end up in the next issue of the magazine. He also wrote that we were "clinging to Fellini like barnacles to a hull!"

Suddenly, I felt the thin spaghetti strap on my dress pop. Grabbing the strap with one hand, I held it up coyly as the paparazzi tried to get a shot of my exposed boob. Not shy, I continued posing and teasing them until Fellini ambled away to his awaiting table in the restaurant downstairs.

Composing myself, I dashed off desperately seeking a safety pin to secure my strap into place.

• • •

Having survived the clusterfuck of paparazzi at the entrance to the party, I bolstered up my confidence, held in place by the simplicity of one small safety pin. It was a symbol of how fragile my state of mind had become. Mingling at these press events was an easy task for me; it required very little focus as I could flit from one person to the next much like a bee seeking nectar. I stopped briefly to chat and thank our host for the evening, Dinah Prince from the *Daily News*, when she grabbed hold of my arm.

"Come this way, Tish," she said as she led me over to the roped off area where Mr. Fellini was dining privately with his wife and guests. Wait! Did I really hear what she just said? And before I knew it, I was standing before the table where Mr. Fellini was entertaining his guests in fluent Italian when Dinah interrupted and said, "Excuse me Mr. Fellini, I'd like you to meet Tish Gervais. She's a huge fan of your work."

He rose pleasantly smiling and looked me over from head to toe and exclaimed, "So lovely to meet you. You, *mi amore*, must come to Roma!" He then sat back down and resumed his conversation in Italian.

It was as if everything I had planned for had finally culminated in the maestro's one statement. If he felt I was good enough to go to Rome, then Hollywood surely couldn't be that far out of my sights. Luxuriating in the fantasy in my head, my beeper began buzzing loudly in my purse, beckoning me back into the harsh reality of sex work.

Beeped out of the atmosphere of celebration and creativity, I was being drawn back into the seedy New York underbelly of sneaking in and out of fancy hotels. Summoned by whomever was willing to pay the going price. My next stop was the Waldorf Hotel, where one of my regular clients was requesting my services.

What never occurred to me was the high price I was paying for such a low life.

CHAPTER 17

Recovery

I still wasn't ready to put the crack pipe down. Within weeks after the Fellini premiere, I was right back on the street trolling for tricks along Eighth Avenue in Hell's Kitchen. I practically bumped into this big, burly, blue-collar guy named Joe. I could tell he was on a similar mission. Addicts have a way of attracting each other, like flies to shit. Joe ended up in my small apartment on Forty-Fifth Street and within minutes I was ringing the bell of the apartment downstairs to get some coke.

I'd become a regular Betty Crocker when it came to cooking up freebase cocaine. I loved the whole ritual of mixing and adding, getting it just right. Finding the right combination of baking soda and water and heat made me feel like a celebrity chef creating the perfect meal. But once the rock hit the pipe, the substance itself became the star of the show.

My neighbor across the hall, a beautiful teacher named Debra, must have gotten a whiff of smoke because she rang my bell to and asked to join the party. Debra became a perfect pawn to keep Joe springing for more and more coke. We smoked nonstop for two full weeks before we had exhausted his every last dollar.

When you smoke for long periods of time, you begin to hallucinate. At one point, I heard helicopters flying above the apartment building and I swore searchlights were being flashed into my window. Out in the hallway, I heard heavy-booted footsteps marching toward my door. I was convinced a SWAT team was poised to break it down and take us into custody. Frantic and jittery, I covered up the windows with blankets and sheets from my bed. But the hallucinations didn't stop.

Joe, too, became increasingly paranoid. During a vulnerable moment, he confided that he was a hit man who was hiding out in New York for the time being. He eventually brought over his duffle bag, which included a change of clothes, toiletries, knives, and a gun. Finally, we were out of cash, which was when things got really desperate. At one point, Joe's paranoia got so bad that he told me to take off all my clothes and lie still on the bed as he turned out all the lights. Immediately, I thought, *Well, this is it.* As I lay naked on the bed in the dark, I imagined that any minute he was going to either stab me or shoot me. I lay there for what seemed like hours until finally he flicked on the lights and decided it was best that he move on. Never was I more relieved.

Relieved, yes, but not yet sane. I immediately hit the streets to try to score more drugs. It was almost daybreak and there wasn't much traffic on the stretch of Eighth Avenue where I could usually grab a trick. Except for a few cabs searching for fares, there wasn't much activity.

A homeless man was shuffling up the avenue when he stopped and circled around me like a shark ready to feed. "What's up?" he mumbled, almost inaudibly.

"Not much," I replied. And without any hesitation, I asked, "Do you want a date?"

"Yeah," he replied. "I got a room across the street at that hotel." He nodded to a hotel on Forty-Sixth Street and Eighth Avenue where you could rent rooms by the hour, which was very convenient for the working girls of Times Square.

"Okay," I said. "Let's go. How much you got?"

"Five dollars in change, mostly quarters."

Five fucking dollars, I thought to myself. Needless to say, I went to the hotel with him. He was only interested in doing one of the vilest acts I had ever been asked to do. But when queen cocaine beckoned, nothing was out of bounds.

Completely disgusted by what I had just done, I pulled up my panties, slipped into my jean skirt, my pockets now bulging with change, pulled my T-shirt over my head, and left the hotel to resume my perch on the corner of Forty-Fifth and Eighth. The sun was high and bright and I felt as if it were searing my soul. Not only did I feel filthy, but I hadn't showered and probably smelled as bad as the homeless man I left back in the hotel. My very short denim skirt revealed the tips of my ass cheeks. The black T-shirt I wore slipped off one shoulder as I manically paraded back and forth. Clad in head-to-toe black, I was ready to attend a funeral: my own.

At this time of day, the morning business crowd bustled by, looking fresh and determined with their briefcases proudly slung over their shoulders or tucked securely under their arms. And then as if in slow motion—I don't know if it was the drugs or some kind of spiritual intervention—the crowd seemed to be moving slower and in sync as they passed me. Plastered against the window of a pawnshop, feeling as if my life was in hock, I had a sudden notion that if I didn't do something soon everything would pass me by. I wondered where each person was heading with such intensity and purpose. I questioned why I hadn't ever imagined myself in such a position. And if I had, what would my purpose be? Could I even have one? In that moment, I realized I had to do something, anything. The quarters jingling in my jean skirt pocket seemed like a signal that I should call for help.

I shivered as I slipped a quarter into the nearest phone booth and called the one person I knew I could count on, the person who had been there for me when I left my husband in Brooklyn. I knew the number by heart. I dialed, hoping there would be a familiar voice on the other end, praying for an answer. It rang a few times before a cheerful voice answered.

"Good morning, 13th Street Theater. How may I help you?"

"Eva, it's me Natalia," I said.

"Well, hello!" she replied, and before she could say another word I burst into tears, sharing my entire ugly story of addiction, revealing how sad, scared, and hopeless I felt, and how soon I feared the marshal would be at my door. With no family to rely on, this was the first time I had ever humbled myself and asked for help. Without any judgment or hesitation, Eva offered for me to come back to the Village and take up my old room on the third floor of the theater.

"Don't you worry, honey, we're going to take care of this."

I had never felt more grateful.

• • •

The next day, Eva pulled up in her daughter Jenny's clunky station wagon outside my Hell's Kitchen apartment. With great difficulty, I had managed to put down the pipe long enough to pack the very few possessions I had left.

Settling back into my life in Eva's apartment wasn't easy, but she helped me obtain public assistance and Medicaid by giving me a letter stating that I was staying with her. It was incredibly difficult not to use drugs, but when I applied for public assistance I was straight with the woman who did my intake and she kindly referred me to an outpatient program on lower East Broadway, close to Chinatown. My enrollment was contingent on it, and so I went to the appointment.

Soon after, I found myself sitting in a circle with other drug addicts, along with some who were on methadone treatment. Immediately, my denial kicked in again. *I'm no damn junkie,* I thought to myself. I used heroin and kicked it myself back in the late 1970s, so I certainly wasn't as bad as this group. Also, being a trans woman who was very closeted, I found it incredibly difficult to share anything personal about myself. But I did attend and was thankful that I was at least getting some badly needed assistance from the state.

The groups were hardly enlightening. I wasn't ready to listen or engage with the other people, whom I held in contempt. I was convinced that this was just another phase I was going through. There had been so many. For the first few weeks, attending group did help me abstain from drugs and for the first time I started to feel okay, like, *oh, I got this, I'm not going down like some of the others in my group, I'm fine!* What I didn't know was that I was setting myself up for the classic fall that many people in recovery make early on: a sense of false confidence that doesn't prepare you for the moment when you feel most vulnerable to use.

Meanwhile, things at the theater were going well. I had regained Eva's confidence and our friendship was solid. I got cast in a play called *Passages*, about a woman and her daughter dealing with Alzheimer's. The rehearsals were intense but I was happy to be back on the stage and pursuing an acting career again. Nevertheless, I felt uneasy. It wasn't a well-known fact that I wasn't born female around the theater. There may have been whispers, but with the exception of a few close friends to whom I'd confided, no one knew. I was caught in a crazy conundrum of trying to be my authentic self, but feeling too ashamed to be open about something at my very core. There was still a huge stigma attached to being trans and I found that most people who knew my secret viewed me as an oddity or something they just didn't understand. It reminded me of walking a tight-rope: Being strong, upright, and confident would take me to the other side, but one slip to the left or right could crush me.

It was a difficult thing to hide. Several guys in the theater company flirted and chased after me. One was a very handsome young Italian American actor named Chris, who reminded me of my ex-husband, with the same strong striking features and broad, strong body. Flirting came easily to me but following it up was terrifying as it made me vulnerable to rejection. Everyone loved him, myself included. The closest I ever got to him was when my breasts squeezed by him on a narrow stairway. Later Chris Meloni would become a well-known and terrific actor on the HBO series *Oz* and *Law & Order: SVU*. With a few of the others, I went as far as oral sex, but stopped short of telling them my little secret.

One of the things that didn't change right away was my idea that I could still go out to nightclubs and attempt to revive my career. The invitations trickled in even though I'd been out of commission for a while and I was foolish to believe that I could function in that environment. After a few close calls, I decided it was best that I give it a rest. In the back of my mind, I knew I was tempting fate and eventually, if I weren't careful, I'd end up right back where I had been.

One night after rehearsal, a few fellow actor friends and I closed up the theater and went next door to a bar to bitch about the theater, the state of the production, other actors, and so on. The actors ordered beer while I drank ginger ale. The bartender asked if I'd like another drink and without thinking twice I answered, "Sure. I'll have what he's having." At the time, I didn't consider alcohol to be part of my problem. Even though I had done my fair share of drinking, I wasn't a blackout drunk, however my drinking had escalated to more than just taking the edge off or to be social. Although alcoholism was rampant in my family, it never occurred to me that I might have had a problem with it. I was in such denial because I preferred drugs to booze.

The bartender poured me a nice cool draft beer and placed it squarely in front of me. I took a sip, then another, and finished about half of it when I got a slightly fuzzy feeling that felt all too familiar.

I never finished that drink. Within minutes, I had excused myself, saying I was tired and had to go home. Go home I did, but not to the apartment. Instead, I went into the box office, opened the unlocked box where the receipts were kept, and grabbed a fistful of cash. Out the door I went, down Sixth Avenue to Washington Square Park, where I knew I could get exactly what I wanted.

It didn't take long. Within minutes, a tall guy with dreads approached me, recognizing my desperate expression and frantic pace. "Follow me, mommy," he said. On the other, less populated side of the park, I gave him forty bucks and he gave me four vials of crack. Drugs in hand, I ran to the cigar store on Sixth Avenue to buy a stem and a screen, which they sold like loosies. On my way, I figured it was late enough that no one would be in the women's bathroom in the park. With my stem in hand I slipped into the bathroom realizing my hunch was correct.

Entering the last stall, I fastened the latch and proceeded to drop a rock into my stem. My heart pulsed as I anticipated the feeling I was about to experience as my cigarette lighter heated the tip of the stem. Slowly, I sucked the smoke deep in to my lungs and was hit with that familiar rush one gets from the first puff. Time stood still as I continued to scrape and smoke, scrape and smoke each remaining crack rock I dropped in. The sun would be rising soon and it didn't even register to me that I'd been in a stinky bathroom stall for hours getting high.

Eventually, as all good crack addicts know, once you run out, the chase begins. You begin looking and looking for just a little bit more, sometimes dropping anything that slightly resembles crack into your pipe and hoping to regain that initial blast. When I realized I was out, I left the bathroom and ventured outside to look for my friend with the dreads.

"Over here, mommy," he yelled. Fresh out of cash, I knew if he didn't front me some more I'd have to be more resourceful. The theater was a five-minute walk from the park and I asked him if he was going to be here for a bit. He nodded, and I headed double-time back to the theater, which had now become my own personal ATM. Quietly, I crept into the theater, which was still closed, headed straight for the box office, and took what-ever money was left.

Back in the park, I handed over a bundle of cash to my new friend, and he gave me what I was after.

"Would you like to come smoke with me and my buddy over there?" he asked, pointing to another guy by the entrance. *Hmmm, free*, I thought, and in a snap we were headed under the steps by NYU. The spot was marked by the fresh stench of urine and some broken bottles, trash, and milk crates, evidence that someone thought this out.

The taller guy sat down, put a rock into my stem, and lit it up.

"Pull on it, mommy, that's it, suck it good," he said. He then started to unbuckle his belt and motioned to me to get down and give him head. Since the drugs were free and I still had my stash, I figured, *what the hell*. Then the other guy came around the back of me and started to play with my ass, talking about giving up some pussy. I thought *the only pussy they were getting was not any pussy they wanted*. Now I knew I was screwed. Thinking fast, I protested that I was on my period.

"Okay, well keep doing what you were doing," he said, forcing my head down.

Eventually the other guy grew more insistent and aggressive about getting "some pussy." I protested, but then he pulled out a knife.

"Bitch, you think we brought your ass down here to smoke all our drugs?"

I panicked. Thankfully, I figured I was close enough to the exit that if I made a run for it, the most they might do was cut me. I survived Mona's slicing back in the day so what the hell.

"Why don't you switch places here so I can just sit on you right here?" I said calmly. As they began to exchange places, I made a mad sprint up the steps, running as fast as I could toward Sixth Avenue. Luckily, they didn't give chase.

At this point the birds were at full chirp, letting me know that daybreak had arrived. Heading back up the avenue, I stopped at a deli and bought a forty-ounce beer. Making my way back into the theater, I slowly opened the door to ensure that no one would hear me and tiptoed into the theater dressing room. It was deathly quiet and I remembered there was a little space under the room where we stored our bigger set pieces. You entered by lifting a hatch, much like a pirate about to enjoy his haul of booty. I descended into the small space and flicked on the dim light bulb. At last I had found some peace and quiet.

The walls around me were made of brick and the dirt floor was damp and cool. I leaned back and dug into my pocket to fish out my supplies. Lighting the first hit, a warm secure feeling came over me and I had the sensation that all was right.

After a few more hits and some swigs of my Colt 45, I heard a tinkling sound coming from above. It was Saturday and the children's shows would be starting soon. Had I really been under the dressing room that long, and how could I have forgotten about the show? Soon I heard footsteps and muffled voices above me. Crates and boxes were being dragged along the floor. The sound of the piano grew louder as children started entering the theater. *Oh, shit*, I thought, *I have to get out of here before it's too late.*

I gave the hatch above me a shove. It didn't move. It must have been weighted with props. *Now what do I do?* Sweat dripped from my brow.

If I didn't get out, I would be stuck for at least several hours until the shows ended.

When the entrance music began for the kiddie show *Snow White and the Seven Dwarfs*, my anxiety reached its peak. I tried again to open the hatch, this time using more force. It clanged open and a crate of dishes and silverware came crashing down. The actors' heads swiveled around from their dressing tables to see me climbing out of the hole and running onto the stage. The poor kids screamed. I must have scared the life out of them as I bolted off the stage and ran up the steps to the back entrance of Eva's apartment.

Back in my room, I was so rattled I began to imagine all sorts of horrible scenarios. "Oh God, oh God, what am I going to do?" I said out loud as I paced back and forth.

A little voice whispered, *Jump, just jump out the window.*

My teeth chattered. I was frightened and still high as a kite. For some reason, even though I wasn't raised religious, I started pleading for divine help. "Oh God, oh God, what have I done? Oh God, please let me calm down and fall asleep. I swear I will never do this again." I lay in my bed and rocked myself to sleep, hoping my foxhole prayers would work.

Thankfully, Eva was not home during all this but downstairs attending to the theater. I didn't see her until I awoke the next morning.

"Well, you had quite a night," she said as I stumbled out of the bathroom. Before I could respond, she addressed me flatly. "Natalia, I know you took the money from the box office, so what are you going to do about your little problem?"

Little problem, I thought. *She has no idea, even if she had been married to an alcoholic.*

As I started to speak, she cut me off. "Listen to me now, Natalia. You have to do something about this. You're going to have to get some help because I can't let this go on. You have too much going for you and it wouldn't be right for me to stand by and keep quiet."

No one—except for Paulie—had ever spoken to me this way, with such concern.

"I care too much for you to watch you throw your whole life down the drain," she said. "Either you're going to get help or you're going to have to leave."

As she issued this ultimatum, tears fell down her face. Sobbing, I apologized and swore I would seek help.

Both of us cried, we hugged, and she said it again, "I care too much about you."

The shock of being caught paled in comparison to hearing someone say they cared about me. It was a staggering realization.

After our conversation, we decided to look for support. The next day, after I felt more rested and recovered from my devastating relapse, we looked in the telephone book for support groups. We found a listing for a Recovery support group. Tentatively, I dialed the number. As luck would have it, there was a group that met right down the street at the Lesbian and Gay Community Center (no B, T, or Q back then). Groups were held every day of the week and one started at 6:15 p.m.

Since it was a short walk down the block, I arrived a little early. As I entered the center, I felt my usual skepticism and apprehension, not knowing what to expect. The meeting was held on the third floor, in what used to be a classroom, and a circle of chairs had been placed in the center of the room. Around it, people milled about, talking and laughing.

I whipped off my scarf and sunglasses and stuffed them in my bag. I removed my vintage blue cashmere coat and placed it over the back of my chair. I adjusted my lilac turtleneck. My hair was still loose and wild. I was about to sit when I heard someone call my name.

"Natalia, over here. It's Dodi." I turned to see a woman with whom I had worked years before at the Third Avenue Bazaar. She had been a window decorator, and we would bond every time she and her gay friend Matt came to dress the windows. Dodi gave me a big, warm hug and explained a little bit about how the meetings worked.

Feeling relieved, I raised my hand when the person running the group asked if there was anyone new to the meeting. "My name is Natalia and my friend thought I should come here because I have a problem with drugs," I said.

The whole room answered, "Hi, Natalia," and burst into applause.

It did seem a bit jarring but as I listened to people talk, not only did I relate to what they were saying, I felt that I was finally somewhere I could begin to be myself. At the break, a woman who said her name was Carolyn, a beautiful, soft-spoken fair-skinned woman of Latina descent, asked if anyone would like to surrender his or her disease and get a hug and a chip.

"White is the sign of surrender and on one side of the chip you can place a quarter to call someone if you have the urge to use," she said.

People weren't shy about getting up. So I did too, to more applause and hugs. Hey, this wasn't so bad after all. I had been so used to people treating me badly that it was reassuring to know that I'd found a friendly place. The war was over and my surrender was an auspicious beginning.

After the meeting, people came up, shook my hand, hugged me, introduced themselves, and offered their phone numbers. At first, I was suspicious, wondering what these strangers wanted from me. But it seemed their intentions were good: they just wanted me to stay clean and sober for one more day. Everyone told me to call.

That evening Dodi walked me home with her girlfriend at the time, a striking Cuban woman named Yvonne, who later became another mentor and dear friend. Before saying goodbye, Dodi handed me her phone number and asked me to call her to let her know that I was okay. She also said if I wanted she would be willing to be my sponsor, the person who would guide me in my recovery. Having nothing to lose and feeling so welcomed, I gladly accepted. Dodi offered to take me to another group that met on Saturday and I agreed. At the entrance of the theater, we said our goodbyes and closing the door behind me, for the first time in a very long time, I felt that, somehow, I would be okay.

In the morning I woke early, had my coffee with Eva, and regaled her with the details of the meeting. She was as ecstatic as I was.

Once I fell into my new routine, things started to get a little better. Dodi, my new sponsor, was my rock. On occasion I would call her, hysterical, and she would ask, "Did you read the first three steps today?" referring to the first three steps in the recovery workbook.

"Not yet."

"Well, call me back when you do."

It wasn't tough love but structured love, something I wasn't used to. I was fortunate to find someone so sensible and so willing to share her hardwon wisdom. I was also fortunate to have found a group that felt like family. And even though it entailed the requisite family drama, the experience taught me things my family never did. One of the most valuable lessons I learned early on was to be of service to others. My sponsor invited me to help her make coffee before the meeting and to put out the chairs and place ashtrays around. I was told this is where my spiritual awakening would begin. If I was going to seek a power greater than myself I might find it hanging around the coffeepot for starters. Most addicts are self-centered by nature and since I had never really thought of anyone but myself this was a hard-earned but essential lesson on the road to recovery.

• • •

On February 8, 1987, I reached my ninetieth day of sobriety, a huge milestone for anyone suffering from addiction. In this short time, I was beginning to fathom a sense of myself that I had never known before. A fellow addict had invited me to celebrate at the Friday meeting in the tiny church kitchen on West Fourth Street. While I had my shared some of my experience before, this was really an occasion to celebrate.

Eva's daughter, Jenny O'Hara, was in town visiting her mom. She had become like a big sister to me; I adored her and was so in awe of her talent as an actress. She was getting ready to do the all-female version of *The Odd Couple* on Broadway with the legendary Rita Moreno. When Jenny heard my good news, she asked me what was I going to wear. I'd managed to save very few of my nice things and told her I would wear a black stretch wool dress that Paulie had made for me. She then went to the closet and came back with her full-length mink coat.

"I think this will be perfect, too!"

My jaw dropped at her generous offer. Just three months ago, I couldn't be trusted and now I had earned the trust of Eva and her incredible daughter, Jenny, who was now my dear friend too.

Friday arrived fast. The meeting was packed and when I walked into the group everyone was glad to see me. Some addicts are triggered by milestones and use again, or let fear keep them away. Not me, although I was feeling quite emotional for the tremendous amount of support of the group and my friends.

After being introduced, I stood up to a thunderous round of applause. I could already feel my eyes well with tears. It was the most overwhelming experience I had ever known. I never thought I would feel so accepted.

Feeling like a million bucks, for dramatic effect I slipped off Jenny's fur, took my seat, and began to tell my tale. I can't remember my words exactly, but it was the first time I was honest not only with my group but with myself. What a relief it was to not be living a life of active addiction and to gain the trust of friends new and old. I wasn't naive enough to believe that everyone was entirely supportive, but it didn't matter because I believed that for the most part many of my peers and fellows in recovery recognized the good in me, the good that I had lost so many years ago. For the first time, I felt capable of love. They always say in the meetings, *let us love you until you can love yourself.* Well, it was a start and a very strong one at that.

After ninety days came ninety-one and, before I knew it, I was celebrating a year of recovery. Throughout the year, I had also benefited from individual therapy, which had been recommended by some of my fellow addicts in recovery. What happened during this process was not something I had ever imagined or expected. Having the privilege of honest self-appraisal is something that is reinforced in the recovery program, but some of us need more.

While I was clean and sober, I was still feeling very depressed about my gender identity. Since I wasn't medicating my symptoms with drugs or alcohol, I could no longer pretend that living between two genders wasn't taking a toll on me. The feelings I had were real and I knew that I had to deal with them or face the consequences of repression.

Finding work as a trans woman still proved to be especially challenging and Dodi, my sponsor at the time, suggested temp work as a way to get out of the sex work arena. Half serious, half joking, she said, "You'd be the perfect Kelly Girl." Taking suggestions was something uncomfortable for me but slowly I was learning that it wasn't such a bad thing. So I made an appointment with the temp agency she recommended. Certainly, I was smart enough to answer a phone and give general advice and file things alphabetically when needed.

Managing to get a few corporate gigs, I'd dress conservatively and show up on time. Even taking the bus was a new experience. Bravely facing the challenges of adjusting to joining the daytime work force wasn't without its own pitfalls. Being clean and sober, I was becoming more present and in touch with my feelings. Spending the better part of life during the daytime wasn't especially new to me, but I couldn't escape the fishbowl effect that living as a trans person often invited. Although my passing privilege was great, there still were occasions when people would stare or whisper in a way that was disapproving and embarrassing to me. It happened on the bus and sometimes at the various work sites I temped at. There were many days when I could be found on any Manhattan street corner not looking for a trick but clinging onto a phone booth in tears calling my sponsor for support. It was an awful and consistent feeling that was becoming increasingly difficult to bear sober.

Back in my first ninety days of recovery, a friend gave me a referral to a mental health clinic at Beth Israel Hospital, but I was hesitant. As a person of trans expression, my prior interactions with the medical community had been less than favorable. The last time I had tried to seek help for my substance abuse problem, at Odyssey House in the East Village, I was rejected outright due to my gender orientation. The intake coordinator told me I would be "too much of a distraction for the rest of the clients."

Hearing the word "distraction" flashed me right back to 1974 when I was arrested for the first time back in Providence at the age of nineteen for loitering for prostitution. The prison system didn't know what to do with me back then either. I had spent the night in the precinct and the next morning they transported me to the Adult Correctional Institute. After the strip search, I just wanted to screw with the guards. So when they asked my sizes, I ordered pants that I knew would be figure hugging. Instead of buttoning up my shirt, I tied it into a twist so that I could show a little cleavage. They were so perplexed about what to do with me that they kept me in the captain's office while I tried to make bail. At one point, they decided to give me a tour and herded me up to the general population cellblock. Inmates of all shapes and sizes were yelling, whistling, and begging the guards as choruses of catcalls ensued, "Let her in here!"

Eventually, I contacted a family friend, Helen Robinson, a jolly Armenian woman who was my confidante and was sworn to secrecy not to let my mother know what had happened. Helen was one of the few people I could talk to about my transition and she always lent a sympathetic and non-judgmental ear. She would come to my rescue on more than one occasion and was one of the first people I came out to in any way as a teenager.

So back then my gender identity had worked to my advantage, but now I was trying to save my life by seeking treatment. Following up on another referral, I had no idea what to expect when I arrived at the clinic. It was embedded in me to believe the more you told people the worse off you would be, so I had never taken therapy seriously.

But my leap of faith paid off when I met Dr. Erin Newman. She was soft-spoken, plainly dressed, and had a very inviting smile. What was noticeably obvious about Erin was that she was wearing a wig. Having worn a few wigs myself, I could tell. As it turned out, Erin was an Orthodox Jew. My initial reaction was one of surprise and trepidation. But just as I was learning to trust, so was I learning to be open, as the program suggested. After all, hadn't I been judged enough in my life to know how it felt?

Over the course of my therapy, I related my story to Erin as honestly as I could. It was liberating to talk about all the things that I had kept bottled up inside. For the first time in my life, I felt heard. I could tell that not only was she listening intently, she was doing so in an open, non-judgmental way, which made it less painful to recall some of the trauma I had experienced in my young life.

I told her in detail about how my father beat me mercilessly with a rubber hose as I begged him to stop. I told her of the sexual abuse I suffered at the hands of adults and the anger I had felt when no one protected me from the violations. I told her of my suicide attempt and how I had had to go to that extreme to alert my family of the serious confusion I was experiencing with my gender identity. Over the course of my treatment, I didn't leave much unsaid.

After a few months had passed she also suggested that I get my medical house in order. So I agreed to be tested for HIV at the Stuyvesant Polyclinic on Second Avenue where I had gone for a general check-up. My sexual past was checkered to say the least, but somehow because I wasn't having sex with gay men I thought I would be fine. The day approached when I was ready to receive my results. I clearly remember confidently walking up the steps into the clinic feeling the test would certainly be negative.

When the doctor came into the office to talk with me, my gaze was drawn to the big gold cross with Jesus dangling from his neck. He sat down and looked at me across his desk.

"Hello Ms. Gervais, I'm Dr. Lopez and I will be giving you your results today," he said. Without missing a beat, he then proceeded to tell me. "Your test came back positive for the HIV virus," he said, devoid of any scintilla of compassion. "You're not surprised, are you?" he asked. "Given your history of prostitution and IV drug use you are at a higher risk."

Wait. Did he really just say what I think he did? I thought. *Did he really in a roundabout way say it was my fault?* If something like that happened to me today I'd be more than equipped to handle it, but then I was so vulnerable that I had no idea how to fend for myself against such ignorance. Mistakenly I had gone alone to the clinic. After hearing the news, I went numb. Not having any idea what this meant or even how I was supposed to process this news, I left feeling stunned and disoriented. I called a friend who luckily picked up the phone for support. My life was about to change in a way I had never even once considered.

Thank God Erin continued to be a safe harbor to dock in from what had been a very violent and turbulent storm. She was there when I was diagnosed as HIV positive at a time when the prognosis was not good.

She witnessed my grief first hand over a mother whom I had accepted did the best she could, but at the same time felt it was never enough. She understood how my spirit as a young boy had been broken not by my own hand, but by a society that was intolerant of anything that strayed outside the norm. She consoled me when I talked about how my biggest dreams had been squashed by a family incapable of being there for me just as no one had been there for them. She listened to me express, for the first time, my anger and disappointment at being dismissed by mostly everyone in my life.

And through it all, I stayed the course, kept my appointments with Erin, made my meetings, and showed up for my life the best way I could, even though there were days when I curled up in a ball on my bed in Eva's apartment and cried into my pillow. Prior to recovery, I had no direction and no guidance, but little by little I was learning.

Because I was new to recovery, it was strongly suggested to not make any major changes in my first year. I took this seriously as I knew I wasn't able to withstand emotionally the challenges that come with major decisions. By witnessing others before me make that grand mistake, I avoided relapse and its attendant consequences, the biggest one being death, a common occurrence among recovering addicts. But another common occurrence was growth and moving forward. It took painstaking patience and perseverance to put my life back together. I first had to understand that what happened to me wasn't my fault. No longer did I need to blame myself and endure the punishment that outside forces had tried so hard to inflict on me. I had choices. My life could look like anything I believed it should, or wanted it to be. At times my negative feelings were so overwhelming that I had to resort to a slower, more laid-back pace, which was difficult for someone with such an active mind and spirit. I wanted it to be over.

In my own naïveté, I believed that my problems were because of drugs and alcohol and other forces outside of myself. Imagine my surprise when I began to understand that not only did my problems begin with me, they could end with me as well. As I became stronger and gained more time away from drugs and alcohol, I was developing a new set of coping mechanisms, which I never had before. If I wanted to achieve something, it wasn't just a matter of wishing it into existence and hoping for the best. No. I had to work for things in order for them to materialize, and work for them I did. Sometimes cheerfully, but mostly begrudgingly, I did it myself, and I became stronger and stronger because of it.

Deep down, because of the work I had been doing, I knew that eventually a decision had to be made. Although my depression was manageable, at times it could be debilitating. Something had to shift. Meanwhile, my sessions with Erin had taken on an exploration of the notion of gender and what that meant to me. What was female? What was male? I had never asked these questions before, but now they seemed crucially urgent.

Would I give in to external pressure to undergo gender confirmation surgery in spite of some of the negative outcomes I'd witnessed? Many of my friends from the early days had had surgery but were unhappy with the results, which often led them to suicide. On the other hand, could I accept the duality of my gender and be free and open with my body the way it was? Or should I just fold my tent and go quietly into oblivion? Oncoming trains at the local subway stop had begun to seem appealing sometimes, but the messiness of it all scared me too much to go through with it.

Finally, I began to wonder about another option. Would it be possible to reverse what I had done and re-transition back to my assigned gender at birth? Or was Brian, who had been replaced by a much larger and more colorful personality, already too far gone?

All of these ideas held equal weight, but it was up to me to decide—not any outside force, not my therapist, my sponsor, my good friends, or my peers. Me. It was entirely up to me. Earlier I had made such life-altering changes impulsively, for fun or for attention. And almost always I had been under the influence of drugs and alcohol. I had been so fearful that friends would reject Brian, saying that I just "went along to get along," as they say. But now that I was thinking clearly, I needed to take a good hard look at the direction in which my life was heading.

CHAPTER 18

Transitions

Now barely six months into my recovery one beautiful day in May of 1987 I was getting ready for my regular meeting down the street when the phone rang. Picking up the receiver I could hear my sister Sheila sobbing as she told me. "Mommy died." Del's long battle with heart disease and lung cancer had finally taken her at age fifty-seven. I knew she had been ill and was planning to go back to Rhode Island to see her, hoping she could hang on just a little bit longer so I'd have enough time to get there. Unfortunately, it was too late.

We had spoken over the phone a few times recently and the last time she had called me for the first time that I can ever remember. She had even asked me, "How are you doing?"

"I'm fine, Mom," I'd said. "Things are really getting better." I chose not to disclose to her that I had recently tested positive for HIV—that probably would have killed her sooner. I kept it to myself and it was some time before I even told my siblings.

"Good. I'm glad to know you're okay," she'd replied hoarsely.

It had been a rare occurrence and one that comforted me, knowing that she had been conscious that her time was limited and wanted to be sure I was okay.

After trying to console my sister, I hung up, shocked and numb from the painful reality that I would never see or hear my mother again. While our relationship was extremely turbulent and complicated at times, deep down I knew she truly loved me. And although she never said so, I knew that she was proud of me.

Eva was a rock, offering her usual loving and comforting consolation when I told her of my mother's death. Sheila mentioned that plans for the funeral and wake were being handled begrudgingly by my older brother, Randall. He never once consulted with any of us about decisions regarding the arrangements. I ran to my recovery home group and shared the news of my mother's passing. While the support and love from my group members was tremendous, some strongly suggested I carefully consider my recovery first when deciding whether to attend the wake and funeral. But how could I not say a final goodbye to my own mother?

Once the meeting ended and I had received the best hugs, I left the Center feeling shaken but satisfied and supported by so many of my new friends. However, as I strolled back home to the theater my mind was flooded with so many unpleasant memories of my life in Providence. Because I wasn't using drugs or alcohol, it wasn't uncommon for this to happen. While it felt awfully uncomfortable as I relived the experience, I was also grateful to be able to feel.

• • •

The next day as I boarded the Amtrak train headed to Rhode Island, I knew I was walking into a viper's nest. I didn't feel prepared to handle any mistreatment from my own siblings. Proudly clean and sober, I had picked out a somber navy-blue ankle-length wrap dress, a wide red belt, and matching red kitten pumps. It was important to me that I looked chic and respectable for my mother and myself.

My brother Randy limited the wake to family so none of my mother's friends, including her best friend Helen, were able to attend. Years later, Helen confided to me through tears how hurtful it had been to be excluded.

Del was the first of her sisters to pass and all three of her surviving sisters attended. Wakes are usually somber affairs, but in my family this wasn't the case. The three sisters sat in the back cackling loudly as if they were having coffee and donuts, which was odd to me.

After the burial, I had the good sense to invite my aunts back to my mother's apartment for real coffee and donuts. It wasn't much but it was the appropriate thing to do, as Randy hadn't even bothered arranging any type of reception. Entering my mother's apartment, my aunts and I found my youngest brother David passed out on the bed from a night of drug use. He hadn't even bothered to make it to the wake or the funeral. Sheila was also staying at my mother's apartment as well. Once I turned the key and entered, I was stunned by how my sister Sheila snatched my mother's house keys so violently out of my hand as we arrived back at Del's apartment. It was symbolic of our complicated relationship. It felt as if I was being cast falsely as an outsider who had no right to be there.

As soon as my aunts left, I knew to get the hell out of there. Clearly, my brother was actively using drugs and it was a potentially loaded situation for me to linger behind and get caught up in his insanity. Jeffery was still in prison for selling drugs and wasn't able to get a pass to say goodbye to Mom. I also sensed a seething resentment from my two older brothers, Joe and Randy. My siblings were connoisseurs of blame and maybe because of my own mixed feelings about my gender I felt it pointed in my direction.

Quickly looking through my mother's things, the only item I cared to have was a photo album she made of my childhood photos. Gathering the album, I called a taxi and headed to the train station for the next train to New York. I felt incredibly angry, sad, and disgusted by the treatment I received from my siblings. While we were never particularly close, I fool-ishly believed our shared common grief over the loss of our parent would bring us together. It had only split us further apart.

Arriving back in New York, I processed my grief using the support of my therapist and my recovery group, and I resumed my fearless moral inventory of my life. It was becoming clearer to me that many of the things I had most desired were far from my reach as a trans woman. In examin-ing my motives in such a profoundly deep way, I understood my present reality was built on a foundation of sand. I was young, fairly attractive, and had continued working as an actress, in Off-Off-Broadway shows. I was successful from an external standpoint. But the cruel, hard fact was that I might never find acceptance in society for what I so deeply loved doing: acting. On top of that, there was also this nagging notion in the back of my mind that, somehow, I made a huge mistake and correcting it would take a Herculean effort on my part. Blind faith had been the only thing that had gotten me so far within my first year of recovery. But I would come to rely on it more than ever before.

It was always easy to talk to Erin as I began to pour my heart out in a way that was frightening, yet refreshing. Soon I realized that things were about to get real in a way that I never imagined possible. The deeper I went with examining my history of physical, sexual, and emotional abuse, the clearer it became to me that many of the choices I made in my life were based on living up to other people's expectations of me. It was more important what others thought of me than what I did myself.

Deep down, I was a frightened little boy who did what anyone suggested, as I feared that I would be rejected, judged, or disliked by others. It was a core theme I began to explore with Dr. Erin. One of the most important relationships of my youth, my friendship with Paulie, provided a perfect example of how easily led I could be in order to please.

Growing up, I never had a really good friend. Basically, friends I did have put up with me because on some level I think they felt sorry for me. Boys from the neighborhood I hung around with constantly ridiculed me and always undermined my confidence. Throughout my education, the friends I did make never turned out to be the type that would endure many ups and downs of life. My best friend in junior high was my now sister-in-law, and even she abandoned our friendship once I introduced her to my brother. There was no long-term friendship, nothing like the one in *Thelma and Louise* between Geena Davis and Susan Sarandon. Not for me.

In Paul Bricker I had not only found a friend for life, but someone who loved me in a completely unconditional way. His friendship was so pure and meant everything to me. It was he who instilled a tiny seed of confidence in my very broken and unstable consciousness. The fear I felt that he might reject me in the same way that countless others had for so many years was the most terrifying thing to me. When I needed them the most, even my own family rejected me in the most cruel, unimaginable ways.

The further I went during my early transition, the more Paulie encouraged me. I sought his approval in what today I recognize was such an unhealthy and reckless way. Even to this day, I'm paying the price for some of those life-altering decisions. It wasn't as if he held a gun to my head to do any of these things, although he certainly did adore the brash and unapologetic way I went about transitioning to a female identity. I often wonder what he would think about how things turned out. No doubt he would approve, but he might be surprised at just how much I've accomplished, as his mother Gloria always reminds me.

My sessions with Dr. Newman varied from week to week, but once we got through processing and acknowledging the trauma I had suffered in my early years and the struggles of living as a trans woman for nearly half of them, we were able to focus on the present. There were many options available, but the one I couldn't help considering was suicide. I had to be careful about how I spoke about it because Erin could make a call and lock my ass up within minutes if I even so much as hinted at a plan. However, I did feel it was a vital option because I kept feeling that I would never be as happy and content as my friends.

We kept returning to this question: What was it like for me to experience life as both genders? Not many people have the luxury of inhabiting the other gender identity to the extreme in which I did. It involved not only a physical change, but also a sociological and cultural change. How many cisgender men ever get to truly know how a woman is treated or may feel in modern-day society on such a profound physical and emotional level? Not many do, nor would they even care to, in my opinion.

The idea that we are born with both masculine and feminine influences in our early development was another idea I paid special attention to. We are conditioned at an early age to act or feel a certain way based on our gender assignment at birth. If we are little girls, we're taught to be soft and vulnerable and to focus our attention on family and motherhood or homemaking.

On the other hand, if we are assigned male at birth, we are immediately pre-conditioned to follow along to the script of what it is to "be" a boy. We're taught to be strong no matter what and God forbid we should ever express our feelings about anything! Then we are ridiculed as weak or less masculine. This was especially difficult for me in a household with five brothers, all of whom were hypermasculine and physically imposing. While I tried time and time again to keep up, it was next to impossible. Physically, I never measured up, and they liked to shame me at every opportunity. Given my early history of breathing problems it makes perfect sense that I had been metaphorically holding my breath my entire life—even when it came to who I was going to be.

I'm not sure exactly when it happened, but there was a definite moment when I realized that I clearly embodied both male and female characteristics and there was nothing wrong with that. It's also important to note that I now understood that gender was fluid and that it flowed more easily when I allowed it to. The realization that gender identity was not as fixed or binary as I'd been led to believe my entire life was one of the most profound moments of my therapy sessions with Erin. It felt that a gigantic burden had been lifted and that I was suddenly free and clear to be the decider in my own choices moving forward. I no longer felt dictated to by societal norms that had been proven to be a lie.

Leaving my therapist's office with this new understanding of gender fluidity, I felt relieved, giddy, and downright gleeful. I pondered the possibilities on my stroll home. Once I arrived back at Eva's apartment, my impulse was to share with my friend the recent developments of my therapy, but instead I practiced restraint, which was an entirely new tool of recovery I was learning to employ. It would be some time before I needed to reveal my new truth to Eva. For those closest to me, prudence was the order of the day.

At another session, Erin brought up the topic of the choices I had as I moved forward in my recovery. Narrowing my options down to four was necessary for me. Living in the solution was also a new concept to me. While I had not always been solution-focused, there truly had been a consistent part of my personality that thrived on resolution and action. I was never one to sit around and wallow in uncertainty or self-pity. The four choices available to me all carried a realistic solution to my dilemma, but each one also instilled an incredible amount of fear and trepidation. Some were slightly easier than others, but all were challenging in their own right.

The first option was easiest: accepting my life as a pre-operative trans woman and all it encompassed, which included facing constant rejection, scrutiny, the curiosity of others, and even the ever-present danger of being killed or assaulted. It was also limiting for me as someone who desperately wanted to continue acting. There just weren't any roles for trans women, even one like me with passing privilege. Also, the relationships I had with men were particularly troubling. Men in general had hang-ups about commitment, but trans-amorous men were even more fickle when it came to relationships. Sure, they functioned well behind closed doors, but expressing their desires in public was where they really fell short. Most of this had to do with their views of their own sexuality, and, of course, society didn't make it any more acceptable for them either. Things were changing, but we still had a very long way to go.

Option two involved having gender confirmation surgery. While some trans women claimed they always felt they were in the wrong body, this had never been my experience. I was in the body that I had created for myself, by myself, and I could never really know what a cisgender woman really felt like. It was beyond my perception. I had never felt I was a girl, only that I was feminine-inclined and I presented what I thought a woman should be. It was an idea steeped in stereotype and misogyny from a very early age.

The physical aspect of the surgery itself was complicated. Many of my trans women friends in the seventies and eighties who had undergone gender confirmation surgery had privately confessed their disappointment about it to me. Some committed suicide and many became heavily drug addicted. While medical advancements had been made, surgery was still a scary proposition for me. Also, I didn't despise my penis in the way some trans women described. Even though the conflicting feelings of shame and self-loathing I constantly felt when being objectified by men as a woman with a penis wasn't enough to convince me otherwise.

Re-transitioning back to my male identity was the third, seemingly impossible and most difficult choice. That said, I was never one to shy away from anything challenging. Having spent most of my adult life going against the norm, an outlier in so many countless ways, I was more resilient than most folks. Increasingly, I was becoming more aware of the many different types of gay men in my community. There were so many shapes and sizes and levels of masculine and feminine presentation. In fact, there was one fellow who attended my regular group who had a pretty face and a very strong muscular body. We could have been siblings. We looked similar in a way, except he obviously lived in the gym. I'd find myself studying him intensely. If I were to re-transition back to my male identity, might I resemble him?

Lastly, suicide was still not out of the question. It was a very viable solution in my mind. Receiving an HIV-positive diagnosis with no clear path for medical treatment weighed on me heavily. It was further complicated by my gender dilemma. I was haunted by how callously the doctor at the Stuyvesant Clinic had delivered my test results. Having experienced discrimination firsthand from both the gay and straight community, I could only imagine the horrors I might encounter as a trans woman facing an AIDS diagnosis, and this terrified me more than anything—even more so than the thought of losing Tish.

My transition to female, I realized, had been a great source of strength for me. Miss Tish had kept me alive all these years and it was almost as if I had needed to become her just to survive. What would it be like to say goodbye to such an old friend? That thought alone nearly snapped my mind shut like a steel trap. In the seventies, there hadn't been a broad category for gender expression. It was a simpler time when if you identified as gay or lesbian, you were butch or femme. It was the same for both sexes. All you had to do was pick a lane. Or if you were what we labeled "trans," it meant you were a drag queen or had had a sex change. If you fell into a feminine gay spectrum, like I did, it wasn't unusual for you to think of switching gender. Why live your life as a lonely, effeminate gay queer when you could have more options for love in your life being trans?

I truly believe that if the AIDS epidemic hadn't wiped out an entire generation of men my age, my story would be as common as salt. Historically, too, there hadn't been any gay rights or marriage equality. It was a time of incarceration and ostracization of gay men and lesbian women everywhere. During my life. the needle had moved ever so slightly toward acceptance, but things were nowhere near equal. Yet, I managed to always be who I was in spite of the sometimes cruel and vicious consequences.

One bitterly cold morning in January of 1988, I arrived for my appointment with Erin. I had reached a decision.

"So how has your week been since our last session?" she asked.

"Well, I've been looking at the choices that are available to me, and it hasn't been easy," I replied.

"Can you say a bit more about that?" she gently inquired.

"I just don't think I can continue with things the way they are. It's so painful, all the time. All I want is a little relief. I've thought about it long and hard. I prayed. I shared about it with my sponsor and after what I feel is more than enough consideration it may be time to just be me."

"Well, what do you mean by that? Aren't you already who you are?"

"Yes, but I'm talking about who I came into this world as. I'm no longer feeling trapped in an act of my own design. I want to be Brian again."

"I completely support your decision, but we might what to look at what steps it would take to get there." And, as usual whenever we got to a very intense moment in our session, our time ran out. However, I was relieved that I spoke my truth for the first time.

But at thirty-one, I felt a sense of urgency about coming to terms with the status of my gender identity. Remaining clean and sober for a year was a miracle considering so many of my friends in recovery were either dying from AIDS or relapsing. It was the height of the crisis, a brutally harsh time to get clean and sober, and so many of my friends and acquaintances were getting sick or dying. First to go was Donnie, a sweet and talented man who worked for the Mr. Kenneth Hair Salon. Then Curtis, Eric, John, Charles, Antonio, George, Jimmy, Timothy, Cindy, Loic, Bobby, Arthur, Paulo, Cookie, Carl, Michael, Bill, Bo, Roger, Monica, Laverne, Johnny, Ivan, Nicky, Juan, Fred, David, Willy, Carol, Barbara, and even Paulie's lover Stanley. The list continued to grow longer every day. There wasn't any treatment available and what "medicine" did eventually come down from the National Institute of Health was as toxic as poison. It made people even sicker than they were before taking it.

Looking back at this tumultuous and scary time, I'm grateful that our community had been able to channel its outrage and anger into a movement called ACT UP (AIDS Coalition to Unleash Power). If it hadn't been for the brave and sometimes dangerous efforts of activists like Larry Kramer, Peter Staley, and so many other nameless soldiers who joined the group in their resistance to the government's inability to do anything, I wouldn't be writing this memoir today.

Normally I never stuck with anything too long. In many ways being sober was a natural high because everything was so clear and crisp. My feelings had returned and I was experiencing them in an entirely new way. While I was still suspicious of them and fought occasionally to ignore my reality, I was grateful to be present in a way I had never known before.

Not only was I completely confident it was the right thing to do, but it was also essential for my survival. While it would be no easy undertaking, I would return to my assigned-at-birth male gender. Excited about this next phase of my life, I was also very anxious about how this re-transition would happen and how my family and friends would react. I thought that I had been tested before reaching this decision, but nothing would prepare me for the looming obstacles and further discrimination that I was about to incur. But I was just trying to secure some sanity and serenity around my identity as a human being in this mixed-up, complicated world.

CHAPTER 19

Life of Brian

If I've learned anything in life, it's the cold, hard fact that if you want something bad enough, you had better work damn hard to get it. While I knew my transition back to Brian was going to be challenging, I wasn't prepared for the pushback I was about to receive from the medical community that I needed as an ally in my re-transition. Since I had no money and was living on public assistance and Medicaid, I was left to the mercy of doctors less sensitive to my needs as a trans person. That's putting it mildly.

Back then, trans folks were still considered a medical anomaly. There wasn't much training involved in how to give fair and equal care for trans women. I needed seven hundred and fifty dollars to have my implants removed. Once again, Eva came through and loaned me the money. Dr. Messier was still practicing and as Eva and I sat together in the waiting room, I looked around in horror at some of the overly-done plastic surgery patients. I had no choice but to return to him since he had done my original procedure. It disgusted me that he could get away with such butchery. At the same time, my fingers were crossed that my procedure would go off without a hitch.

Eva was kind and reassuring as I sat there trying to remain calm. While she knew this was the first major step of restoring my body, I knew

I had a long, long way to go. Looking at me, she sensed my nervousness. "Are you having second thoughts?" she asked.

"No. I've never been more certain. Looking around, though, doesn't give me much confidence."

"Don't worry, honey. You're going to be just fine and I'll be right here when you're done."

After the procedure, I woke up from the anesthesia and looked down at the bandages that reflected the reverse of my initial breast augmentation. I cried. My breasts were gone, and I had invested so much in them. How had I summoned up the nerve to actually go through with taking them away?

The next phase would prove to be much more difficult and nearly impossible. After fifteen years of hormone shots and silicone injections, my skin had stretched and I still had small breasts. Just as some trans men did, I began wearing an ACE bandage to bind them flat (though it is much safer to use binders specifically created for this purpose nowadays). Feeling tightly bound on a daily basis was a consistent reminder that I required a second operation. My options were pretty limited because I was without a steady income, although I had managed to secure my first part-time job as a man. Another lovely friend in recovery alerted me to a job filing 35-millimeter images of celebrities at a photo agency.

This part-time job led to a full-time position with benefits, something I had never had before, as well as a path to a career in photojournalism. Not only would I excel in this position, but also one day I would be running the whole operation. It seems my nightclub days had given me an inadvertent crash course in pop culture that would serve me well in photojournalism.

My first foray into seeking someone to perform the breast reduction surgery, also known as a double gynecomastia, was a referral for a consultation at a plastic surgery clinic at the Eye Ear and Nose Hospital on West Fourteenth Street. It was a teaching program I found through a friend. I was optimistic they could help me.

Arriving at the clinic, I was instructed to change into a gown so I could be examined from the waist up. Okay, standard procedure, I thought. I entered a room that felt much like a classroom considering that there were about a half-dozen medical students and the instructor watching me. The instructor asked me to remove my medical gown. As I lowered it, the students came up to get a closer look, asking my permission to poke and prod at my chest like some mad scientific experiment. Finished with their up-close and personal inspection, they returned to their seats. Then the inquisition began.

"Why, after so many years, would you want to reverse your gender? It seems so unusual," one student said, which immediately put me on the defensive. I felt judged for what I believed was a sane and sober decision.

Then more insulting questions were hurled at me.

"How did you pay for this in the first place? Were you a prostitute?" asked another particularly snarky student.

Then another asked, "Were you ever a drug addict and did you take IV drugs?"

It hit me where they were going with the questioning. It was the height of the AIDS crisis. The medical community was discriminating heavily on what types of procedures they could do on HIV positive folks. They were trying to discourage me from participating due to their fear of contracting the AIDS virus through what would certainly be a very bloody procedure.

Putting two and two together, I slipped up my gown, thanked them very much, and said, "I didn't come here to be judged or made to feel dirty by your line of questioning. Thanks, but no thanks."

I headed back home. Eva was home with her daughter, Jenny, who was visiting from California. I recapped my experience in lurid detail and both of them were equally upset at my treatment. Jenny suggested I try the private referral route and offered to cosign a loan for me. I saw her mouth moving but my ears couldn't believe what she was saying. This was the best news I could have heard.

My doctor at the time gave me a referral for a gay plastic surgeon on Park Avenue. Moving quickly, I booked an appointment and met with Dr. Levends who was pleasant, respectful, and professional. He took "before" photos of me as he explained what the procedure entailed. He said he could do it for about "five." Completely ecstatic, I made the appointment with his secretary. She requested that I send her a check a few days before. As the day grew closer, I received a call at work from the receptionist. She said she had received my check but asked me when I would be sending the remaining balance.

"Balance? What balance?" I asked. "I thought the five hundred dollars was the total fee?"

There was a very pregnant pause.

"Dr. Levends's fee is five thousand dollars, not five hundred."

"I'll have to call you back," I said and hung up. I didn't know whether to throw up, as I felt sick, or laugh hysterically at the absurdity of the situation. I did both. Immediately, I called Jenny and explained the mix-up. She cheerfully kept her word and said she would cosign for a loan with me.

Soon Jenny and I were sitting before the loan officer at Citibank. I rescheduled my appointment with Dr. Levends and all the papers had been drawn up and ready to sign. The loan officer asked us both for IDs. I handed over my New York license and Jenny gave him hers.

"Are you a California resident, Miss O'Hara?" he asked.

Jenny replied, "Yes, I'm bicoastal."

The loan officer sat stone-faced and then said, "I'm so sorry, but we can't approve loans for out-of-state residents."

Jenny tried to reason with the banker while my jaw was scraping the floor. We looked at each other dumbfounded and feeling as if I had been kicked in the stomach, I collected my things and left.

This now seemed like some cruel joke the universe was playing on me. First, there was a miscommunication about the amount and now a glitch over residency. Jenny tried to assure me that there was a way it could be done and she would do some more research. All hope wasn't lost, but it certainly felt like it.

Devastated, I called my sponsor in tears. She dispatched me to a meeting where my flailing hand was the first to be picked. Sobbing throughout my share, I described how humiliating it was to be treated like a leper misfit by these allegedly professional surgeons. I felt helpless and was faced with the very real possibility that, because of my HIV status, I wouldn't be able to move forward to become Brian again. Crying like a baby, I slumped back into my hard metal folding chair.

After the meeting my new friend, Cindy K., walked up to me and gave me a big hug. "Don't you worry," she said. "My credit is stellar and I'd be honored to help you out. I'll cosign your loan."

Stunned by what she'd said, I became a blubbering mess once again, amazed by her generosity. One day I would look back and appreciate the incredible kindness and faith that others showed to me and in me, and the sense of confidence they were willing to invest in my new character. One of my proudest moments was the day that I finished paying Cindy back every penny. Unfortunately, she was one of the unlucky ones who didn't make it through the AIDS crisis and passed away well before the cocktail of drugs became available.

Checking into the hospital and having the procedure done was a cakewalk compared to the funding fiasco. However, it was a long, slow painful recovery with not one, but two tubes draining from my chest for more than two weeks in St. Vincent's Hospital.

It was a cold and wintery day, but I remember it like it was yesterday as I finally was discharged from the hospital. The light snow falling covered the streets in a powdery substance that transformed the bustling city streets into a white oasis. The bandages wrapped around my chest felt snug, like when I had received the implants so many years ago. Moving more slowly than usual, I boarded the R train back to my little Astoria studio apartment. Happily the elevator was working. Arriving on my floor I flicked the key to the left end entered my home. Suddenly a new sense of calm had come over me as I removed my heavy overcoat and placed my small suitcase on the bed. Slowly, I began to unbutton my crisp cotton shirt one button at a time. My heart began to race as I realized I was about to see myself for the first time. Once I removed my shirt I stepped into the bathroom to face the full-length mirror. Gently lifting off my T-shirt and revealing the bandages that remained there reminded me that the end of my long journey was what lies beneath. Slowly I began to unwind them. As if in slow motion I watched as the final bandage dropped to the floor. I stood there in awe of what I saw. It felt as if time froze as I stood there staring, poking at my bruised chest. In that moment I finally felt complete in a way that there are no words to describe. There were no tears now, only a great sense of relief and gratitude.

Friends were especially kind during my convalescence, bringing food and fellowship out to my new small studio in Astoria, where I had found a quiet respite from the bustling city.

Slowly I returned to my work routine and began my new life without being bound by ACE bandages. But while I was finally at peace physically, I found myself at the beginning of a long road to reclaim and recreate my male identify. Being Brian was something I had abandoned many years ago, so in many ways it was like getting reacquainted with an old friend who had been away for too long.

It was difficult for my friends and family to adjust as well. They were being asked to accept the changes I was now making in the same way I had so desperately sought their acceptance of my female identity earlier. But I was now living my life one day at a time and had to treat each relationship the same way.

• • •

One of my coworkers during this time was always encouraging me to keep acting and one day she read about an audition in *Backstage* for a new film directed by legendary filmmaker Sidney Lumet. He was seeking actors to play transvestite characters for his new film. I managed to get an appointment with the casting director, Joy Todd. When I arrived, her assistant handed me sides to read as I sat patiently going over the scene in the waiting room.

She called my name and I entered her office and read the scene with her. It was a role as the villain in the film. She said, "You did a really good job, thanks for coming in. I'll be in touch." As I left, I went out to the elevator and pushed the button. Just as I was stepping into the elevator, Joy came running out to the elevator area and asked me to come back in.

"Brian," she said, "I'd like you to read something else," as she handed me a side for another scene. "Take a few minutes to look it over." I did and then read again with her.

"You know I think this is something that just might work for you." Now I was more than excited that she had stopped my exit and that I had a second chance to read again.

"Let me make a few calls and I'll get back to you this evening," she said. I left feeling confident and happy that I was being considered for my first professional acting gig. Later that night she called and asked if I was available the next day to audition for the director. She told me I'd be reading with him. This would be the first time I was ever auditioning at this level. She gave me a great direction. "Remember, Brian, whatever you do, be as still as possible. You are terrified for your life." Well, that was easy. Terror? I had that down in spades.

When I finished, director Sidney Lumet looked across the desk at me and instead of unbuckling his pants, he smiled broadly and said, "That was great, really, really nice. I think I'd like you to do the part."

I nearly fell off the chair. As a male actor, I was having more commercial success then when I was trans. My first big role was in a film directed by Sidney Lumet and acting with Nick Nolte—granted, I was cast as Sophia, a transvestite prostitute, but nevertheless I did get my SAG card. The strangest thing of all was that the scene was filmed on the very corner on Ninth Avenue I had spent years hooking on.

Another rewarding experience in New York theater was back in November of 1991. I had been living as Brian for four years when I auditioned for and got cast in *Bluebeard* with the incredible Ridiculous Theatrical Company. I was recreating the role of Lamia, the Leopard

Woman, who was a sex change experiment gone awry . . . type casting perhaps? This was the same Ridiculous Theatrical Company that I had seen so many years ago when I first arrived in New York at eighteen and was so inspired by.

• • •

Details magazine asked me to do an interview about my decision to re-transition. My friend, Michael Musto, did a full three-page interview including before and after photos of my transition. He arrived with a photographer in tow to Eva's home where she let us do the shoot. Once the interview was published, it saved me from a lot of awkward potential encounters with my nightlife friends and acquaintances. The interview set off a firestorm of media inquiries and requests for TV appearances. For a while it seemed that I was always explaining my re-transition over and over again. Soon I was on the talk show circuit on the *Geraldo Rivera Show* and the *Joan Rivers Show*, as well as local reality news programs like *People Are Talking*. I traveled to California, Seattle, Philadelphia, and back to New York. It was incredibly challenging being a guest on those talk shows because there still was an inordinate amount of ignorance about trans issues. In true tabloid TV fashion, the hosts were most concerned with my Army marriage, my breasts, and my sex life, in that order. It was an interesting lesson in how to convey my life story in the way *I* wanted.

Healing physically, I needed to begin an exercise routine to strengthen my body and build up muscle. It had been years since I saw the inside of a gym, let alone a male locker-room. With a couple of gay male friends, I joined a local gym on Houston Street. I was about to join the world of gay male muscle queens. While I never expected to become Arnold Schwarzenegger, luckily my strong genes gave me good basic muscle mass. I would definitely need it for my second body transformation.

It would take some time, but before long I became more comfortable with my new old identity. It was as an awkward chubby teenager the last time I identified as anything male. Brian was but a memory, and finding my way back to him wouldn't happen overnight.

As my friends and I approached the entrance to the gym, we pressed the ground level elevator button to get up to the gym. Emotions were running high, and at the same time I was excited and terrified about this new experience. It immediately brought me back to my school days when I entered the boys' locker-room on the brink of puberty. It was just as confusing back then as it was at that moment. I had never really fit in. My body had been soft and pudgy. As the elevator door slid open onto this mecca of muscle mania, I felt that old feeling of inadequacy casting its ugly spell.

Looking over the vast collection of work out equipment and weights I felt instantly overwhelmed. Not once did either of my friends even get the slightest hint of my anxiety. I was still good at hiding. Then, as I viewed all the activity as if in slow motion, we headed to an area identified by a large sign: MEN'S LOCKER-ROOM. My feet felt heavy as I trudged along following my friends. They had done this hundreds of times, so it wasn't any big deal to them.

But for me it packed a huge emotional wallop. Slowly, I immediately recognized the smell of fresh towels, chlorine bleach, and manly sweat. Without warning, a beautifully fit, naked man popped out from the shower, dragging his towel off the rack and proudly displaying his exquisite physique. So here I was, after fifteen years, in a men's locker-room feeling far from confident and less male myself.

Deal with it, I said to myself.

I stumbled to a locker and imitated what my friends did. I stripped off and changed into my workout clothes, all the while peeking at all the many different male forms parading in and out. My face was still pretty— it will always be pretty, no matter how much facial hair I try to grow or how much eyebrow pencil I use. In those early days, I looked quite androgynous, sort of like a trans man during the beginning of his transition. While it bothered me, I was still content with the idea that I was letting go of the trappings of my former female identity. Just as difficult as it was to transition to female, the road back to Brian wasn't going to be any easier. Being in this environment only amped my reality.

Recovering from the shock, smells, and sights in the locker-room, I made it out into the workout area. My friends helped me untangle the complicated maze of exercise machines and were trying to instruct me on what to do. They got a big chuckle watching me trying to figure out how to use the exercise equipment. This lightened the situation, which for me was already traumatizing enough.

When I was diagnosed as HIV positive, there was a very strong possibility that I would die a similar horrible and painful death as so many of my friends and acquaintances. I lived each day as if it might be my last and was amazed when I woke up healthy and sober the next day. Being HIV positive instilled in me great grace and hope that it might be possible to make it through what I consider to be one of the most devastating times in human history.

• • •

For the first ten years of my recovery, every day was precious to me. What was happening around me was so terrifying. Everywhere I went someone was getting sick and dying from AIDS. When I would go to my regular home group, I dreaded seeing my fellow recovering addicts raise their hand at the break for fear it was going to be more bad news. One by one, so many of some of my closest friends were being decimated. Sometimes, it really felt as if some alien being had come down and snatched them off the earth.

I became numb with the quantity of death that surrounded me in those first ten years. Witnessing so many losses in such a short amount of time was stressful, sad, and devastating. For me, it really was one day at a time.

As a long-term survivor of HIV, I had to do whatever I could to get health insurance to be vigilant in monitoring my health status. Through that early kindness of my recovery friend, I was able to keep working in the photo industry. The work at that little photo agency not only opened up what would become a career in photojournalism but it provided me with the necessary stability I needed as a person in early recovery.

Establishing credit, moving out of the theater and, most importantly, securing health benefits was essential for my survival.

During this time, I was also able to find a place to live back in the city. One of my friends from the nightlife scene was getting married and moving in with her new husband. Her apartment on Rivington Street on the Lower East Side was rent stabilized. While the apartment I had in Astoria was sufficient for a small studio, I jumped at the chance to be back in Manhattan. The small one-bedroom railroad flat would be fine. My rear window faced out onto a school courtyard, in which, after school let out for the day, the local junkies and prostitutes would use this space to shoot up heroin and turn tricks: visual proof and a daily reminder of where my life could lead if I wasn't careful. Then the neighborhood was far from the swanky gentrified area that it is now. There were no Starbucks or four-star restaurants, and rents were still relatively low for the neighborhood. Unlike today when a couple of thousand dollars might get you a tiny studio. But I was grateful to have a place and a lease of my own.

Also, during this time my father, who was eighty years old, had taken a turn for the worse. His diabetes had finally gotten out of control and his kidneys were shutting down. The doctors told my brother Jeffery he was too old for dialysis and that he would eventually not have long to live. This time I made sure I got there in time to say goodbye. Seven years sober, I had successfully re-transitioned back to Brian and worked as the Bureau Chief of London Features International, where some years earlier I had cut my teeth in the photo business.

Having some sober experience made it less difficult to navigate the minefield of dysfunction that my family always seemed to thrive on. But it couldn't remedy the past burdens and disappointments they had suffered. I was financially solvent and stayed in a hotel, which provided me a safe haven from my siblings. Most of my dealings with them were at the hospital. My Aunt Doria, who was married to my father's older brother Peter, came to visit on a day I was there. She had only heard stories about me and I hadn't seen her since I was a boy, when my Dad would bring me over for the Jewish holy days. My father had always chided me to be more like her son, my cousin Michael. He was a successful football jock who later went on to die from years of heroin use. Glad I didn't take his advice.

Doria was surprised to see me looking so well. I remember wearing a suit and tie whenever I went to the hospital because I wanted to present myself in the best possible light for my dad. Even if he never would acknowledge me for it, I was going to give him the comfort in his last days that one of his sons was doing all right. As it turned out, my aunt was especially inquisitive in front of my dad. I got to explain to her in detail as he listened about the measure of my recent success. Boy was she impressed. From the look on my father's face, so was he.

The last exchange I had with my dad went like this. It was time for his lunch and he was struggling to feed himself. So I sat on the bed and slowly helped him eat. His hands were shaky so he couldn't really hold the fork very well. I thought, *Well, this is a huge change of events. Here I am feeding the man who brought me into the world.* As I continued to feed him, he was taking big bites of salad and I said, "Slow down, Dad. You don't want to choke, do you?" Instead of taking my advice he continued to gulp a big serving of food.

"You're so stubborn. Now I know where I get it from," I said, chuckling to myself.

He then said, "You don't get that from me."

"Oh really?" I said.

"You get it from your mother."

"Well, what did I get from you then?" I asked.

He pointed to his head. "Brains," he said with a smirk.

In that instant, all the years I felt that my father never cared for me, or understood me, disappeared. It was in that moment I knew for sure that, for the first time ever in my life, he was proud of me. I didn't need to imagine it any other way. It was the way he looked into my eyes and smirked in a confident way—almost like a wink without winking—that I knew we were good. It was a blessing that I will always cherish and, while I didn't have it with my mom, it gave me faith that she too felt the same way. None of the noise in my head ever mattered again.

Dad's funeral was a traditional Hebrew service and he was buried in a plot his brother Peter had bought him in an amazing act of kindness. I couldn't help but think: Why hadn't that kindness been passed down to my own relationships with my siblings? When my mother died, my brother David was passed out on the day of the funeral and Jeffery couldn't get a pass from prison. This time was no different as Todd, who did get a pass from prison, arrived handcuffed and in police custody. As always there was another drama at play even in the most somber moments in our lives. Each of my father's children was asked to grab a handful of dirt and throw it into the grave. The reality that I would never see my dad again sank in. Finally I was able to unleash the tears I had been holding back for this man whom I'd had such a conflicted and difficult relationship with. It was a different kind of grief from my mother, with whom I had no chance for closure. It was more peaceful and accepting that I had finally done the right thing by showing up in the way I did. That was also the last time I would ever see my older brother Randall, his wife, and his two boys. That was in 1993.

With both parents gone it was time to move forward with my life. I was comforted by the knowledge that in their own way, they had loved me.

CHAPTER 20

Sterling Place

One day I was invited to a friend's apartment in Brooklyn. He was moving in with his boyfriend in Manhattan. I was familiar with the area because in 1983 I had lived there with Denny. The apartment was a block from the subway in one of those great brick postwar buildings. It was a huge one-bedroom, nearly twice the size of my little flat on Rivington Street in Manhattan.

"What are going to do with this place when you move into the city?" I asked.

To my surprise, he said, "I'm just giving it up."

"Really, just like that?" I said. "Would you consider giving it to me?"

And just like that I inherited a big, beautiful Brooklyn apartment for nearly close to what I was paying for the one in Manhattan: $324 a month! It was an easy commute to where I worked. Since that auspicious day, I've always believed my new address on Sterling Place was a great place to be. It was quieter than the city but not too far away. The fragrant linden tree-lined block in summer was intoxicatingly delicious when in bloom. One day on my way home appreciating the view around me—the colors, the sounds—it occurred to me that my life was at a sterling place indeed.

Now a seasoned photo agency professional, I was working at an international French photo agency, Gamma Liaison. It was a much faster paced company and heavily focused on news. I'd been there for about three years when I was approached by the owner of London Features in its new location in the Meatpacking District of Manhattan, still another non-gentrified area that retained some of its seedy charm. The owner made me an offer I couldn't refuse and I agreed to return to head up the agency as its Bureau Chief. I grinned to myself that first day finding it highly ironic that it was on these very cobblestone streets, many years ago that I'd stumbled around trying to turn tricks in the night. With a spring in my step, I made my way to the office as the company's new manager. My savvy expertise took it from a floundering business to the top of a crowded field of photo agencies. Pushing forty, I'd managed to carve out a comfortable living for myself and earn a decent salary. The photographers I worked with appreciated the work I did for them and I continued to excel in my career.

One photographer in particular was an ambitious young man from Long Island who got his start sneaking into a Billy Joel concert with his camera and getting his images published in the local paper. Handsome and charming, he resembled a young Tom Cruise; he'd set the female photo editors' hearts aflutter. Kevin Mazur was a diamond in the rough and I could tell from those very early days that he would succeed. He became one of the most successful rock and roll photographers of his time. *Rolling Stone* dispatched him to every possible music venue they needed to cover for their readers and Kevin began his ascent to the top of celebrity photojournalism.

After leaving London Features a second time I went to work directly for Kevin Mazur Photography as his studio manager and agent. It was the early nineties and things in the photo industry were moving at a breakneck speed. During those years, I was at Kevin's side at some of the swankiest events in the entertainment industry. I had to pinch myself whether I was on the red carpet at the Academy Awards, or hanging backstage at the Grammy Awards and MTV Music Awards. Then there were live concerts of all kinds: the Rolling Stones, U2, Sting, Madonna, Mariah Carey, Sheryl Crow, Billy Joel, and Elton John, to name a few. Finding myself caught up in this wave of celebrity at times was overwhelming, of these situations at times was overwhelming, but being clean and sober I appreciated every moment.

Unfortunately, after three years with Kevin I wasn't able to continue as studio manager. Earlier that year I had been diagnosed with hepatitis C and was undergoing the grueling treatment that, in those early days, involved daily injections of Interferon and pills twice a day that knocked me for a loop.

Leaving Kevin was a difficult decision, but one I had to make. My health was my main priority. It was one year of treatment and, while I tried to work throughout most of it and hung in there as long as I could, eventually I couldn't keep up with the demands of the fast-paced world of celebrity photography. The medication was making me incredibly depressed and suicidal. At one point, I found myself on the window ledge of our office on Twenty-Third Street with a little voice whispering to me, *jump, jump, jump.* It was one of the worse years of my life. I never thought I would make it through the grueling regimen. But as with most things in my life now, one day at a time, one shot at a time, I made it to the end of my treatment and to this day I'm in remission from Hepatitis C.

Unemployed and finished with my treatment, I was itching to get back to work. It was now the year 2000. My experience with Kevin and the A-list clients we worked with led me to apply for a position my good friend Ramiro told me about. There was an opening as a photo-researcher at *People* magazine. He felt it would be a natural progression for me from my work in the trenches of photojournalism. The great relationships I had cultivated over the years had also given me a bankable and solid reputation as someone who was reliable, smart, hardworking, and fair.

During my time at *People*, I worked in an intensely creative and stimulating environment. With no formal college education, it was a bit of an anomaly that I could land in such a bastion of Ivy League-educated colleagues. One of my friends asked, "How did you like working there? It must be such a cool place to work," he said. I replied that it felt very much like, "I was clawing my way to the middle." If I were to do it all again, perhaps I would do some things differently, but I was incredibly grateful for the opportunity and I learned so much about thriving in a corporate environment.

During the seven years I spent there, I never gave up entertaining the creative side of my personality and with my good friend Kent Green I wrote and performed in a one-man show titled *Boys Don't Wear Lipstick*. In the fall of 2000, and after several years of workshops and limited trial runs at different venues, we ended up getting produced Off Broadway at the Players Theater in the heart of Greenwich Village.

It ran for a few months with great reviews. After the curtain call for the opening night performance having received a standing ovation from an audience packed with friends and loved ones, I returned to my dressing room and spontaneously burst into tears. I couldn't believe I'd come so far and worked so hard to get to that point creatively. My tears were a messy mix of gratitude and grief for the life that I had lived, which I was now portraying on stage every night. It was a cathartic and intensely personal performance, one that left me drained physically.

Hoping to strike while the iron was hot, I made the rounds of the New York talent agents in hopes of finding representation as a working actor/ writer. The harsh reality even in the year 2000 was that the entertainment industry was still incredibly homophobic and ageist. After my Off-Broadway play I managed to get an interview with a potential agent. I was so excited—at least until he looked across his desk at me and said point blank, "Well, Brian, you are a bit too gay. And although you're only forty, it's still a bit old." I can't remember his name, but I can see his face. The moment I heard that from a handsome, masculine-looking gay man, I realized that what I was up against was much bigger than any great interview or audition I could give.

So identifying as male got my boot in the door, but as a queer male back then, it was still an uphill fight.

Once the excitement of being a produced playwright and Off-Broadway actor wore off, I came back down to earth and returned to *People* with a more serious eye toward retirement. I began to think more about the future and what that might hold. Knowing my talent and creativity would never leave me, it was integral for me to find a way to make a living and sustain a level of financial security. Keeping my health benefits was my number one priority. And so, reluctantly and with a great deal of sorrow, I accepted the limitations of the acting industry and instead happily focused on my career as a photo editor at *People*. I was grateful that it met my needs financially and fulfilled me creatively.

With the new drug regimen I was on, it looked like I might even possibly have a future. The current regimen of drugs known as "the cocktail" had rendered the virus undetectable in my blood. That is, as long as I was compliant with my daily medication. I came to appreciate the handful of pills I took each morning as opposed to resenting them.

• • •

My relationship with love was at best sporadic over my many years in recovery. My first serious boyfriend in recovery broke my heart, but at the same time made it stronger. After that, it was a series of fits and starts. Each experience taught me something new. Still I hadn't met Mr. Right. Back then I was more in the Mr. Right Away frame of mind. Sex as a gay man hadn't become any less complicated than it was back in the 1970s, especially not if you were HIV positive. I realized not much had changed at all. Men were extremely promiscuous. Hooking up often stoked the fantasy that something might happen, but it never did for me. Most of the sex I was having in the nineties was anonymous. In bookstores, porn theaters, sex clubs, gyms, restrooms. My addiction switched to sex as a substitute. I even became a trick of my own, hiring hustlers whenever I felt the urge. It was easier to pay for sex than face rejection from potential partners. It also provided me a different view of the men who had paid me for sex for so many years. I still had a deep desire to love.

• • •

At that time, I had an adorable little Jack Russell Terrier, Bricker, whom I had named after my best friend, Paulie Bricker. I still struggled with depression and felt that I just couldn't take living another day. One day I had this crazy idea when I got home to enter the shower with a belt. As I wrapped the belt around the shower nozzle to test how strong it was, I heard the pitter-patter of puppy paws on the tile floor. Bricker then looked at up me like *what the hell are you doing?* All I did was take one look at him and I knew I couldn't leave him ownerless. I came out of the shower, put the belt back in my drawer, and laid on the bed cuddling my little friend till I fell asleep. It was Bricker who saved my life during the depths of my depression from the Interferon treatments for my hep C.

Surviving the horrid attack on 9/11 instilled in me serious priorities. While I was lucky to not have been anywhere near the World Trade Center that day, as usual I got up and went about my morning routine. Every morning I would take Bricker out for his walk and that day was no different. It was a perfect fall day: blue, blue sky so clear you could see for miles. Walking the dog down Sterling Place and along Seventh Avenue, I noticed smoke in the distance. I thought to myself, *that's odd*, and hoped they were able to put the fire out. As I reentered my home, where I'd left my TV on, I saw on the news that a plane had crashed into the first tower. As I watched, the second one hit. I never made it to work that day as millions of New Yorkers and people all over the world were stunned by the horrific events.

CHAPTER 21

A New Happiness

One year later in 2002, I was walking Bricker after work as usual on a hot, sultry August evening. Headed over to Flatbush Avenue from Eighth Avenue with Bricker leading the way (I was on the phone and have no memory of to whom I was talking). Standing and waiting for the light to change, I noticed a tall, dark haired man glancing across the avenue in my direction. He has since reminded me that I was wearing a white athletic tank top and khaki pants and that the phone was glued to my ear. Never one to ignore male attention, I thought, *Hmm, this looks interesting.* He kept turning back to see if I was crossing the street.

The light changed. I put more of a sprint in my step to see if I could catch up with this handsome stranger. He looked back again as he turned the corner headed over to Plaza Street, which was the same direction in which I was headed.

As I turned the corner, there he was. He'd stopped and waited for me to approach, no doubt. In true Brian fashion, I boldly stepped up to the challenge and introduced myself to this fellow.

"Hi, I'm Brian."

"I'm Jim, headed to the gym."

"Jim, headed to the gym, that's funny."

We chuckled as he bent down to pet Bricker, who was more than happy to get a free rub from a stranger. Like father, like son, I suppose. I don't know why I felt the way I did, but I was immediately smitten with Jim. He was tall, dark, and handsome in a swarthy Daniel Day Lewis kind of way. His eyes were a beautiful steely blue, his smile was sanguine and sweet. There was an instant spark. I know he felt it too. After a few minutes of chitchat, I said that I was headed home around the corner to Sterling Place and wanted to know if he would like to join me. He never made it to the gym.

Back at my apartment, our tête-à-tête became physical and we made love for hours. It was well past midnight before he left, and we exchanged phone numbers. He'd mentioned that it was also his mother's birthday and I thought, *well, that's a good sign.* How nice it was of her to send me her son on her birthday. Before he left I reminded him, "Don't forget to call your mom. Birthdays are very important."

I took the lead and made a date for a romantic dinner at a local Brooklyn restaurant and we began a whirlwind courtship that included many fun evenings, concerts, beach days, and just plain old-fashioned falling in love. After six months of dating, things started to become more serious.

Initially, I was hesitant to tell Jim about my infamous past as a trans woman and the day I got the courage to bring it up, he shrugged it off as no big deal, because in his words, "I googled you when you told me you were a playwright." This was a testament to his stellar character. Rather than be turned off, which had been my experience with some other gay men, he appreciated it and found it fascinating. The other big secret I loathed to reveal to anyone back then was my HIV status. And of course, that too turned out not to be an issue for him.

Since that eventful day in August 2002, we've been together ever since. We were married in 2013 once marriage equality became law. Not only did I meet the most fantastic man I could have ever dreamed of, I also inherited his amazing family who has, in many ways, become mine as well. They more than make up for the lack of closeness I have with my own family today. We are partners for life and I love him more than any other man I have ever been with. He teaches me something new about myself every day, and is the cool counterbalance to my fiery nature.

Jim is just a few years younger than me. He was born on Long Island, but grew up in Hawaii, where he relocated after his dad passed away in a fatal automobile accident. His aloha spirit is one that jives so beautifully with my daily goal of keeping serenity in my life. My wellbeing and happiness are dependent on it, as it's an important part of my continuing recovery. The day we met I just knew we would be together as we are now. While it took lots of practice and many different instances of heartache, rejection, and disappointment, my higher power had something really special in store for me as long as I continued to have hope that one day it would find me. And it did.

The massive downturn of the economy in 2007 led to huge job cuts at every magazine title owned by Time Inc. *People*, the behemoth money earner was last on the chopping block but wasn't spared. I was offered a golden parachute and I jumped headfirst. Within the severance package, there was money available for education. Barely on the other side of fifty, I was presented with the opportunity to decide what direction my life was going to take. Since it now looked like I might actually be living for a while, I had the opportunity to do something that I wanted to do. I knew only one thing: Never again did I want to be put in a position where I was selling something that I didn't believe in. Whatever new career path I chose, it had to be in an area that benefitted others in some way.

My research led me to look into the other thing I'd become passionate about: the field of recovery. Being incredibly grateful for the changes that had occurred in my life as a result of giving up drugs and alcohol, I knew it might be a natural fit for me. Doing the legwork, I found some information about a specialty credential to become a credentialed alcohol and substance abuse counselor. Locating a training facility, I signed up to audit one of its classes. My instinct was correct. I found it incredibly fascinating and rewarding to make positive change in another individual's life. One class at a time, I finished the requirements and became a credentialed alcoholism and substance abuse counselor for those who are struggling with addiction.

Taking it a step further, I went back to college after recklessly abandoning my education in my twenties and received a Bachelor of Science degree in Health and Human Services. Presently, I'm working on a master's degree for mental health counseling. If I can make a small difference in people's lives, I believe this is what I've been put here on this earth to do.

· · ·

Today, after more than three decades of sobriety and entering my sixth decade of life, there's no way I could have ever imagined life as it is. It would be another book entirely if I were able to detail the incredible things that have occurred over the last thirty years. It would be hard for me to imagine my life today so many years ago as a mixed-up, gender-confused young person.

On more than one occasion, it looked as if I might not even make it to thirty. The simple truth of learning to live life one day at a time has been the greatest blessing for me. Living in the moment, in the here and now, I benefit fully from the immediacy of the present. Doing so brings all the value and attention each day deserves. If I'm consumed with thoughts of the future or thinking about tomorrow I'm not honoring the importance of living life in the moment to its fullest capacity. While it takes practice, and sometimes I still fall short of trying to align myself with this simple truth, the great thing is that I can always pause or take a deep breath and get back in the day or the moment at hand. While it sounds like one of the simplest truths, it nevertheless takes commitment and consistent practice to achieve.

As someone who never gave much respect to commitment or practice, I've been the lucky beneficiary of those qualities that most people take for granted. For those who are not challenged with the disease of addiction, it is the natural order of things. This isn't to say that folks not in recovery don't have struggles, because we all do have life's challenges to bear. But for addicts, it is especially hard to maintain. We're not the most patient group and when the universe was passing out the tolerance and acceptance gene, most of us, myself included, were not inclined to receive it that day.

· · ·

My mother dispensed an occasional pearl of wisdom every now and then. One was "Patience is a virtue," and I never understood this simple principle in my early life. But today it allows me to not have to act on impulse or indulge in the fear that may rule any given situation. As someone who was raised to be afraid of everything, it is such a gift today to know that living fearfully is a false way to live life. I understand that I haven't accomplished some groundbreaking major achievement like finding a cure for cancer, but instead, knowing that I've found the remedy for my own unhappiness is more than enough.

Faith was another foreign concept for me, one that I ignored like a vampire does garlic. Living your life believing the worst will happen becomes a way of not accepting that you are deserving of anything good. As a survivor of sexual and physical abuse, I was always waiting for the other shoe to drop and it's something I still struggle with. It was almost as if I expected and willed the worst to be. Today, that's not the case. The faith that I have gained by instinctively knowing I will be taken care of is an act of simple humility. I've been cared for in ways that, at times, seem unimaginable.

For example, whether it was faith, God's grace, or coincidence that led me to the therapist I met in early recovery, I will never know. Dr. Newman was a gentle and soft-spoken soul. To this day I feel as though I couldn't have been luckier to occupy a seat opposite this lovely, caring, and generous woman. Or was it faith that led me to the steps of Grace Church in Providence, Rhode Island when I met that longhaired, beautiful stranger who showed me such compassion and kindness at a very low point in my life? Or was it faith that sent me the amazing miracle of recovery when I needed it the most? Questions like these I leave to more qualified persons to answer. For me I accept it as the grace of some power greater than myself.

This way of life is manifested today by the example of thousands of others who have weathered some of the most difficult life circumstances. By staying "woke," as the kids now say, and paying attention not so much to what people say but what they do, I've become stronger in my resolve that I too can make it through my own difficulties with the same persever-ance and grace that allowed others to do so.

While today I have a civil relationship with my siblings, it's my family of choice that brings me the most joy and gratitude. These are the people in my life who believe in me, and I in them. They are able to show up for me during times of great achievement and also deep despair. Over the past thirty years it has been the collective wisdom and experience of these known and sometimes anonymous voices that has contributed to the solace, serenity and wisdom of my life. It's this simple way of life that I owe an eternal debt of gratitude.

Acknowledgments

There are so many people past and present who have guided me along the way, but first I'd like to thank everyone who ever told me "no" for adding additional strength and resilience to my character. I want to express deepest gratitude to my agent, Tom Miller at the Carol Mann Agency, for his keen expertise, perseverance, and belief in me. Caroline Russomanno, my editor and the entire Skyhorse team. Thank you Susan Randol for opening the door and inviting me in. My BFF Ramiro Fernandez for constantly bugging me to finish my book. Keith Greer for everything. Eva O'Hara for being a lifesaver and great friend, Jenny O'Hara for her incredible kindness and generosity. Cindy Kergoat for signing on the dotted line. Rebecca Paley for her book savvy, humor, and graceful guidance throughout. James Mulqueen who kept Tish alive in a box under his kitchen table for decades. Matthew Carnicelli for his initial editing expertise. My besties, Michael Musto, Richard Ottens, Everett Quinton, Karen Bernstein, Colleen Meenan, Deb Makin, Gabriel Rotello, Nelson Sullivan, Ethyl Eichelberger, M. K. Schilling, Bobby Reed, Paul Caranicas, The Estate of Antonio Lopez and Juan Ramos, Donna Cohen, Hope and Steven Klein, Cheryl Perry, Felipa Lopez, Dr. Stephen Dillon, Dr. Benjamin Medrano. My sister, Sheila Belovitch, the Hochberger family—Liz, Fred, Marjie, Colleen, and Andy, along with Charlie and Ruth Russell for all their loving support. All the brave, bold and beautiful transgender women who inspired and paved the way for the current generation—Monica, Monique, Rusty, Dina, Laverne, Kimiko, April, Pebbles, Jesse, Leslie, Chanel, Taxi, Ava, Vivian, Melissa, Yvonne, Bianca, Crystal, Portia, Chrysis, Cody, Raquel, Tiny, Mara, Candy, Liz, Jackie, Marsha, Sonia, Nikki, Holly, Candy, Pinky, Carol, Marlene, Collette, Naomi, Sandy, Wilhelmina, Lola, Monique, Kim, Paige, Samantha, Vanessa, Sandy, Easha, Octavia, Angie, Venus. Diana Ross & the Supremes for keeping me hanging on. My degree from the Bette Davis School of Drama. ACT UP, Larry Kramer and Peter Staley who are my real heroes. H. P. and his notorious FOBs. Paul E. Bricker for instilling in me the wonder of possibility and the true meaning of friendship. Gloria Walker for always believing in and loving me no matter which gender I lived in. Thank you Martin Norregaard for your infinite wisdom, unconditional love and friendship. And lastly, my brilliant husband, Jim Russell, who brings the aloha spirit into my life every day and challenges me to be a better, more compassionate version than the day before with his enduring love and support.